The Origins
of Hertfordshire

The Origins
of Hertfordshire

Tom Williamson

Hertfordshire Publications

an imprint of the

University of Hertfordshire Press

First published in Great Britain in 2010 by

Hertfordshire Publications

an imprint of the

University of Hertfordshire Press

College Lane

Hatfield

Hertfordshire

AL10 9AB

British Library Cataloguing in Publication Data

A catalogue record for this book is available from the British Library

ISBN 978-1-905313-95-2

Design by Mathew Lyons

Printed in Great Britain by CPI Antony Rowe

Contents

Figures

Abbreviations

BAR	British Archaeological Reports
CBA	Council for British Archaeology
CUCAP	Cambridge University Committee for Aerial Photography
EPNS	English Place-Name Society
HALS	Hertfordshire Archives and Local Studies, Hertford
HER	Historic Environment Record, County Hall, Hertford (accessible online via www.heritagegateway.org.uk)

Note

Grid references are given to six figures and preceded by the Ordnance Survey grid-square letters: e.g. TQ097995.

Preface

This is a new, largely rewritten and considerably extended version of a volume which was originally written over a decade ago. When the University of Hertfordshire Press first discussed with me the possibility of republishing the book I realised that drastic revision of the original text would be necessary. There were two reasons for this. Firstly, during the last ten years my own views on many of the matters discussed in it have changed, sometimes considerably. More importantly, archaeologists and historians have discovered many new things about Hertfordshire's past, and while some of these discoveries have confirmed arguments and suggestions made in the original text, others have served to undermine them. Among the most important of recent contributions have been Julia Crick's invaluable edition of the Anglo-Saxon charters of St Albans Abbey and Ros Niblett and Isobel Thompson's masterly summary of the archaeology of St Albans, *Alban's Buried Towns*.

A brief note on my own background might be helpful. I was born in Hemel Hempstead, spent my early life in Bushey, and was educated at Watford Grammar School. But I have not really lived in Hertfordshire since I went to university at the age of eighteen, and this book is therefore really the work of an outsider, looking in. Others might have made a better job of it: the county is fortunate in having so many local historians and, in particular, archaeologists of great ability and reputation, and much that is written here rests firmly on the research of Ros Niblett, Isobel Thompson, Jonathan Hunn, Stewart Bryant and others. Nevertheless, there may be some merits in the views of a landscape historian who, having lived and researched elsewhere for many years, returns to look with fresh eyes at places he once knew well. But Hertfordshire people will be the best judges of that.

Many people have helped in producing this volume, providing information, encouragement or advice. I would like to thank, in particular, Stewart Bryant, Brian Perry, David and Bridget Howlett, Isobel Thompson, the staff of the Hertfordshire Archives and Local Studies Centre, Robin Harcourt Williams of Hatfield House archives, and above all Anne Rowe, who also read and commented on the revised text. Phillip Judge drew the maps and diagrams. Figures 11 and 58 were provided by the Cambridge University Committee for Aerial Photography; Figures 7, 40 and 57 by English Heritage; and are reproduced with permission. Figures 9, 13, 29, 35, 51, 61, 63, and 65 are by Anne Rowe. Figure 61 is reproduced with permission of Hertfordshire Archives and Local History, and Lord Verulam; Figure 63 with that of HALS alone. My wife, Liz Bellamy, and my children, Jessica and Matthew Williamson, provided (as ever) understanding and support. Perhaps this book's greatest debt, however, is to the people who many years ago first encouraged my interest in Hertfordshire's past: my late mother, Jean Williamson; the late Tony Rawlings of the Watford and South-West Hertfordshire Archaeological Society; and the late Grant Longman, who worked for many years uncovering the history of the parish of Bushey.

Chapter 1
The Identity of Hertfordshire

Introduction

This book is about the early history of one English *shire*, or county –
Hertfordshire. It will explore how both it, and its ancient subdivisions, came
into existence; and it will examine the subtle and complex relationship
between natural topography and the development of territorial organisation.
These are matters of more than merely antiquarian interest. The patterns of
settlement and territory established in the period before Domesday
continued to mould the development of Hertfordshire for centuries: indeed,
they continue to do so, to some extent, today. Moreover, it is impossible to
understand the history of any district without some knowledge of the
administrative structures within which its inhabitants lived, and the shire
was a unit of immense significance in the lives of our ancestors from the time
of its emergence in the later Saxon period until well into post-medieval times.

In the early Middle Ages the shire was the principal subdivision of the
English kingdom, and it had financial, judicial and military functions. Its sheriff
– 'shire reeve' – was responsible for collecting the taxes owed to the king and
for organising local defence. Each shire had its own court, and continued to be
the main unit of judicial organisation even after itinerant justices developed in
the course of the Anglo-Norman period. But the shire was more than an
instrument of central government. In time it became something which gave
people a sense of identity, not least because it formed the basis for parliamentary
representation. Even today, most people can tell you which shire they live in, or
were born in. And this, in part, is a consequence of the remarkable longevity
and stability of shires: their boundaries changed little over the centuries, until
the alterations effected by the Local Government Acts of modern times.

English shires had a variety of origins. Many in the south-east of England, and in East Anglia, bear names which attest to their beginnings in early tribal territories and ancient kingdoms. Essex, for example, perpetuates the name (and in part the territory) of the East Saxons; Sussex, that of the South Saxons; and Middlesex, that of the Middle Saxons. The name of Kent is ultimately derived from the Iron Age tribe the *Cantiaci*, more immediately from the early English kingdom of Kent. Surrey is the 'South Region'; Norfolk takes its name from the North Folk, an ancient subdivision of the East Angles; Suffolk from the South Folk. In the far west of England, Devon and Cornwall, too, have their origins in post-Roman successor states, Dumnonia and Cornubia (Winchester 1990, 61–4).

In south-central England shires also have early origins, but not as independent polities. Instead, they began as administrative subdivisions of Wessex, the ancient kingdom of the West Saxons, and their names are derived from the royal estate centre from which they were governed: Wiltshire, for example – 'Wiltunscire' – is the 'shire governed from Wilton'. Different again are the shires of Midland England. These are comparatively late and obviously 'artificial' creations which bear little relationship to early tribal kingdoms or ancient administrative divisions. Most take their name from their present county town: Buckingham, Northampton, Cambridge, Bedford and the rest. These shires came into existence only in the later Saxon period, during or after the re-conquest of eastern England from the Danes by King Alfred's successors (Winchester 1990). They represent an attempt to impose the established West Saxon system of administration on what had formerly been the kingdom of Mercia and adjacent areas conquered from the Danes. They were created, that is, as part of the unification of England under a single West Saxon dynasty. Some of these new administrative divisions seem to have been formed by throwing together a number of ancient territories; but others appear to be almost entirely artificial in character, their boundaries cutting across earlier units, so that, for example, the tribal territory of the *Magonsætan* in the West Midlands was divided between Shropshire and Herefordshire (Winchester 1990, 63). Hertfordshire, as its name suggests, falls firmly into this third category, of artificial 'Mercian' shires. Unlike its neighbours to the south and east, Essex and Middlesex, it does not bear a name indicating a prior existence as an independent kingdom or the territory of an archaic folk-group. It is simply the shire governed from, and attached to, the town of Hertford.

Shires were subdivided into units called hundreds (in the south of England) and wapentakes (in the north). Like shires, these had both legal and fiscal functions. Each hundred had a court which met (originally in the open air) every four weeks, and which was responsible for pursuing criminals within its boundaries. Each hundred was responsible for the collection of the geld, the main tax in the tenth and eleventh centuries, which was levied on a unit of land called a *hide*. Originally there were notionally a hundred hides in each hundred. Hundreds were not, in themselves, very ancient. Like shires, they seem to have emerged in the tenth century, as part of the growing apparatus of the West Saxon state, and the details of their boundaries were often changed in subsequent centuries – sometimes fairly drastically, as we shall see in the case of Hertfordshire. Nevertheless, hundreds sometimes incorporated, and preserved, elements of the more ancient territories out of which they were created.

The lowest level of medieval local government and taxation was represented by the *vill*, or township, a unit which generally (although by no means invariably) developed into the civil parish of the nineteenth century. Vills had individual names – generally that of the most important settlement within them. They were not necessarily units of ownership; indeed, in the Middle Ages an individual vill might contain several separate estates or *manors*. Over most of southern England and Wales, but less frequently in the north, many vills were the secular equivalents of ecclesiastical parishes, and shared their boundaries.

The character of Hertfordshire

Hertfordshire is one of England's smallest counties: covering a mere 632 square miles (1,638 square kilometres), it constitutes little more than 1 per cent of the total land area of England and Wales. Bounded to the south by Middlesex, to the east by Essex, to the west by Buckinghamshire and to the north by Bedfordshire and Cambridgeshire, its boundaries are only loosely related to the broad sweeps of regional topography. It does not correspond neatly to any drainage catchment and, while its long northern boundary follows, very roughly, the line of the Chiltern escarpment, and much of its eastern the line of the Rivers Lea and Stort, its others seem largely arbitrary. In the words of the editors of the EPNS volume for the county, published in 1938, 'There can hardly be a county in southern England which is more obviously artificial than Hertfordshire' (Gover *et al.* 1938, xiii). Moreover, the county has an odd, arbitrary shape. It takes the form of a lozenge, with short sides orientated north-west–south-east and long sides running south-west–north-east; but this shape is distorted by three marked 'salients', or projections (Gardiner 1967, 1–4). Two extend northwards, beyond the Chiltern escarpment and out onto the Midland plain: one, in the north-west, contains the parishes of Tring and Puttenham; the other, in the area to the north of the town of Baldock, comprises Hinxworth, Ashwell, Radwell, Bygrave, Caldecote and Newnham. A third 'salient' projects southwards, deep into Middlesex – or at least it did so until boundary changes in 1974 modified the county's ancient topography. This contains the parishes of Arkley, Totteridge, Monken Hadley, East Barnet and Chipping Barnet. At the time of Domesday a number of other places, now in the county of Bedfordshire, were included in Hertfordshire: Barwythe, Caddington, Kensworth, Meppershall, Polehanger and Westoning. As these were detached at an early date I will say no more about them: my discussion will concern itself with the county as it was constituted immediately before the boundary changes of 1974, thus including the southern 'salient' embracing Totteridge and the rest, but excluding South Mimms, which was transferred from Middlesex at the same time (Figure 1).

In terms of landscape, Hertfordshire is a county without an identity – or at least, without a clearly defined character of its own. The phrase 'the Hertfordshire landscape' is almost entirely meaningless. The landscape of east Hertfordshire forms a continuation of that of the claylands of Suffolk and north Essex: the scenery is seamless, flowing across the county boundary without a break. To the west, the landscape of the Chilterns – a level plateau cut by deep valleys, with broad arable fields and beech woods – is the same in Hertfordshire as it is in south Buckinghamshire and south Oxfordshire. To the south lies London, outside the county and not a part of it, yet arguably the greatest single factor in its history. Certainly, it is the most important influence on the modern landscape, for much of the south of the county is engulfed in its outer suburbs, and once again this landscape – like the distinctive London Clay countryside which it has largely replaced – continues without interruption across the county boundary into Middlesex.

Yet it is also important to note that, to the north, Hertfordshire does not flow quite as easily into Cambridgeshire or Bedfordshire. Here there is more discontinuity. The Chiltern escarpment (and its more muted north-easterly continuation, often referred to as the East Anglian Heights) not only forms the approximate northern boundary of the county, but also constitutes a

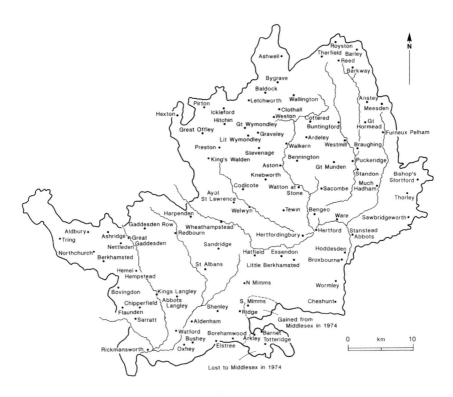

Figure 1. Hertfordshire: boundaries, boundary changes and principal places mentioned in the text.

fundamental divide in the cultural landscape of southern Britain, separating the metropolitan counties and the south-east sharply from the central and southern Midlands. The latter districts have a landscape dominated by nucleated villages, one in which outlying farms and hamlets are a subsidiary and often comparatively recent addition to the settlement pattern. The fields are generally rectilinear, defined by straight hedges of hawthorn or sloe which contain comparatively few other species. Most were created in the period between the seventeenth and nineteenth centuries when extensive, hedgeless 'open fields' were enclosed by the agreement of the principal landowners, or by parliamentary acts.

The two 'salients' of Hertfordshire which extend north of the escarpment lie within the Midland plain and the villages here had field systems, and settlement patterns, approximating to this Midland norm. Immediately to the south-east, on the chalk scarp of the Chiltern Hills, similar nucleated villages, with their attendant open fields, could also be found. But over most of the county the medieval landscape was very different. In many places open fields did exist but they were of complex, 'irregular' form, and usually intermixed with closes held in severalty: that is, with small fields which had always been enclosed by hedges and cultivated on an individual basis. Most of these open fields had disappeared before the start of the eighteenth century, although in a few places they lingered longer. The bulk of the county is thus characterised by fields which do not derive from planned post-medieval enclosure. Field patterns like this, in Hertfordshire as elsewhere, are usually associated with a fairly dispersed pattern of settlement, consisting of numerous isolated farms and hamlets as well as – and, on occasions, in place of – the compact villages which dominated the landscape of the Midland plain. The bulk of the county, to use Oliver Rackham's term, is thus characterised by *ancient countryside*:

> The land of hamlets, of medieval farms in hollows of the hills, of lonely moats
> in the clay-lands, of immense mileages of quiet minor roads, hollow-ways, and
> intricate footpaths; of irregularly shaped groves and thick hedges colourful
> with maple, dogwood, and spindle (Rackham 1976, 17).

As we shall see, different regions of the county display their own particular variants of this common theme. But, as already intimated, none are unique: all continue without the slightest interruption across the county boundary into Essex, Middlesex or Buckinghamshire. Moreover, such visual identity as the county ever possessed has been steadily eroded in the course of the twentieth century, not only by the steady outward expansion of London but also by the establishment of various New Towns and Garden Cities (Hatfield, Letchworth, Welwyn, Stevenage and Hemel Hempstead), and by the inexorable suburban growth around other long-established settlements. Except in the north-east, Hertfordshire's countryside now survives as pockets between various types of urban and suburban landscape.

Neither urbanisation nor the economic influence of London are new; and the core of most of Hertfordshire's principal urban settlements still usually retain something of the air of the market town, with a large medieval church, numerous timber-framed or Georgian buildings, and often a marketplace. St Albans, Hertford, Hitchin, Ware, Baldock, Royston, Bishop's Stortford, Hemel Hempstead and Berkhamsted – even, although to a more muted extent, Watford – still retain their historic cores. All of these towns had medieval origins. Some, as we shall see, first rose to prominence in Saxon times; some have yet more ancient roots.

The physical background

Physical geography underlies the historical development of Hertfordshire, a hidden hand moulding landscape and territorial organisation in innumerable, often complex, ways. True, there are dangers in taking too 'determinist' an approach in matters of human history: but the natural environment needs always to be considered first when attempting to understand the genesis of a region. Early societies were primarily agricultural and so the quality of the soil – the ease with which it could be worked, its fertility, the extent to which productivity might be limited by such factors as poor drainage – was of crucial importance. So too was the availability of a reliable supply of water. The natural environment provided, at the very least, a stage upon which the dramas of local and regional history could unfold.

Underlying the whole of the county, although often at considerable depth, are thick deposits of chalk. These form the northern part of a great trough of sediments, at the central and lowest point of which lies London and the River Thames (Gardiner 1967, 90–2; Sherlock 1962). The southern limits of this trough are formed by the North Downs; the northern by the Chiltern Hills and their north-easterly continuation, the East Anglian Heights. These ranges of hills also form part of a much longer chalk escarpment which continues all the way from Salisbury Plain north-eastwards to Cambridgeshire and beyond. In Hertfordshire, the highest point on this escarpment can be found a little to the west of Hastoe Farm in Tring, close to the county boundary with Buckinghamshire, where the ground reaches 804 feet (244 metres) OD. The Chiltern Hills *sensu stricto* – that is, the area to the west of the Hitchin Gap – are dissected by a number of deep, parallel valleys, trending north-west–south-east at right angles to the escarpment. Some of these contain streams and rivers, but many are dry. The largest of these break through the escarpment to the north, providing natural lines of communication through the hills. The higher ground between these deep gashes forms a slightly tilted plateau, or dipslope, falling in height from north-west to south-east (Figure 2).

The great basin of chalk was later filled with other deposits, of which the surviving remnants are principally of Palaeocene and Eocene date – that is, they were laid down between fifty and sixty million years ago (Gardiner 1967, 92; Curry 1992; Millward *et al.* 1987, 10–12). These, in turn, have been removed by erosion, and mainly survive in the south of the county: their northern boundary roughly follows a line running through

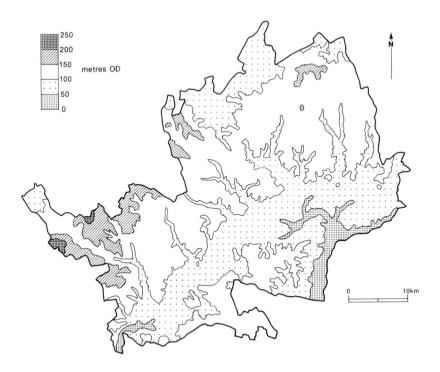

250
200
150   metres OD
100
50
0

Figure 2. Hertfordshire: relief.

Rickmansworth, Watford and Hatfield, then east of Hertford and west of Bishop's Stortford; although a series of outlying 'islands' shows how they originally extended further to the north, filling much of the basin. The lowest and oldest are the Woolwich and Reading Beds, often now known as the Lambeth Group – mottled, plastic clays and light sands, frequently containing masses of pebbles. The latter are sometimes cemented together by silica from percolating water, forming the hard conglomerate known for centuries as 'Hertfordshire Pudding Stone'. Lying above these deposits, and covering a much greater area of ground, is the London Clay, a thick blue clay weathering on exposure to a dull brown (Thomasson 1969; Millward *et al.* 1987, 14; Curry 1992).

Except in this southern area the underlying 'solid' geology of the county – the Chalk and Palaeocene/Eocene deposits – is mostly obscured by thinner and later materials, 'drift' deposits which are the direct or indirect results of the successive glaciations which have affected Britain over the last million years (Gardiner 1967, 93–5; Sherlock 1962, 26–37). Capping the London Clay in

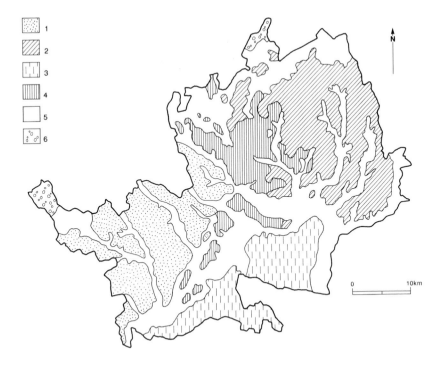

Figure 3. Hertfordshire: soils. Key: 1. Leached, moderately pervious soils of the Chiltern Dipslope (Batcombe, Marlow and Sonning Associations); 2. soils formed in chalky boulder clay (Hanslope Association); 3. poorly draining and infertile soils formed in London Clay; 4. leached and waterlogged soils of the Hornbeam Associations; 5. well-drained soils formed in chalk, head or gravel; 6. clay soils of the Midland vales.

places are spreads of sands and pebble gravels, laid down in Quaternary times, which occupy tracts of the higher ground in the south of the county, from Oxhey through to Hertford Heath. In the north-west of the county the chalk is obscured by the 'clay-with-flints' and 'pebbly clay': the former a fairly permeable clay containing large numbers of flint pebbles, the latter a more complex mixture of stony clays, sands and gravels. Once thought to be the insoluble residue left behind by the weathering and solution of huge depths of chalk, these two formations are now generally regarded as the remains of a more diverse range of parent materials, especially the Palaeocene and Eocene deposits, which have otherwise (as already noted) been erased from the central and northern parts of the county. In the north-east, in contrast, the chalk is largely blanketed beneath a rather different material – the so-called boulder clay, a deposit left behind by glaciers moving across the county 400,000 years ago. Because the ice passed over the Wolds of Lincolnshire and Yorkshire (and over associated deposits in the basin of the North Sea) during its journey south, these clays generally contain fragments of chalk and thus give rise to calcareous and rather fertile soils, except along the western edge of the plateau, in the country between Stevenage and Welwyn, where (as we shall see) less fertile, more acidic soils occur (Gardiner 1967, 98).

Glacial action had other effects on the geology of Hertfordshire. The streams and meltwaters running out from the ice fronts transported large quantities of sand and gravels that were deposited in the valleys running through the Chiltern Hills and, in particular, in a broad lowland belt of country – the Vale of St Albans – which runs east–west through the centre of the county, along the northern fringes of the London Clay and Reading Beds. In the Chilterns, permafrost conditions caused solifluxion to occur: the ground surface became waterlogged during the summer months because the subsoil was permanently frozen, and soil flowed down slopes, scouring out deep steep-sided valleys, to be redeposited on lower ground as a material generally described by geologists as 'head' (Gardiner 1967, 96–7).

The relationship between solid geology and drift geology is complicated by the action of the county's rivers, which have in many places cut valleys through the latter to expose the former in narrow strips. Overwhelmingly the flow of Hertfordshire's rivers is with the dip of the chalk, from north-west to south-east, the only real exceptions being in the far north of the county, where the chalk escarpment, and the two 'salients' projecting beyond it, are drained by rivers which either flow into the Thames via the Thame or (in the vicinity of Hitchin) flow northwards into the Ouse, and eventually into the Wash. The vast majority of the county, however, drains into the Thames via two south-flowing rivers, the Colne and the Lea (Gardiner 1967, 100–3).

The former river rises in the London Clay uplands but flows for most of its course through the Vale of St Albans. It is fed largely from streams flowing off the Chilterns: the River Chess has its source outside the county, near Chesham, and forms for only a limited distance the county boundary with Buckinghamshire before joining the Colne at Croxley Green, between Watford and Rickmansworth; the Bulbourne, which has an ill-defined source somewhere near Tring Station, joins the Gade at Two Waters near Hemel Hempstead; the Gade itself rises near Studham (in Bedfordshire) and flows via Gaddesden, Hemel Hempstead and Cashiobury to Croxley Green; and, lastly, the River Ver has its source at Kenworth Lynch in Bedfordshire and,

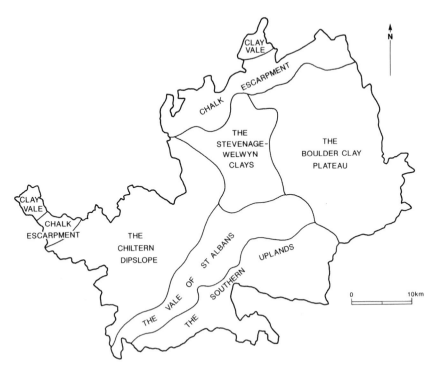

Figure 4. Hertfordshire: principal landscape regions as discussed in the text.

flowing along one of the deep Chiltern valleys, passes St Albans and enters the Colne near Bricket Wood station.

The Lea drains the eastern side of the county and, in contrast to the Colne, takes its waters largely from the boulder clays of the north-east (although it its own headwaters lie in the Chilterns, and its tributary the River Mimram takes most of its water from the Chiltern dipslope). Its principal tributaries do not have single, if shifting, sources like the Chiltern rivers. In this watery land, numerous minor watercourses, taking the water from innumerable field ditches, gradually join to form named rivers: from west to east, the Mimram; the Beane (with its tributary the Old Bourne); the Rib (with its tributary the Quin); the Ash; and the Stort (Gardiner 1967, 102–3).

This rather simple account of Hertfordshire's topography helps us to define a number of broad zones which together account for the majority of the county's land area (Figure 4). The first of these is the *Boulder Clay Plateau* in the north-east, which occupies around a quarter of the area of the county and constitutes in essence the dissected dipslope of the East

Anglian Heights. In the larger valleys – which generally trend north–south – the soils are fairly freely draining because the underlying chalk is exposed, or mixed with boulder clay to produce a relatively light loam, while the gradient allows for easy removal of surface water. On the level interfluves between, in contrast, the soils are heavier and poorly draining. It is important to emphasise, however, that in most cases these interfluves, while running for long distances north–south, are not very wide: that between the valleys of the Rib and the Ash, for example, forms a long thin finger of higher ground which is nowhere more than three kilometres in width despite extending for nearly twenty kilometres all the way from Meesden to Ware. In many places, therefore – as, for example, around the Mundens – the appearance of the landscape is less that of a plateau cut by valleys, more that of gently rolling countryside. Most of the soils in this region, occupying the sloping sides of valleys, can thus be cultivated with the kind of technology available from later prehistoric times, and amply repay the effort. By the end of the Iron Age the area was already quite densely settled and in later Saxon times (to judge from the information in Domesday Book) it carried a population density above average for England, and certainly much higher than in other parts of the county. The settlement pattern today features a mixture of loosely nucleated villages, often straggling beside the roads which run along the valley floors, hamlets, which often cluster around the small greens from which they take their names, and isolated farms, often moated. Numerous ponds, streams and moats testify to the poorly draining nature of the more level areas of plateau clay. This is the most rural region of Hertfordshire: the countryside is still extremely attractive, despite the impact of intensive farming in this overwhelmingly arable district, the proximity of major towns such as Stevenage or Hertford, the presence of major roads and the noise of aircraft heading for Stansted airport, just across the county boundary in Essex.

A second main region, that of the *Chiltern Dipslope*, occupies the western quarter of the county (Figure 4). Here, too, the terrain takes the form of a low tilted plateau dissected by a number of valleys; and, once again, the key to the landscape is the contrast between valleys and interfluves. The steep-sided valleys contain light, easily worked soils formed in chalk, gravel and 'head'. The plateaux between are blanketed with clay-with-flints and pebbly clay, interspersed in places with spreads of gravel, which give rise to soils which are moderately leached and acid. It is possible that the character of these upland soils has changed over time: there is evidence to suggest that large areas of the uplands were originally covered with a thin layer of *loess*, wind-blown material deposited during the glaciations, which provided more fertile soils (Catt 1978; Holgate 1995, 13). Traces of such deposits remain in places; but if they were once widespread, they were almost certainly eroded by agriculture at an early date, and by later prehistory had probably ceased to be a major factor in the development of settlement.

Although they are technically described as 'clays', the deposits blanketing the uplands are more porous than the boulder clays in the east of the county, and there are relatively few ponds or streams on the uplands. In addition, the interfluves between the principal valleys are often very wide. That between the Gade and the Ver, for example, is generally between five and six kilometres across; that between the Gade and the Chess reaches eight kilometres. This, then, is a landscape in which major valleys – well-watered, and with easily farmed soils – are separated by wide tracts of relatively waterless, relatively infertile land. Not surprisingly, most of the major nucleations of settlement were, and are, to be found within the principal valleys, with more dispersed settlement strung across the interfluves between. The latter includes, as in the boulder-clay region of the north-east, not only isolated farms but also loose agglomerations of farms and cottages, often clustered around greens and commons: good examples include Chipperfield Common and Sarratt Green.

Less clearly defined, and often neglected altogether in discussions of the county's topography, is an area sandwiched between the two distinct regions discussed above. In the country around Stevenage and Knebworth, extending westwards as far as Kimpton, southwards to Welwyn and northwards almost to Hitchin, is a region characterised by soils, derived in part from the clay-with-flints and in part from the boulder clay, which are more acidic than those in the region to the east and less well drained than those of the Chilterns to the west: soils of the Hornbeam 2 and Hornbeam 3 Associations, to use the jargon of the Soil Survey (Hodge *et al.* 1984, 219–25). This, as we shall see, is an important district, with its own particular history. Although by the time of Domesday it was nearly as well cultivated as the main area of the Boulder Clay Plateau to the east – and more densely populated than the Chiltern Dipslope region to the west – in earlier times it appears to have been occupied by extensive tracts of woodland and waste, and even today is still noticeably well-wooded

(Gardiner 1967; Hodge *et al.* 1984, 221). The district has no name, official or otherwise: in the chapters that follow I will refer to it, for convenience, as the *Stevenage–Welwyn Clays* (Figure 4). This district is crossed by the Hitchin Gap, which forms the technical dividing line between the Chilterns proper and the East Anglian Heights. It is a major line of communication which is followed by both the main railway line from London to Peterborough, York and beyond, and by the Great North Road.

The last main topographic region comprises the extreme south of Hertfordshire and extends into the old county of Middlesex: this I shall refer to as the *Southern Uplands* (Figure 4). Here the main features of the landscape derive from Palaeocene and Eocene deposits – London Clay, Woolwich and Reading Beds (Lambeth Group) – although also from the Quaternary Pebble Gravels. As already noted, the latter occur in patches on the higher ground, overlying the London Clay which occupies the majority of the region (Gardiner 1967, 99). This in turn overlies the Reading Beds, which outcrop only in a relatively thin band on the lower ground, along the northern and eastern fringes of the region, in the Vale of St Albans and the valleys of the Lea and Colne. The London Clay is highly impervious and, as a result, this is a district of abundant surface water; there are numerous ponds, and many streams, which sometimes disappear suddenly where the clay has been dissolved and washed down into the underlying Upper Chalk, forming a 'swallow hole'. This combination of acid, pebbly gravels and waterlogged acid clays ensured that the Southern Uplands were not an area much favoured for early agriculture. In spite of widespread urbanisation in the course of the twentieth century, fragments of its rural landscape still survive, forming another distinctive variant of 'ancient countryside', with patches of woodland, anciently enclosed fields and a settlement pattern which features some nucleated settlements, numerous isolated farms and various forms of irregular hamlet. Until the early nineteenth century extensive tracts of common and heath, including Cheshunt Common, Northaw Common and Bushey Heath, survived on the higher ground.

These four main topographic zones together account for the majority of the county's land area. But a number of other regions, smaller in area yet of immense importance in the early history of the county, need to be mentioned. These are areas of light, well-drained soil more extensive than the clay-free valleys already discussed. Firstly, the Southern Uplands are divided from the other regions by the *Vale of St Albans*, which runs from Watford in the south-west to Hertford in the east (Figure 4). The western section of this broad, low-lying region contains the valleys of the River Colne and the lower Ver; the eastern, that of the middle reaches of the River Lea. The Vale was the original course of the Thames before that river was diverted south in glacial times, and has been aptly described as a 'wide trough scoured out of the chalk by running waters ages ago and used later by nature as a sort of rubbish or detritus tip' (Gardiner 1967, 100). This rubbish included, crucially, extensive spreads of freely draining sands and gravels, as well as patches of brickearth (relatively light and fertile clays): the chalk itself is also exposed in places. The Vale formed an important area of early settlement in the county, and many of the county's historic towns – St Albans, Hatfield, Welwyn, Hertford and Ware – are found within or beside it. It also constitutes a kind of nodal area into which other valleys flow, most notably those of the Ver, the upper Lea, the Beane, the Mimram and the Rib.

A second extensive area of clay-free terrain exists in the north of the county, almost completely separated from the Vale and its associated valleys by clay-covered uplands. The Chiltern escarpment between Hitchin and Royston, and the light free-draining deposits at its base – the Vale of Baldock or Wringtail, and the northern part of the Hitchin Gap – together form a district of moderately fertile and easily worked soils, watered by a number of streams which flow northwards onto the clay vale which largely lies beyond the county boundary. Another string of major towns is today associated with this area of light soil: Hitchin, Baldock, and Royston (together with that great addition of the twentieth century, the Garden City of Letchworth). To the south-west of Hitchin the county boundary swings south of the Chiltern escarpment and this strip of amenable soils therefore lies outside the county, within Bedfordshire and Buckinghamshire, except for a small area in Hertfordshire's north-western 'salient', to the north-west of Berkhamsted (Figure 4). As we shall see, both the main scarp zone and this smaller, detached area were key areas for early settlement.

Lastly, attention must be drawn to two tiny parts of the county comprising the far northern 'tips' of the two 'salients'. These extend beyond the chalk escarpment out onto the level plain to the north, which is occupied by poorly draining, tenacious Gault clay. Here, Hertfordshire just reaches into the clay vales of the Midland counties.

It might be useful at this point to summarise the foregoing discussion. The bulk of the county is covered by clay soils which are, to varying extents,

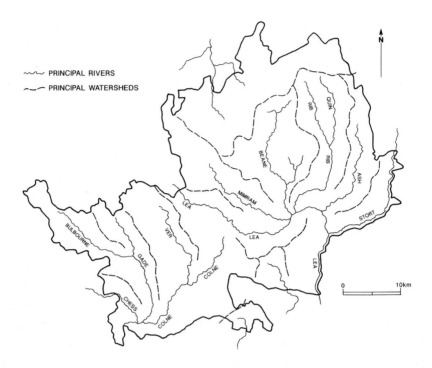

Figure 5. Hertfordshire: principal rivers and watersheds.

poorly draining and were unsuitable for early agriculture. But areas of lighter, better-drained soil also occur, both as ribbons of lower ground within the main clay areas, and as larger blocks – the Vale of St Albans, and the chalk escarpment in the north and north-west (Figures 3 and 4). Most are associated with good supplies of running water and thus, as we shall see, formed the primary areas of early settlement. The various clay uplands which lie between them display considerable variation. The Boulder Clay Plateau is well dissected; its soils are comparatively easy to cultivate and highly fertile. Moreover, settlements can be established in many places with relative ease owing to the perched water table found where the plateau is most level. The clay-with-flints and pebbly clay on the Chiltern Dipslope, in contrast, are relatively easy to cultivate but – once any overlying deposits of *loess* had been removed – were only moderately fertile, while the absence of reliable water supplies away from the principal valleys would always act as a disincentive to the spread of settlement. Lastly, the Southern Uplands and to a lesser extent the Stevenage–Welwyn Clays are characterised by soils which are both difficult to cultivate *and* comparatively infertile. These were districts in which, for the most part, arable cultivation took second place to grazing and wood production in prehistoric and early historic times, and which, as we shall see, were often exploited by communities living at some distance, in more favoured zones.

River and wold

The strong topographic contrast encountered over much of the county – between valley areas, well-watered yet with well-drained soils, and higher, clay-covered ground – is found across much of England, and its significance in English history has been discussed by a number of historians, especially those of the 'Leicester School' (Everitt 1977; 1979; Phythian-Adams 1987; 1993). They have argued that the distinction between 'river and wold', or valley and watershed, was vital not only in the development of settlement, but also in that of early communities and territorial patterns (Figure 5). According to this model, the earliest settlements in England tended to be located in the principal river valleys. When population levels were low the intervening uplands (or 'wolds') were used for grazing and pannage (i.e. the practice of grazing pigs on acorns, nuts and other woodland resources) and exploited for wood and timber from subsidiary settlements which were often only seasonally occupied. Only as population levels rose would such settlements become permanent, as land came to be used more intensively. But these places would nevertheless often remain part of valley-based territories, and even when sundered from them some traces of earlier dependence might often survive in the form of archaic administrative or ecclesiastical arrangements. Moreover, because the interfluves continued to be comparatively sparsely settled compared with the valleys, and because the 'primary' settlements often developed as administrative centres and market places, the inhabitants of a valley – or system of valleys – tended to interact with each other to a greater extent than they did with people in neighbouring, but separate, river systems. Drainage systems, in other works, were not simply topographic entities. They often approximated to social ones.

This is only a model – a conceptual structure, 'good to think with' – but it is one which I shall employ on a number of occasions in this volume. However, it is a model which, especially in the case of Hertfordshire, has a number of limitations in practice. Although early patterns of social contact were strongly influenced by the configuration of the natural topography, other factors might also be important, overriding the dictates of valley and watershed. In particular, while many of the main communication routes within the county – both today, and throughout recorded history – followed the major valleys or the light soils of the Chiltern escarpment, others cut right across the grain of the topography: most notably, the Roman military road called Watling Street, established in the middle of the first century AD. Entering the county from the north, this initially follows – sensibly – the line of the Ver valley. But to the south of St Albans it strikes off bravely against the topography, cutting across the Southern Uplands *en route* for London. Other roads in the south of the county, probably of some antiquity, do likewise. What is now the A411, for example – the Sparrow's Herne Turnpike in the eighteenth century – passes over the high, windswept ground of Bushey Heath, an area notorious for highwaymen in the eighteenth century. The pattern of major valleys in the centre and west of the county tends to funnel roads in the general direction of London, but as they proceed southwards the Colne swerves to the west, and they are forced to break through the constraints of topography. This is one of many ways in which the presence of London has had a determining effect on the development of Hertfordshire.

It is also important to emphasise that it was not only at a local level that patterns of cultural and social identity, and the chronology of settlement and colonisation, were moulded by the structures of physical geography. At a much larger scale, situations in which contact and communication between individuals and groups of people was easy and regular tended to engender if not a measure of social or political identity then at least some sharing of beliefs, language and material culture. Where contact was restricted, in contrast, there was more divergence in social and cultural development. Entire river systems and drainage basins might thus constitute, albeit in certain periods more than others, 'cultural provinces' within which ideas, styles and fashions were exchanged with relative ease from group to group, person to person. Conversely, the peripheries of river catchments would often be at the margins of social and political territories, the last areas to be settled and cleared, and might always remains sparsely settled territory, almost regardless of the character of the local soils. The concepts of 'river and wold', in other words, operated at a regional and national, as well as at a local, level: and in this context it is useful to consider Hertfordshire's position in terms of the great river systems of England.

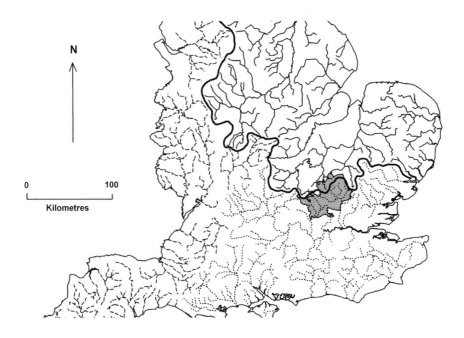

Figure 6. Hertfordshire's location with respect to the three drainage 'provinces' of England (comprising rivers draining into the North Sea, the Thames and Channel, and the Irish Sea/Atlantic respectively): the heavy line represents the watershed between the first of these, and the second and third.

In broad terms, England can be divided into three great drainage 'provinces', whose waters make their way into the North Sea, the Irish Sea, and the Channel and the Thames estuary respectively (Figure 6). The watersheds defining their boundaries are varied. Sometimes they correspond with dramatic ranges of hills, obvious barriers to contact and communication; sometimes to more muted topographic incidents. Hertfordshire, with its principal rivers draining south to the Thames, lies largely within the 'Channel Province'. Only its northern extremities – the chalk escarpment, and the main northern 'salient' containing Ashwell and its neighbours – extend over the watershed into the 'North Sea Province'. Such a location hints that the northern sections of the county, at least, were always in some senses marginal: and it is possible that the well-wooded nature of the Chiltern dipslope in early historic times, and of the high ground running along the top of the Chilterns and the East Anglian Heights, reflects this peripheral character, on the margins between the Thames basin and the

Midlands, as much as any more local characteristics of soils and topography. Certainly, the *cultural* contrasts between the two provinces, and Hertfordshire's position relative to them both, shows up sharply – as we shall see – in certain periods of history, and especially in the immediate post-Roman centuries.

Chapter 2
Before the Saxons

The earliest settlement

Much about the character of early prehistoric settlement in Hertfordshire remains obscure. In part this is because in many parts of the county (especially in the south and west) the potential for fieldwalking – the systematic examination of the ploughsoil for the spreads of pottery and other debris indicating the location of settlements – is limited by the extent of urban development, and by the fact that much of what open land there is lies under permanent pasture. Moreover, some of the most important areas for early settlement in the county – especially in the Vale of St Albans – have experienced sand and gravel extraction on a massive scale in the past, leading to the wholesale destruction, often completely unrecorded, of archaeological sites. Similar factors, coupled with the unresponsive nature of the clay soils which cover much of the county, also mean that the contribution made by aerial photography to our understanding of Hertfordshire's past is often limited. Nevertheless, a number of important fieldwalking surveys have been carried out and a surprising number of cropmarks and soilmarks have been plotted in the county, the latter partly as a result of the recent National Mapping Programme supported by English Heritage. Moreover, changes in planning legislation in the 1990s – the advent of 'PPG16' – have ensured that all major building and road-construction projects over the last decade and a half have been preceded or accompanied by archaeological reconnaissance, and often by large-scale excavation. In short, although the spatial distribution of our archaeological knowledge is uneven, the broad lines of the development of early settlement within the county are comparatively clear.

The earliest settlers in Hertfordshire were hunter-gatherers who have left
no real above-ground traces and no durable monuments. A scatter of sites
are known from the Palaeolithic – the immense period of time leading up to
the end of the final glaciation some 12,000 years ago (Holgate 1995, 5–8;
Roe 1981, 184–200). At Gaddesden Row, on the Chiltern Dipslope north of
Hemel Hempstead, an important Lower Palaeolithic site discovered at the
end of the last century produced more than fifty hand axes as well as many
other flake tools, all of flint. But most known sites are in the principal river
valleys. In particular, large numbers of Lower Palaeolithic finds have been
made from the Colne valley near Rickmansworth (at Croxley Green and Mill
End). Although the tools had been transported from their original site by
subsequent movements of ice, they had probably not travelled far and
presumably came from hunting sites positioned beside river channels (Roe
1981, 176–7, 189). A number of Upper Palaeolithic sites have also been
recovered, most notably at Broxbourne, again apparently representing
hunting sites beside water – in this case, the River Lea (Jacobi 1980, 18–19;
Holgate 1995, 6–7).

With the end of the glaciations – or, perhaps more accurately, with the
start of the present interglacial period – the quantity of known settlement
sites increases significantly. A number of early Mesolithic sites are known,
principally from the valleys of the Colne and Lea, representing waterside
hunting camps existing within an environment of birch and pine woodland
(Holgate 1995, 8). Many more examples are known from the later
Mesolithic, the period after c.6500 BC when England had become cut off
from the European mainland and denser deciduous forest dominated the
landscape. This was a period in which population density in England as a
whole appears to have been increasing, leading to the more intensive
exploitation of more restricted territories than previously (Jacobi 1978;
Darvill 1996, 43–7). Once again, most known sites in Hertfordshire are from
river valleys, although they are now more numerous, and more widespread,
than in earlier periods. They are found higher up the valleys of the Lea and
Colne, and also in the valleys of the latter's tributaries: in Robin Holgate's
view, 'almost the entire lengths of these valleys were exploited during the
later Mesolithic period' (Holgate 1995, 9). A few sites even appear away
from the rivers, on the dipslope of the Chilterns, especially around the
headwaters of the River Lea, where they perhaps represent specialised
stations for the exploitation of particular resources (Holgate 1995, 8–10;

Holgate 1988, 376). Some sites from this period have been excavated. That at Tolpits Lane, Moor Park, close to the River Colne, produced more than 2,000 flints and bones from wild cattle and deer, presumably the principal quarry of the camp's inhabitants (Holgate 1988, 216). At The Grove, in the valley of the Gade to the north of Watford, scatters of tools, a possible hearth and quantities of deer and cattle bones were recovered from various places during extensive excavations of a complex multi-period site. The excavator noted that such finds, although quite sparse, fitted in well with the emerging picture for the local Mesolithic 'of small communities of well-organised hunter-gatherers making expert use of a resource-rich landscape' (Le Quesne *et al.* 2001). We can indeed envisage communities of hunter-gatherers exploiting defined territories, and doubtless with a keen awareness of landscape and topography; and, while we can know nothing for certain about the configuration of these territories, the distribution of known settlements strongly suggests they were based on river valleys.

The early fourth millennium BC was a period of radical social and economic change in England: communities began to herd livestock and to some extent cultivate the land, as well as hunting and gathering their food. This Neolithic period has produced a number of sites in the county. Some were permanently occupied settlements, others places where specific tasks (especially tool production) took place. They have left fairly ephemeral traces. Many have been discovered by chance, during the excavation of later settlements – which suggests that the known sites represent the tip of a much larger iceberg. At Gorhambury, near St Albans, for example, excavation of the Roman villa revealed a hitherto unsuspected early Neolithic site consisting of two rectangular structures defined by slots and gullies cut into the subsoil (Neal *et al.* 1990). Similarly, at Blackhorse Road in Letchworth, excavations of a Romano-British settlement revealed ten pits, a post-hole and a gully which produced sherds of late Neolithic Peterborough Ware, Grooved Ware and Beaker pottery (Moss Eccardt 1988). Other examples of such unintentional discovery include Foxholes Farm near Hertford (Partridge 1989, 8) and Old Parkbury in St Albans (Holgate 1995, 12). More extensive remains, in the form of pits, areas of burning and post-holes defining lengths of fencing and roofed structures, were recovered during the excavations at The Grove (Le Quesne *et al.* 2001). Sites of Neolithic date have also been recovered during some of the fieldwalking surveys which have taken place in the county. In the south-west, in the Chess valley, large numbers of stray flints and many dense concentrations of flintwork attest to considerable activity, although some of these may date to a slightly later period, the early Bronze Age (Stainton 1995, 126–8).

Sites of both early and late Neolithic date occur in locations away from the main rivers, especially on the clay-with-flints of the Chiltern dipslope: examples include the remains discovered during the construction of the A41 bypass at Oakwood, south-west of Berkhamsted (MacDonald 1995, 122). It is possible that early farmers exploited deposits of *loess* soils in the Chilterns, leading to their gradual erosion and deterioration (Catt 1978). But, judging from the available evidence, it seems that the main areas of settlement – and the cores of social territories – remained in the principal river valleys, and on other areas of light calcareous soil such as the Chiltern escarpment: the areas most amenable to farming communities with a comparatively simple technology. Not that all Neolithic sites were necessarily involved in farming: hunting and gathering continued to play a significant role in the economy, and at Blackhorse Road, Letchworth, the assemblage of animal bones recovered included not only domesticates – cattle, pig and sheep/goat – but also wild cattle and red deer (Moss Eccardt 1988).

There is little doubt that the more sophisticated economy and technology of Neolithic times were able to sustain a significantly higher population than was the case in previous periods. It is partly for this reason that Neolithic communities, unlike their predecessors, were able to erect a range of ceremonial or 'ritual' monuments substantial enough to survive to the present. Hertfordshire does not score well in this respect, however. It has nothing to compare with the great monuments of Wessex, such as Avebury or Silbury Hill. The county still has only one certain example of a 'causewayed enclosure' – a form of early Neolithic monument consisting of an area defined by lengths of intermittent ditch, which seem to have functioned primarily as seasonal meeting places. This is at Sawbridgeworth, straddling the county boundary with Essex, and does not survive as an upstanding earthwork but was revealed from the air as a cropmark (Wilson 1975, 183). Similarly, there is only one certain example of that other characteristic early Neolithic monument the long barrow – rectangular mounds of earth covering groups of disarticulated internments – within the county. This is on Therfield Heath, near Royston (HER 40; Holgate 1995, 10). What is probably the remains of another stands on Pegsdon Common, on the county boundary with Bedfordshire in the west of Pirton parish (HER 7312); while three others may be indicated by cropmarks, two near Ashwell and one at Hitchin (HER 7883, 1698, and 6161; two other possible examples are less convincing). Nor is the county well endowed with monuments from later Neolithic times, a period which saw the replacement of causewayed enclosures by monuments called henges – enclosures defined by a substantial earthwork bank and ditch continuous except for entrances. One example exists just over the county boundary into Bedfordshire, at Walud's Bank in Luton (and even this is atypical in having the ditch outside, rather than inside, the enclosing bank); another probable example has been suggested, as a denuded earthwork, between Baldock and Weston (HER 2583: TL250319). Moreover, no certain examples of cursus – long, cigar-shaped enclosures, defined by banks and ditches – have yet come to light in the county, although one possible example has been detected as a cropmark near Sandon (HER 7718), and two perhaps related monuments have been discovered through excavations: the curious arrangement of forty parallel ditches, ranged roughly east–west, found during the construction of the A41 bypass at Bottom House Lane near Northchurch on a terrace above the Bulbourne valley; and the parallel ditches excavated in 1963 at Norton Road, Baldock (MacDonald 1995, 121; HER 9449). There seems little doubt that more monuments of Neolithic date, long levelled by later agriculture, will come to light in future years. Nevertheless, Hertfordshire was clearly an area in which few large monuments were erected. This almost certainly reflects the fact that, compared with some other areas of England (such as Wiltshire), the region had a relatively low population density in this period, presumably because of the heavy and/or poorly draining nature of most of its soils.

The comparatively meagre evidence we have for settlement in the early Bronze Age – roughly, the period from *c.*2300 to *c.*1700 BC – seems to suggest that population levels in the county remained relatively low. This may, however, be a misleading impression, resulting from the low visibility of the relevant archaeological material in field surveys: for if we see little trace of the living in this period, we find ample signs of the dead. Large numbers of round barrows – characteristic burial mounds of the period, raised (usually) above single interments – are known from the county. Most survive not as upstanding monuments, but as the distinctive cropmarks called 'ring-ditches' – circular features representing the filled ditches which once surrounded the levelled monument, clearly visible (in the right conditions) from the air. Important concentrations of upstanding barrows

Figure 7. Therfield Heath barrow cemetery, near Royston, from the air. The cemetery, on the crest of the chalk escarpment of the East Anglian Heights, includes Hertfordshire's best-preserved long barrow, as well as several round barrows (by courtesy of English Heritage).

survive on Therfield Heath near Royston (Figure 7), and in general the majority of known sites are on the light soils of the Chilterns and the East Anglian Heights.

The sparse evidence for settlement in Hertfordshire in the Neolithic and early Bronze Age means that we can say little with any confidence about the main theme of this book, the development of territorial organisation. Some hints may, however, be provided by the distribution of the various kinds of 'ceremonial' monument briefly described above. It has been suggested by a number of archaeologists, working elsewhere in the country, that some of these features may have been erected on the margins of social territories (Spratt 1989). Both long and round barrows may have been prominently placed in peripheral positions in order to legitimate claims to land by communities or their elites, by marking the boundaries of their territories with the 'bones of the ancestors'. Burial grounds may also have occupied marginal locations for religious reasons, the dead being most fittingly and safely placed at a suitable distance from the principal abodes of the living, perhaps in areas of upland grazing which were visited and occupied only on a sporadic or

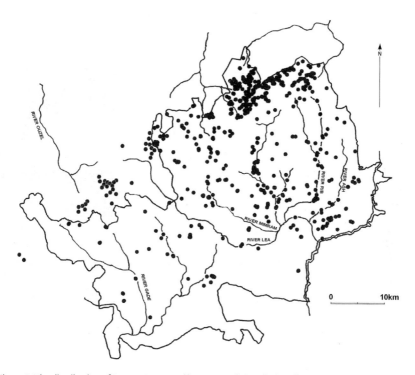

Figure 8. The distribution of Bronze Age round barrows and ring-ditches (from HER and Holgate 1995).

seasonal basis: 'where the living resided and where the dead reposed might be two completely different areas' (Parker Pearson 1993, 91). Other types of monument may also have been erected on boundary zones, but for different reasons. Causewayed enclosures and henges may have served as points of contact and exchange between neighbouring social groups, and would thus have been erected where the natural topography provided a limited area of contact within what was otherwise a zone of separation.

The distribution of Hertfordshire's Bronze Age round barrows (Figure 8) is only partially informative when considered in these terms. The main concentrations lie in a band along the Chiltern Hills, close to the watershed running along their crest, with particular concentrations around the headwaters of the River Lea, in the vicinity of Hexton, Lilley and Little Offley; in the area to the south of Letchworth, close to the headwaters of the Purwell; and (the largest) in the area around Royston. At the centre of the first and last of these clusters stand probable or certain Neolithic long barrows, at Pegsdon and Therfield Heath, while slightly off-centre of the second is the cropmark of

Figure 9. Bronze Age round barrows on Chipperfield Common stand close to the watershed between the rivers Gade and Chess.

a probable long barrow at Hitchin; this all suggests some continuity of ritual geography over a very long period of time. There is *some* indication that these clusters mark significant boundary zones between drainage systems north and south of the Chiltern escarpment. The first concentration thus lies in the interfluve zone between the Ivel and the Lea; the second in that between the Hiz/Purwell and the various western tributaries of the Beane; and the third between the drainage basin of the Cam and those of Rib, Quin and upper Beane. They occupy, moreover, places where the interfluves are comparatively narrow – and where we might expect competition for upland grazing, or other forms of interaction, between neighbouring communities to have been most intense. This said, many barrows and ring-ditches are known from low-lying, valley sites: while they may sometimes have been erected in liminal zones, there were clearly many exceptions. Moreover, the distribution of known barrow sites in the Chilterns has only a tangential relationship with their original distribution. Long-levelled barrows are revealed as cropmarks only where the soils are freely draining. Where the chalk is overlain with clay-with-flints, pebbly clay or boulder clay such sites are unlikely to be revealed in this way. Indeed, the general paucity of known barrow sites from elsewhere in the county – where exposures of light soil are more limited – may in part be due to such factors, rather than to a real absence of such monuments in the past. Nevertheless, it is noteworthy that the few examples of barrows which *are* known from such places are also located – definitely, almost emphatically – on watersheds. The two round barrows on Chipperfield Common (Figure 9: HER 4261 and 4290) thus stand almost exactly on the watershed between the Rivers Gade and Chess, which lie three kilometres to the east and south-west respectively – a location most unlikely to be coincidental. Some eight kilometres to the north-east, engulfed now in the outskirts of Hemel Hempstead, another barrow (HER 54) stands on the precise line of the watershed between the Gade and the Ver. Field names apparently indicating long-lost barrow sites in this district hint at a similar pattern. Money Hill, a common term for a barrow, appears as a field name on the 1842 tithe award map for Watford (HALS DSA4/111/2; HALS 111/1–1/6/8). The field in question occupies a position at TQ097995, just to the north-west of Gammons Farm (near what is now Gammons Farm School), almost exactly on the watershed between the Colne and the Gade.

Other kinds of early monument might, as already noted, have served as meeting places between neighbouring groups, where topography encouraged a measure of contact as well as separation. It is in this context that we might usefully consider the location of the causewayed enclosure at Sawbridgeworth, on river gravels slightly above the flood plain of the Stort. That river is a substantial watercourse with a wide and originally marshy valley which is likely to have formed a significant barrier to communication, and thus a territorial boundary, between communities occupying the amenable soils of the opposing valley sides. In a similar way, the Walud's Bank henge is located suggestively close to the only point in the Chilterns for many miles where well-watered valleys (of the north-flowing Flitt and the south-flowing Lea) approach close to each other from either side of the waterless scarp, another location forming a likely point of contact between neighbouring social groups.

Late prehistoric expansion

In the later Bronze Age and the Iron Age farms and fields become more visible in the archaeological record. Before this, it is ceremonial monuments and activities which are most obvious: settlements have generally left only ephemeral traces and most land appears to have been unbounded. Later prehistory was also a time in which the population continued to increase, and settlement appears to have expanded into new areas. But expansion and growth were not continuous everywhere throughout this long period. There is evidence, for example, for some decline and retrenchment (most notably on the Chiltern dipslope) in the middle of the first millennium from *c.*600 BC to *c.*300 BC (Le Quesne *et al.* 2001). Important insights into the development of the landscape in this period comes from the excavations carried out in the late 1990s by Charles Le Quesne at The Grove, in the Gade valley just to the north of Watford (Le Quesne *et al.* 2001). Here, the evidence for the later Bronze Age included traces of two roundhouses located on the edge of the plateau above the valley and a series of post alignments and boundary ditches marking their associated fields. By the Middle Iron Age a more pastoral landscape may be indicated by the construction of two large enclosures, probably for stock. But this was followed by the layout of further fields, some on the same orientation as the late Bronze Age boundaries, in the later Iron Age. These were organised in the distinctive brickwork pattern which archaeologists often describe as 'co-axial'. Numerous other settlements of late Bronze Age and early/middle Iron Age date have been located within and, in particular, immediately above the valley of the Gade, including those at Leavesden (HER 10048), Gadebridge Road in Hemel Hempstead (HER 7981) and a whole string of sites discovered on the line of the King's Langley–Berkhamsted A41 bypass, such as those at Rucklers Lane in King's Langley (HER 9959) and Crawleys Lane in Berkhamsted (HER 11479; MacDonald 1995, 121–2). Similar concentrations of sites are apparent in and above other major valleys in the county, including the Lea (as at Turnford (HER 6484) or Hertingfordbury (HER 9748)); and the Stort (as at the Dunmow Road site in Bishop's Stortford (HER 509216), or Thorley, where rescue excavations in 1994 revealed an extensive area of late Bronze Age settlement and an associated network of long, narrow fields (Bryant 1995, 22)). Several early and middle Iron Age sites are known from similar locations on the edge of the boulder-clay plateau in the north-east of the county, such as those at Wood End and Raffin Green (Bryant 1995, 24).

By the later Iron Age, settlement was expanding out across the more difficult soils of the clay-covered interfluves at some distance from the valley edges, although sites of this date are poorly represented in some fieldwalking surveys because they appear on the surface only as scatters of small, poorly fired pottery sherds, which tend to disintegrate in the more acidic soils, especially where these have been under cultivation for a long period of time. The failure of the fieldwalking survey carried out by the Chess Valley Archaeological and Historical Society to recover much evidence for later prehistoric settlement (in marked contrast to the large quantities of material recovered from earlier and later periods) was plausibly explained as a consequence of the fact that 'late prehistoric pottery seldom survives the rigours of the plough soil' (Stainton 1995, 128). The later prehistoric expansion is better documented by fieldwalking on the boulder clays in the extreme north-east of the county, around the county boundary with Essex, perhaps owing to the more alkaline nature of the soils in this area. Many settlements are found on the heavier soils at some distance from the principal valleys in upland parishes like Meesden and Nuthampstead (Williamson 1986). Similar densities – more than one per square kilometre – have been discovered further south in Essex, just across the county boundary around Stansted (Brooks and Bedwin 1989), while stray finds from elsewhere suggest that settlement was widespread on the boulder clays by the time of the Roman conquest. Many of these places continued to be occupied into the Roman period (Williamson 1986).

Particularly important evidence for the character of the later prehistoric landscape comes from the survey carried out by Angus Wainwright in and around the Ashridge woods in the far west of the county, on the clay-with-flint soils of the Chiltern Hills. Here, almost uniquely in Hertfordshire, an extensive tract of land survived unploughed throughout the medieval and modern periods in the form of common grazing or woodland (Figure 10) (Morris and Wainwright 1995). Although some of the surface finds associated with the earthworks of scattered farmsteads may date from the early and middle Iron Age, most appear to be of later Iron Age date. Here, too, many sites continued to be occupied into the Roman period. Even the inhospitable Southern Uplands were being occupied by the time of the Roman invasion, although most known settlements, as at Priors Wood (Partridge 1980), Foxholes (Partridge 1989) and Hertford Heath (Holmes and Frend 1959), seem to have been located on deposits of gravel and pebble rather than on the London Clay itself.

Nevertheless, the extent to which any of the clay-covered interfluves were settled in this period should not be exaggerated. The main areas of settlement

Figure 10. Iron Age and Roman settlement in the Ashridge area (after Morris and Wainwright 1995).

clearly remained on, or beside, the lighter soils and the principal valleys. It is here, as we shall see, that the most extensive settlements, the so-called *oppida*, had developed by the end of the Iron Age. More importantly, we should not assume that all settlements located on clay uplands represent farms and hamlets practising a mixed economy, or even that they were occupied throughout the year. Some may well have been specialised establishments, used perhaps on a seasonal or sporadic basis, for the management and exploitation of grazing and autumn pannage, the production of wood and charcoal, pottery-making or iron-smelting (Hill 1999, 201). It is noteworthy, for example, that in the Ashridge woods the settlements discovered by Wainwright are generally surrounded by small groups of fields and are separated from their neighbours by extensive areas, presumably uncultivated, which are largely devoid of earthworks (Figure 10) (Morris and Wainwright 1995) and must represent areas of open grazing land and woodland. The presence of slag indicates that several of the sites were involved in iron-smelting, and thus large amounts of wood used to produce the required charcoal must presumably have been available. A number of lanes, again surviving in earthwork form as 'hollow ways', apparently connect the settlements, and also run down from the high plateau onto the lower ground, in which form they presumably represent droveways for the movement of stock. This relict landscape of scattered settlements and islands of enclosed fields set within wider tracts of woodland and pasture may provide a guide to the character of later prehistoric settlement in other areas of upland clay in Hertfordshire, where upstanding earthworks have not survived the pressures of later land use. Nevertheless, the large numbers of stray Iron Age sherds found in the fields of the boulder clays of north-east Hertfordshire – sherds which were probably carried out from settlements with other rubbish, to manure the fields – perhaps suggests a greater extent of arable land use on these more fertile soils (Williamson 1986, 123).

Iron Age territories and monuments

Following a period in which comparatively few large monuments of any kind had been erected, the late Bronze Age and early Iron Age saw the appearance of substantial embanked enclosures which archaeologists usually refer to as 'hillforts'. These have traditionally been interpreted as defended strongholds which, during the middle and late Iron Age, grew steadily in strength and sophistication. Some served merely as refuges in time of trouble, perhaps in particular for livestock, but many – especially the later ones – contained storage facilities and/or large settlements, and may have formed 'central places' for warlike tribes. Hertfordshire's hillforts – like the ceremonial monuments of earlier prehistory – are neither large nor numerous by Wessex standards. Indeed, there are only four sites which certainly, or almost certainly, fall into the 'hillfort' category: Arbury Banks in Ashwell (an unimpressive example); Wilbury Hill in Letchworth; The Aubreys at Redbourn (Figure 11); and Ravensborough Castle in Hexton. To these, however, we can add the fort at Wilbury, two kilometres to the south of Bishop's Stortford, but just over the county boundary with Essex; Ivinghoe

Figure 11. The Aubreys, Redbourn. There is little evidence that this substantial Iron Age enclosure, often described as a 'hillfort', was ever occupied on any scale (© CUCAP).

Beacon, some three kilometres north of the county boundary in Buckinghamshire; the possible example at Widbury, near Ware (a doubtful contender, indicated by little more than a place-name and an enigmatic earthwork bank); and Gatesbury, near Braughing. This last is a particularly important site, and its status currently a matter for debate. It is a sub-rectangular earthwork which surrounds a small wood crowning the hill on the opposite side of the River Rib to a large late Iron Age settlement or *oppidum*. It has long been considered a possible hillfort, presumably the *oppidum*'s precursor. However, doubt has recently been cast on this interpretation. Fieldwalking in the surrounding area has produced no middle Iron Age pottery, and only very worn late Iron Age and Roman sherds. More importantly, an earthwork survey has suggested that the 'ramparts' are no more than particularly substantial examples of woodbanks of medieval date (medieval woods in Hertfordshire, as elsewhere, were usually bounded by large banks and ditches to protect coppices from grazing livestock) (Cushion 2008). But, against this, it should be pointed out that many Iron Age enclosures were not permanently or intensively occupied, as we shall see, and so the absence of pottery is not necessarily damning evidence. More importantly, the earthworks can be interpreted in a number of ways. They consist of a smaller outer bank, which does indeed look like a woodbank, and a larger but more diffuse bank immediately inside it, which does not. Double woodbanks are extremely rare – almost all woods have only one around their perimeter – and a number of features suggest that the two banks are not contemporary. In particular, the outer bank, as it runs along the south-eastern side of the wood, first diverges from the inner and then, turning northwards at the corner, appears to cut through it. In addition, at the eastern end of the wood is a complex arrangement of banks and a very substantial ditch, which can have nothing to do with the wood itself. On balance, it is perfectly possible that when the site was enclosed as a wood in early medieval times a woodbank was constructed around a defunct and degraded pre-existing earthwork enclosure. The name Gatesbury, applied both to the adjacent farm and the wood itself, is intriguing and hard to explain if the earthwork is indeed no more than a woodbank. First recorded in the twelfth century, it is an Old English name meaning 'Gæta's *burh*', or fort (Gover *et al.* 1938, 190).

Other hillforts may well have existed in the county which have failed to survive or remain unrecognised. One possible example is the curious earthwork within Caley Wood, south-west of Little Hadham. The southern part of the wood comprises ancient, semi-natural hornbeam coppice, albeit modified by nineteenth-century planting. The north, in contrast, has grown up since the late nineteenth century over extensive gravel workings. At the junction of the two areas is a massive earthwork bank, running east–west and mutilated in places by gravel extraction. Towards the east it turns northwards, continuing in a smooth curve along the eastern margins of the newer section of the wood: its flanking ditch is here partly water-filled. After a short interruption, the earthwork reappears – less massive, but still substantial – and runs from east to west beside the road between Piggs Green and Westfield Farm. It begins to curve south, but then disappears again – this section was apparently destroyed before the nineteenth century. Three sides of an oval covering over four hectares are thus defined. The area is described as 'the Castell alias Cales' in a Chancery deposition of 1575, and as 'Castle

Field' on a plan of 1767 (HER 797), but a ringwork on this scale would be associated with the caput of a major barony, and Little Hadham was never one of these. The names are almost certainly the result of later folk etymology, and on balance the site – which commands magnificent views down the valley of the River Ash – is more likely to be Iron Age. Another possible example lies in Great Gaddesden parish, at TL041094. The noblewoman Æthelgifu drew up her will around 980 and left an estate here to St Albans Abbey, the bounds of which are described in an appended document, probably drawn up some time later (Crick 2007, 158–61). One section of these bounds, apparently following the line of the present parish boundary between Great Gaddesden and Hemel Hempstead, passes northwards along the River Gade and then turns west at a point 'to the south of the *byrig*' – the Old English term for a fort, often a hillfort. Just to the north of the point where the parish boundary turns west aerial photographs show a large circular grassmark enclosing an area of some three hectares occupying a prominent spur overlooking the valley. This may well be the site of the lost fort.

To many archaeologists, the proliferation of defended enclosures in this period proclaims the emergence of more stratified and complex societies – 'chiefdoms' – geared to warfare in an increasingly crowded landscape. This was a process which culminated in the last century BC with the development, across much of southern and eastern England, of large tribal kingdoms (Cunliffe 1968; 1995, 59–87). While some of these ideas are still shared by most archaeologists, others – in particular, those concerning the role and function of hillforts – have been questioned. Some scholars, most notably J.D. Hill, have suggested that these enclosures may not all have been primarily defensive strongholds, or 'central places'. A number, especially in eastern England, may have had mainly ceremonial functions, and been more akin to Neolithic henges than to medieval castles. They may thus have been occupied, at least initially, on a spasmodic rather than permanent basis (Hill 1995; 1999; Hingley 1984).

Not enough is known about Hertfordshire's hillforts to throw much light on these matters, but where sites of this type have been excavated in the county the sequences of construction revealed are often complex and discontinuous, and occupation (where located) is often confined to limited areas of the interior. At Wilbury, for example, occupation was restricted to 'one or each side of a thoroughfare running up through the south gate', and the excavator noted that the fortifications were 'strong in proportion to the intensity of occupation behind' (Applebaum 1949, 28). Here, fairly typically, the enclosing bank displayed a complex sequence of construction, with three main phases:

> The first a fortification that was begun and never completed. But a timber
> revetment made at the rear of the unfinished bank was completed and occupation
> continued on the site for a considerable period (Applebaum 1949, 31).

At a later stage a new bank was dug on the line of the old, and this time finished, although the ditch was soon allowed to silt up and occupation to spread across it. At the Aubreys, similarly, the absence of pottery and other finds from the interior indicates, in the words of the Hertfordshire Heritage Environment Record, 'seasonal, not permanent, occupation' (HER 25).

Some of these monuments may have been located not at the centres but at the margins of territories. Ravensborough lies within the major concentration of round barrows around the headwaters of the Lea and the Ivel, while Wilbury is associated with the cluster of barrows to the east of Hitchin, around the headwaters of the Purwell. Both 'forts' occupy positions to one side of the barrow concentrations, beside springs which form the sources of the principal rivers draining northwards into the Midland plain. The Burwell, one of the main tributaries of the River Ivel, begins at a spring beside Ravensborough Castle, while the River Hiz has one of its main sources at Cadwell Springs, below Wilbury. In addition, the River Rhee or Cam has its source a few hundred metres from Arbury Banks, while the mysterious enclosure in Caley Wood looks down upon the source of a major tributary of the Ash. Of course, such a choice of location can be explained in practical terms: communities using or occupying these enclosures needed a regular supply of fresh water. But we also need to note the importance of river systems in the configuration of early social territories, and the undoubted religious significance of rivers and wet places for Iron Age peoples. From the later Bronze Age it became customary to deposit valuable metalwork in such places, although few certain examples of this practice are known from Hertfordshire. Such religious associations are emphasised by the fact that of the few place-names which have come down to us from Iron Age times, most refer to rivers, and at least three of these appear to have a religious significance. The River Brent, for example, which rises in the far south of the county but flows for most of its course through Middlesex, has a name which is cognate with the Old British *Brigantia*, the name of a goddess – quite possibly a river goddess. The early forms of the name of the River Lea – *Lygean*, *Ligean* – similarly mean the 'river dedicated to Lugus', another Celtic god. The River Beane is referred to in a document of *c*. AD 925 as the *Bene ficcan*: the second element possibly incorporates the Old Welsh word *ficean*, 'little'; the first almost certainly the British *ben*, 'goddess'. This river was clearly once regarded as the 'Little Goddess' (Gover *et al.* 1938, 1–5). The sources of such rivers may have held a particular significance, for, as Hill has argued, Iron Age peoples appear to have invested considerable significance in boundaries, edges, limits and beginnings (Hill 1999, 198). We tend to think of the development of prehistoric societies in terms of their agriculture, economy and social structure, and to read the landscapes of this period in essentially practical and functional terms, but here we have hints of another landscape, one of myth and ritual, of sacred rivers and associated enclosures. None of this is conclusive, but it remains possible that some hillforts may indeed have been ceremonial monuments located on the margins, perhaps the magical margins, of social territories, sometimes at places where the rivers which articulated each social territory emerged from the underworld. Indeed, some of these river sources maintained a ritual significance in later times: a spring some 700 metres north of Ravensborough Castle was dedicated in the Middle Ages to St Faith, and it was recorded in the seventeenth century how 'people that come to offer did cast some thing into the well, which if it swamme above they were accepted and their petition granted, but if it sanke, they were rejected' (Dyer 1976, 159). Some kind of ceremonial or religious role for these structures is also suggested by their continued use in the Roman period for burial, as at Wilbury (HER 4452).

Hillforts were not the only kind of large monument constructed in Hertfordshire in the early and middle Iron Age. In the Chiltern Hills there are a number of linear earthworks or 'dykes' – single or multiple banks and ditches, varying greatly in length and scale – most of which appear to date from this period. Such earthworks fall conveniently into two distinct groups (Bryant 1995, 26; Bryant and Burleigh 1995, 92–5). In the extreme west of the county, and lying mainly in Buckinghamshire, are a number of long stretches of bank and ditch which bear the collective traditional name 'Grims Ditch' (*Grimr* being an Old English phrase meaning 'hooded one', an epithet for Woden, 'suggesting that the monument's origins had already been forgotten in Saxon times' (Dyer 1963)). Excavations at Hastoe recovered a single Iron Age sherd from the bank of the earthwork (HER 50), while more extensive excavations of a levelled section, carried out before the construction of the Berkhamsted bypass in 1992, recovered middle Iron Age pottery from the main ditch fill, with later Iron Age and Roman potsherds in the upper fill (HER 11476). The 'Ditch' faces south and runs in a series of straight lines and long, sweeping curves, its course broadly replicating the topography of the Chiltern Hills. It runs along, or close to, the watershed in the spaces between major valleys and gaps, but swings southwards, and sometimes down on to lower ground, when these are reached. How far the various discontinuous sections once formed a more continuous line is unclear; so too is whether all the earthworks so labelled are, indeed, part of the same feature. Doubt has been expressed in particular over whether the section near Potten End, to the north-east of Berkhamsted, is part of the 'real' Grims Ditch (it is much larger and resembles more closely the later Iron Age and Roman linear earthworks found at various places in the county: HER 49). The monument is most plausibly interpreted as some kind of boundary marker, perhaps – given its watershed course – allocating 'upland' resources of woodland and grazing between communities living north and south of the Chiltern escarpment. Whatever its function, the way that it runs in a series of relatively straight sections, changing direction sharply at intervals (at right angles at one point in Great Hampden in Buckinghamshire), hints that when it was originally laid out the landscape was much less wooded than it is today.

Rather different are the 'cross-ridge dykes' found on the light soils of the East Anglian Heights, in the north-east of the county, most of which appear to be of later Bronze Age or Iron Age date. These earthworks run at right angles to the line of the chalk escarpment, and thus perpendicular to the supposed prehistoric routeway (Harrison 2003), known as the Icknield Way, which runs along it. The series begins in the east, in Cambridgeshire, with the Bran Ditch, and ends in the west with the Bedfordshire Dray's Ditches. In 1961 James Dyer proposed the ingenious theory that, together with the Rivers Hiz and Ivel, this series of earthworks served to divide the East Anglian Heights into six territories, each of which contained a hillfort (Dyer 1961, 39–43). Unfortunately, since he wrote, a number of additional cross-ridge dykes, levelled long ago, have been discovered through aerial photography, including those at Punch's Cross, Wilbury Hill, Baldock and Mitchell Hill, rather disrupting the pattern and creating more territories than hillforts

(Bryant and Burleigh 1995, 93). In addition, cropmarks of a number of other multiple dykes which run not at right angles to but parallel with the Icknield Way are now known, especially in the area between Baldock and Deadman's Hill, to the south-east of Ashwell (HER 2317, 295369, 2475, 1664).

Dyer's suggestions about the relationship between the dykes and the hillforts are, as a consequence of such discoveries, now less easy to sustain. Hillforts do not always lie at neat intervals centrally between dykes. On the contrary, they sometimes stand close to the ends of dykes: Wilbury, for example, lies close to the northern end of the Wilbury Hill dyke; the possible hillfort at Limlow Hill in Cambridgeshire lies near the northern end of the Mile Ditches; and Arbury Banks in Ashwell would stand not far from the line of Deadmans Hill ditches, if this had continued some three kilometres further north. Once again we have hints that some hillforts may have functioned not as 'central places' but as ritual or ceremonial features on social boundaries.

In a review of the evidence, Stewart Bryant and Gil Burleigh drew attention to the research by Spratt into similar monuments on the North York Moors (Spratt 1989; Bryant and Burleigh 1995, 93–4). Here, it appears, the earliest territories were bounded by major watersheds and, in the Bronze Age, these were marked by round barrows. But as population increased on the lower ground these territories gradually became subdivided, and additional boundaries were established running up to the watersheds, at right angles to the valley floors. These, too, were marked by barrow cemeteries sited on prominent ridges running between secondary valleys. Later still, presumably as a result of further population growth and competition for resources, territories were more clearly bounded, first with pit alignments (a distinctive form of late prehistoric monument) and subsequently by linear earthworks of varying degrees of complexity. A similar sequence can, Bryant and Burleigh suggested, be discerned in the north-eastern Chilterns. The main dykes here either follow ridges – secondary watersheds – running at right angles to the main scarp, or continue the line of minor valleys up onto the high watershed. In both cases they are associated with obvious 'natural' boundaries. Many, moreover, are associated with major concentrations of barrows on the prominent ridges, which presumably preceded them as territorial markers: this is particularly clear in the case of Dray's Ditches, the Baldock dykes, the Mile Ditches and the dykes on Deadman's Hill (Bryant and Burleigh 1995, 94). When excavated, the east Chiltern Dykes sometimes exhibit complicated histories of development and elaboration. At Mile Ditches, for example, the Iron Age triple ditch apparently developed from a single ditch, possibly of late Bronze Age date (Burleigh 1980). The multiple ditch system on Deadmans Hill may, similarly, have developed from the westernmost ditch, which continues its course alone for some distance to the south (Bryant and Burleigh 1995, 94).

As more boundary dykes are recognised as cropmarks in north-east Hertfordshire it becomes harder to make much sense of them as an overall system of land division, presumably because they were constructed over a long period of time, one replacing another as the detailed patterns of territorial division changed. As so often in archaeology, the accumulation of new evidence not only upsets previous theories, but also makes any overall pattern in the data less easy to discern. Perhaps all we can say with any confidence is that the later Bronze and Iron Ages saw increasing division and demarcation of territory, at least on the light soils of the chalk escarpment, presumably resulting from increasing population and growing pressure on local resources.

Oppida

In the last century BC southern Britain began to be drawn into the political and economic orbit of the Roman world. By the second quarter of the first century BC Italian *amphorae* – presumably containing wine and oil – were being imported into Britain via Armorica (modern Brittany and the adjoining areas to the east). But Caesar's conquest of Gaul between 58 and 51 BC seems to have led to a shift in regional exchange patterns and to a concentration of contacts between Gaul and the areas immediately to the north of the Thames, especially Hertfordshire and Essex. By around 25 BC we have abundant evidence for the import into these areas of high-status goods from continental Europe, including fine pottery, silverware and *amphorae*. Such artefacts are found, in particular, among the wealthy grave goods interred with cremations – often referred to as 'Welwyn' burials, after an important Hertfordshire example, for they are strongly clustered in the valley of the upper Lea. These are normally interpreted as the graves of members of local elites who had grown rich through the control of long-distance exchange. Indeed, according to many archaeologists, this expansion of foreign 'trade' was one of the key factors leading to the development of larger and more sophisticated political units – tribal kingdoms – in southern Britain in the late Iron Age. Some of the names of these polities, and of their rulers, have come down to us either in the accounts of classical writers or because they appear on the coins which began to be produced in southern Britain in this period. Some of the ruling elites of these petty states may have been immigrants from mainland Europe (or so Caesar believed): hence the name 'Belgae', traditionally given by archaeologists to this final phase of the Iron Age, which was characterised not only by new forms of burial and settlement, but also by the use of distinctive forms of pottery, which were tempered with 'grog' (ground-up fired clay) and, a little later, turned on a wheel (Cunliffe 1995).

Of key importance in all this was the emergence of a new type of settlement in parts of southern England, and especially in Hertfordshire and Essex, which archaeologists generally term *oppida* (Bryant 1995, 26–7; Bryant and Niblett 1997; Niblett and Thompson 2005, 23–5). These were extensive but generally discontinuous spreads of occupation, usually defined by and including within their area disconnected lengths of substantial bank and ditch. Such sites often (but not always) display some apparently 'urban' characteristics (metal-working, pottery manufacture and the use and production of coinage), and they often produce evidence for wealthy burials and imports. The most striking example of such a settlement in Hertfordshire is at St Albans (Saunders 1982; Bryant and Niblett 1997, 273–5; Hunn 1994, 26–41; Niblett and Thompson 2005, 23–40). This was called, like its Roman successor, Verulamium or Verlamion – a ruler called Tasciovanus was minting coins bearing the inscription *Ver*, *Verl* or *Verlamio* by *c*.10 BC, although so far the earliest material recovered from the site seems to date from around AD 20 (Figure 12). The settlement was originally thought to have been confined to an embanked site within Prae Wood, to the west of the walled Roman town (Wheeler and Wheeler 1936), but during the second half of the twentieth century it became apparent that this was just one of many distinct enclosures constructed in this period, and evidence for later Iron Age activity is now known to extend over a far wider area, partly beneath the Roman town but mainly on the level plateaux surrounding it. Excavation, fieldwalking and aerial photography have recovered evidence of pits, boundaries, trackways and many individual farmsteads; three main cemeteries, the largest (at King Harry Lane) comprising 140 cremations; and evidence for coin production and some metal-working (the evidence is summarised in Niblett and Thompson 2005, 23–40). Typically, the northern limits of this somewhat amorphous spread of settlement seem to have been defined by linear earthworks – Beech Bottom Dyke, to the north of the

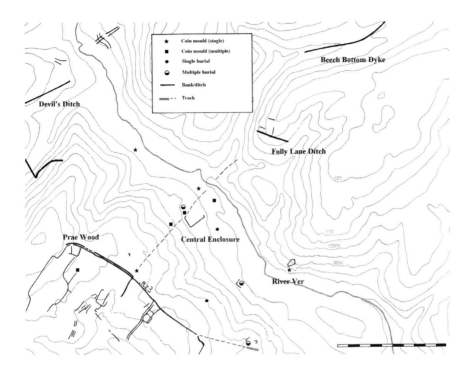

Figure 12. The principal features of the Iron Age oppidum of Verlamion (after Niblett and Thompson 2005).

present town of St Albans, and perhaps Devil's Dyke to the west (Figure 13). Other linear earthworks provided clear internal zoning. In particular, they divided the areas of settlement and domestic production (associated with small, rectangular enclosures) on the plateaux above the valley from the lower slopes of the valley and the valley floor. These dykes are best known (and in places remain as upstanding if degraded earthworks) on the south side of the valley, but are also recorded (in the form of the 'Folly Lane Ditch') to the north. Almost all the local settlement enclosures abut directly upon one of these dykes, which appear to have been kept clean and carefully maintained. On the lower ground below them, high-status burial, various ritual activities, coin production and metal-working took place: the concentration of such things beside the river and associated marshy ground is noteworthy. The name Verlamion may mean 'the place above the pool' (Frere 1983, 5). All known burials in the area were located on the downslope side of the dykes, except for one, of exceptional wealth and importance, at Folly Lane (below, p. 52) (Niblett and Thompson 2005, 36). A substantial

Figure 13. Devil's Dyke, part of the late Iron Age oppidum at Wheathampstead.

deep-ditched enclosure has been discovered near the centre of this area, beneath St Michael's parish church and its graveyard – the so-called 'Central Enclosure'. This was probably a ritual or ceremonial site of some kind (Niblett and Thompson 2005, 38).

Although Verlamion was the largest *oppidum* in the county, it was not the only one and (on present evidence) not the earliest (Figure 14). Another lay to its north-east, in the valley of the Lea around the modern village of Wheathampstead. Here, an area defended by two linear dykes (one of which is at least in part natural) was excavated by the Wheelers in the 1930s and produced evidence for occupation during the first century BC (Wheeler and Wheeler 1936, 16–22) (Figure 13). More recent investigations have suggested that settlement here may in fact have been limited (Saunders 1982), but in the area to the north, on the opposite bank of the River Lea, a number of enclosures and ditches have been revealed as cropmarks and limited excavation has produced evidence for occupation during the early first century AD (Saunders and Havercroft 1982a). This may suggest a shift over time in the focus of settlement from higher to lower ground, but the site remains poorly understood (Haselgrove and Millett 1997, 286–7).

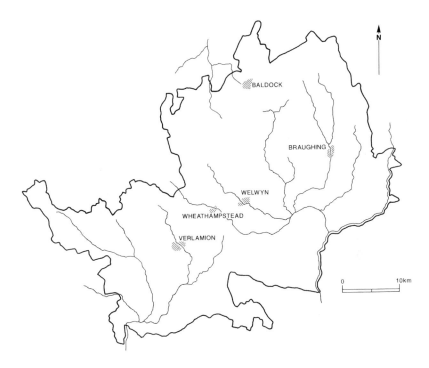

Figure 14. Hertfordshire oppida (after Bryant and Niblett 1997).

Further to the east, in the Welwyn area, no fewer than twenty occupation sites and a number of wealthy burials are now known from the area between the Mimram and the Lea. These were largely revealed during the construction and expansion of Welwyn Garden City between 1920 and 1970 (Rook 1968; 1970a; 1970b; 1974) (Figure 14). Pottery production appears to have taken place on at least two sites. A separate concentration of activity is known to the north of the River Mimram, where observation of a pipeline trench in the 1970s revealed an almost continuous spread of late Iron Age settlement over more than a kilometre. Subsequent fieldwalking surveys have confirmed the scale of occupation, and aerial photographs and archaeological evaluations have revealed traces of long-levelled linear earthworks (Bryant and Niblett 1997, 275–6).

Much larger and more important than these sites, however, was the complex of settlement around Braughing and Puckeridge, in the valley of the River Rib in north-east Hertfordshire. This may have developed from the unexcavated, but probably Iron Age, enclosure at Gatesbury (above, pp. 34–5).

Foreign imports were already reaching the area in some quantities by *c.*25 BC, and by the first half of the first century AD the settlement sprawled over an area of around 200 hectares, with the main concentration of activity perhaps on Wickham Hill (Bryant and Niblett 1997, 276). Large quantities of imported pottery have been recovered from the site – fine wares from Gaul and Italy, and *amphorae* – more than from any comparable site in Hertfordshire or adjacent counties (Niblett 1995b, 16). The bulk of this material seems to date from the period 25 BC–AD 10. Substantial quantities of coin moulds recently recovered from the eroding bank of the River Rib indicate that minting took place here on some scale (Landon 2009). Because it has been studied over a number of decades we can see that Braughing was in many ways a typical *oppidum*. In some places, settlement was dense and effectively of urban character, as at Skeleton Green (Partridge 1981). Elsewhere, as at the site excavated at the Ralph Sadleir School, occupation seems to have been essentially rural and agricultural (Partridge 1977). A discrete area of burial and ritual activity was discovered at Station Road (Partridge 1979, 28–97). This was associated with a length of linear earthwork/boundary ditch, possibly the edge of a religious enclosure or zone, which contained a substantial deposit of broken pottery, refuse from feasting and disarticulated human bones representing the remains of at least sixteen individuals.

Lastly, the Iron Age site at Baldock, in the north of the county, while probably less important than Braughing also conforms well to the traditional model of an *oppidum*. There is evidence for high-status occupation here in the form of wealthy burials from early in the first century BC. By the end of the century a substantial settlement had developed, comprising a number of enclosed farmsteads separated by fields, stockyards and vegetable plots. This extended over an area of at least twenty hectares, but was surrounded by a much wider spread of less intensive settlement which extended over several square kilometres and included a number of discrete enclosures and linear ditch systems (Burnham and Wacher 1990, 281–4; Stead and Rigby 1986; Burleigh 1982; 1995). Within the area of the modern town of Baldock several burials and cemeteries, some with wealthy grave goods, have been recovered, as well as a possible shrine. These were clustered on the fringes of the main area of settlement, mainly on a low ridge to the east, but also, to a lesser extent, to the west.

The available evidence suggests that there were some differences in the characters of the county's *oppida*. Thus Baldock and Verlamion appear to have had major ritual functions which are less apparent at Braughing, while wealthy imports are more in evidence at Braughing than at Verlamion. We should be wary, however, of making too much of these distinctions, given that none of these sites has been (or could ever be) excavated in its entirety, not least because substantial areas lie hidden beneath modern housing. But while *oppida* are a striking feature of the late Iron Age landscape, and one especially characteristic of Hertfordshire and Essex, we should not imagine that the countryside was neatly polarised between sites of this class on the one hand and single farmsteads on the other.

Firstly, various other kinds of site are known from this period in the county. These include the large but apparently nucleated settlement at Ware, on the north side of the River Lea, which was possibly an *entrepot* at which imports were transhipped from large vessels coming up the river from the Thames into smaller ships or land vehicles for the final journey to Braughing (Kiln and Partridge 1995, 25); and the extensive spread of late Iron Age settlement which has been known since the nineteenth century in the area around the Cow Roast Inn, in the Bulbourne valley west of Northchurch (Bryant and Niblett 1997, 271–3) (Figure 14). Excavations here in the 1960s and 70s revealed evidence of large-scale iron production, and separate iron-working sites have been discovered three kilometres to the south-east, at Dellfield in Berkhamsted (Thompson and Holland 1977), and two kilometres to the north-west.

Secondly, and more importantly, it is not entirely clear that the *oppida* sites *can* be neatly divided from the general run of rural settlements. So far as the evidence goes, most have no hard edges but instead fade off gradually into the adjacent countryside, and even their 'cores' seem to have been discontinuous in character, with empty areas and discrete components which cannot easily be distinguished, if at all, from rural farmsteads. As more settlements, ditches and burials come to light as a consequence of watching briefs, fieldwork and the analysis of aerial photographs – much of it carried out by, or under the aegis of, the Archaeological Section of the Hertfordshire Environment Department – it becomes apparent that *oppida* often represent several particularly dense clusters of later Iron Age activity within much wider, more diffuse concentrations.

It is arguable that archaeologists, like scholars working in other disciplines, can become constrained by the terms they use and the models they employ. It is clear that the later Iron Age was a period of demographic growth, economic expansion, increasing long-distance exchange and growing political complexity. What is less clear is how sites of the *oppida* class fit in to all this. Archaeologists have traditionally seen them as essentially proto-urban centres, developing in response to foreign exchange. Imported pottery and other goods testify to their role as *entrepots*, coinage perhaps to an incipient monetary economy, and rich burials to the existence of an elite growing wealthy through the control of long-distance exchange (Cunliffe 1968; 1995, 79–87). But it is also possible that to some extent these various sprawling agglomerations developed under their own, native, momentum (Hill 1999, 194).

Across a wide region of eastern England the later Iron Age seems to have seen the build-up of areas of particularly dense settlement separated by zones of much less intensively settled land (Hill 1999). Some of these concentrations of settlement became prominent centres of import, consumption and manufacture, or the strongholds of tribal chiefs, while others did not. It seems that social groups, while expanding rapidly in size, chose to remain clustered in one location. In part this reflects constraints imposed by contemporary agricultural technology: if we examine the location of the principal *oppida* and other large sites of this period it soon becomes apparent that most occupy major areas of light soils, in the principal valleys or along (and below) the chalk escarpment, while the less intensively settled land between them corresponds to the less easily cultivated clay-covered 'uplands' (Figure 14). Thus the string of sites running through the middle of the county – Verlamion, Wheathampstead, Welwyn – together with the substantial Iron Age settlement at Ware, correspond to the Vale of St Albans and the major valleys leading into this. Baldock is associated with the most extensive spread of chalk soils in the north of the county; the Cow Roast site at Northchurch with the outcrop of similar soils in the far west. Only Braughing appears, at first sight, to break this rule, occupying as it does a comparatively narrow valley which forms a ribbon of light soil surrounded by boulder clay. But as we have seen (above, pp. 11–12), the clay plateau here is well dissected and thus fairly well drained, the level interfluves comparatively narrow. These fertile and calcareous soils were, by late Iron Age times, supporting a substantial population. Yet while environmental factors may to some extent explain these concentrations of settlement, social factors were also clearly at work, for settlement was *more* clustered in particular locations than the dictates of soil types can explain. Perhaps we should envisage demographic growth leading to the emergence of numerous related lineages who clustered beside areas of anciently cleared land, unwilling to forsake these ancestral acres.

Although many of these places are simply concentrations of settlement, rather than centres of political power, the core areas of some densely settled zones – Braughing and Verlamion at least – clearly *did* often develop as the strongholds of tribal leaders. A model of how this might have happened was proposed, in the case of Verlamion, by Haselgrove and Millett. In essence, they suggest that Verlamion began as a ritual focus and meeting place for several social groups on marshy ground beside the River Ver. It was a ceremonial nodal point in a landscape of numerous, but discrete, dispersed farmsteads. Settlement density increased in the immediate vicinity, as 'the place gradually evolved into the recognised focus of the wider grouping, whose identity it came to symbolise. The last stage of the process saw the leading households establish residence there' (Haselgrove and Millett 1997, 285). These households were clustered around the core ritual/ceremonial area, and separated from it by the substantial linear earthworks already described: Verlamion thus achieved a political status and a social one as the residence of a ruling elite.

Iron Age politics

The appearance of wealthy continental imports in graves and settlements came after the area's first direct contact with the Roman world. In 55 BC Julius Caesar arrived in Britain from Gaul, returning the next year with a substantial military force. In his own account of the campaign he describes how, landing on the south coast, he crossed the River Thames and was confronted by a leader called Cassivellaunus, whom he defeated at his main stronghold, 'a place of great natural strength and excellently fortified' which was 'protected by forests and marshes' (Handford 1951, 139). The site has been variously identified with Ravensborough Castle, the Wheathampstead *oppidum* and Gatesbury at Braughing, but its real identity will probably never be known. Nearly a century elapsed before Roman forces arrived once again in Britain, by which time Hertfordshire and the adjoining areas to the north and west formed part of the territory of a tribe called the Catuvellauni. Because this appears, from Caesar's earlier account, to have been the region controlled by Cassivellaunus, it is often assumed that he was king of this tribe. In fact, Caesar does not refer to the Catuvellauni by name, nor does he describe Cassivellaunus as a 'king', instead stating that he had been chosen as overall leader, presumably by a number of separate tribal groups. Caesar gives the names of five tribes who surrendered to him at Camulodunumn (modern Colchester): the Cenimagni, the Segontiaci, the Ancilite, the Bibroci and the Cassi (Branigan 1985, 1–5). Of these, only one – the Cenimagni, who can be tentatively identified with the Iceni of northern East Anglia – appears again in the historical record. There are grounds for believing that the Segontiaci may have been based south of the Thames, and it is clear that much of Essex and south Suffolk was occupied by a tribe called the Trinovantes. The Ancilite, Bibroci and Cassi thus presumably occupied territory in the area of Hertfordshire, Middlesex and south Buckinghamshire. As Caesar tells us that Cassivellaunus had, prior to the Roman invasion, been waging war against his neighbours (Handford 1951, 135–6), it is possible that these groups, and others whom he does not name, were eventually absorbed into a single polity of the Catuvellauni in the period between Caesar's invasions and the Claudian invasion of AD 43 (Branigan 1985, 3). They probably retained some identity as *pagi*, clans or subdivisions, of the Catuvellauni, and the main *oppida* described above – especially Verulamium, Braughing and Baldock – may thus have formed some of their central places. Ros Niblett has suggested that the similarity of Cassivellaunus' name to that of the Cassi suggests that he was a member of that tribe (Niblett 1995b, 15).

Caesar was bent not on conquest, but on acquiring military prestige and political influence, and on achieving the limited practical objective of discouraging British involvement in the wars currently raging in Gaul. He made a treaty with Cassivellaunus, by which the latter agreed not to attack the Trinovantes or their prince Mandubricus (who had sought Caesar's protection following the death of his father at Cassivellaunus' hands). Cassivellaunus agreed to provide hostages and to send regular tribute to Rome. This accomplished, Caesar returned to Gaul (Handford 1951, 139–40).

The evidence of coinage, together with stray references in classical sources, have been used to throw light on the political history of southern Britain during the subsequent decades; unfortunately, as debate continues about how late Iron Age coinage was both used and produced the precise significance of changing types, inscriptions and distributions remains unclear. The earliest coins, dating from the second half of the first century BC, carry no inscriptions but only designs, which are based ultimately on those current in the Graeco-Roman world. Their distribution can be interpreted as indicating the presence of two main tribal groups in Hertfordshire: one based on the

Chilterns, the other in the east of the county. By the early first century AD coins of one type occur over the whole county, suggesting the dominance of a single ruler, Tasciovanus, across much of the southern Midlands – the counties of Hertfordshire, Buckinghamshire, south Bedfordshire and east Oxfordshire, and parts of Northamptonshire and Cambridgeshire. He minted his coins, as already noted, at the *oppidum* of Verlamion, and this was probably his main power base, although little evidence for occupation on any scale as early as this has yet been recovered from the site.

Tasciovanus' rule lasted from *c.*10 BC to *c.* AD 10. His successor Cunobelin was his son, according to the inscriptions placed on his coins (Branigan 1985, 8). Cunobelin seems to have expanded his hegemony by dominating the territory of the Trinovantes and soon made *Camulodunum*, modern Colchester, his main power base, although he also continued to mint coins at Verulamium. Although the distribution of coins should not be read simply as a mirror of political structures (they must in part reflect patterns of economic activity, rather than political power) it is notable that those minted by Cunobelin appear over a very wide area of southern Britain, to the almost complete exclusion of those struck by other tribal leaders (Branigan 1985, 9). Cunobelin (Shakespeare's Cymbeline) was clearly a very powerful leader; the Roman writer Suetonius actually described him as *Rex Britanorum*, 'king of Britain', although he was perhaps a paramount chieftain of a wide area, rather than a king of anything approaching a unified state.

In AD 39 Cunobelin's son Adminus – who had possibly been installed as client ruler in Kent – fled to Rome following a disagreement with his father, and persuaded the Roman emperor Gaius Caligula to intervene. The emperor and his advisers may have been concerned about their increasingly powerful and expansionist neighbour, but the planned invasion was abandoned, perhaps because of Cunobelin's death. He was succeeded by his sons Togidumnus and Caratacus, who probably divided his territory between them. Two years later Verica – ruler of the Atrebates, a tribe occupying the area of modern Hampshire and Berkshire – fled to Rome because of Catuvellaunian aggression, and like Adminus sought imperial aid, this time from the emperor Claudius (Cunliffe 1995, 77). As most readers will be aware, this time the invasion went ahead. Roman troops arrived once again on the south coast and advanced northwards. Within twelve months the Catuvellauni had been defeated and southern Britain – Hertfordshire included – had entered the Roman world.

It is possible, however, that the transition to Roman province was more gradual than this account implies. Roman interest in Britain – and especially southern Britain – may not simply have waned in the period between Caesar and Claudius, as classical sources seem to suggest. Indeed, the empire may have continued to take an active interest in the politics of the region. It is possible, for example, that the Romans supplied the wealthy imports which loom so large in the local archaeological record as an active strategy, to bolster the power and prestige of particular local rulers, some of whom had perhaps (by analogy with practice elsewhere in the empire) spent time in Rome, as the hostages demanded and taken by Caesar. Either way, what is clear is that the Roman empire usually absorbed new territories in one of two ways: either by outright conquest, followed by the erection of numerous garrison forts; or by persuading a local ruling elite (or some disaffected section of it) to accept voluntarily the benefits of imperial protection. In such circumstances a client ruler would normally be put in place, who could administer the area, collect taxes and generally do the emperor's bidding.

It is probable that Hertfordshire and adjacent areas were incorporated within the empire by the latter process. One important piece of evidence in support of this contention was discovered by Ros Niblett during an excavation at Folly Lane, St Albans, in the winter of 1991/2 (Niblett 1992; 1995a; 1999). The site lay within the general area of the Iron Age *oppidum*, although in a location in which few traces of pre-Roman activity had formerly been identified. On the low hill to the east of the Ver, overlooking the site of the later Roman town, a large rectangular ditched enclosure was discovered, within which was a large pit; at the base of this were traces of a complex timber structure. This had apparently served as a funerary chamber for a wealthy individual whose cremated remains had been deposited in an adjacent grave pit. The associated grave goods, considerably damaged by the funeral pyre, included rich metalwork and imported pottery dating to the period *c.* AD 50 – that is, shortly *after* the Roman invasion. Following the burial, chamber and pit had been covered by a square mound of turf. What is particularly striking is that the site appears to have retained some ritual significance long after the interment had been made, for a Romano-Celtic temple was built beside it – within the ritual enclosure – in the later first century, facing the mound, and this remained in existence until at least the mid third century. Niblett has plausibly argued that the grave must be that of a local ruler, a chieftain of the Catuvellauni; and that 'this must have been someone who managed to retain his wealth and status after the Roman Conquest of AD 43', presumably as a client king (Niblett 1995a, 101). The individual in question might even be tentatively identified as Adminus, son of Cunobelin, who (as we have seen) had earlier appealed to Rome for protection (Niblett 1999).

Such an interpretation of the political events of the period would help explain the remarkable dearth of early Roman forts within Hertfordshire and adjacent areas. Some examples have been suggested, on the basis of aerial photographs, but none confirmed by excavation. One was claimed at Verlamion itself, on the strength of a rampart and possible gate of pre-Flavian date excavated in 1966 on the northern edge of the settlement. This, however, could just as easily relate to an early phase of the town's defences (Niblett 1995a, 101; Niblett and Thompson 2005, 148). An absence of early Roman coins here certainly seems to preclude any significant period of military occupation in the wake of the Conquest; and the same appears to be true of the other main *oppida* sites in Hertfordshire, at Baldock and Braughing. Indeed, Haselgrove and Millet, with Niblett (1993), have even argued that the rampart and gate at Verlamion might be 'entirely native in construction and function, demarcating the margins of the expanding settlement in the early years after the Conquest' (Haselgrove and Millett 1997, 294).

The evidence for the early adoption of elements of urban planning here certainly suggest an enthusiastic acceptance of Roman ways. The road which passed through the rampart and gate led to the Folly Lane enclosure, and shares the same orientation as the street grid of the early Roman town. All this, together with the evidence for the rapid adoption of Roman fashions at neighbouring sites like Gorhambury and Parkbury, have suggested to Haselgrove and Millett that the origins of the Roman town are best understood not in terms of a military presence, but as the result of 'indigenous initiative with a pro-Roman elite manipulating their privileged position in relation to the conquerors to their own advantage and indulging in the construction of new forms of display which emulated the Roman manner' (Haselgrove and Millett 1997, 294). Moreover, as Niblett and Thompson have pointed out, probably uniquely in Britain two pre-Flavian masonry buildings were erected in Verulamium (the 'protoforum', a structure of uncertain but probably ceremonial significance at the south-western end of the earlier Central Enclosure; and the bath buildings in Insula

XIX); while, when the southern section of the Central Enclosure ditch was filled in soon after AD 50, the levelling contained unusually large quantities of samian and other imported fine wares. As Niblett and Thompson state, 'here surely we have a clear example of a local elite losing no time in associating itself with the dominant power and demonstrating its wealth and loyalty by the construction of showy "Roman" buildings and the consumption of imported goods' (Niblett and Thompson 2005, 148). Nevertheless, many aspects of traditional culture were strongly maintained: in spite of the adoption of Roman fashions, Verlamion remained, at least for a while, essentially an Iron Age town.

Romano-British geography

Whatever the truth of these arguments it is clear that, while in many ways the Conquest brought upheaval and change, many of the economic and territorial structures of the late Iron Age endured, moulding the development of the Romano-British landscape. Continuity is most striking in the case of the larger settlements (Figure 15). Verlamion thus became the most important Roman town in the region. It was a *municipium*, a place with particular legal privileges, which functioned as the main centre for the Catuvellauni, now reconstituted as a *civitas*, or administrative subdivision, of the province of Britannia. The history of the town has undergone successive revisions over the last few decades. Following the campaigns of excavation by the Wheelers (Wheeler and Wheeler 1936) and Sheppard Frere (Frere 1972; 1983; 1984), it was originally thought that in the immediate wake of the Conquest the town covered around forty hectares and had a grid of streets and a perimeter ditch (discovered by excavation in 1955). But recent investigations and the careful re-examination of earlier excavation reports now suggests a rather different picture (Niblett 1993, 85–6; Niblett and Thompson 2005, 40–165). Although a street grid had been laid out by *c.* AD 50 this in fact covered a much smaller area, of only twenty hectares, around the area of the Central Enclosure and the 'protoforum'. With the two exceptions already noted, the earliest buildings were all of timber and wattle and daub, and were ranged around a small number of streets (those conventionally labelled 14, 18, 19 and 20) which were little more than lightly metalled tracks (Figure 16). The character of the walls and ditches surrounding this initial phase of the Roman town are unclear, but insofar as they existed they were insufficient to prevent it from being sacked by

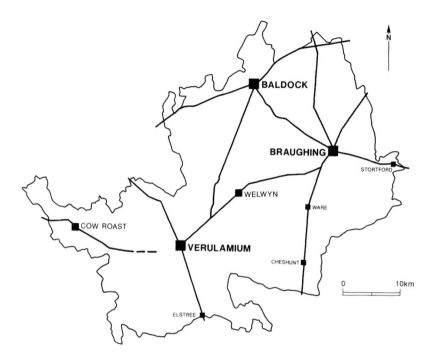

Figure 15. Hertfordshire: principal Roman roads, towns and nucleated settlements.

Boudica's rebels in AD 61, and many of its buildings appear to have been burnt to the ground. It has been suggested that the town was a particular target for the combined Icenian/Trinovantian rebels because of the enthusiastic pro-Roman stance of its inhabitants (Niblett 1995b, 26–7).

The settlement soon recovered, however, and was rebuilt on a lavish scale. Within a few decades of the revolt an imposing masonry basilica, 400 feet long and 95 feet high, was erected: this would have served as the meeting place of the *ordo*, or tribal council, of the Catuvellauni, and the place where magistrates heard court cases. It was completed in AD 79. To its south an imposing forum, or ceremonial town centre, was laid out: an extensive open area surrounded by ranges of offices and shops. Together, forum and basilica formed the largest such complex north of the Alps (Niblett 1995b, 38). Significantly, this two-hectare site overlay the Central Enclosure, the ritual centre of the former *oppidum*. It was at about this time that an area of around forty hectares was surrounded by the ditch that was discovered in the 1950s (Figure 16).

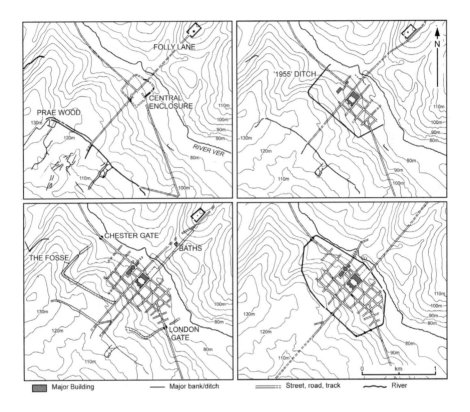

Figure 16. The development of the Roman town of Verulamium (after Niblett and Thompson 2005).
Top left: the town in the mid first century; top right: late first century; bottom left: mid second century;
bottom right: fourth century.

The late first and early second centuries were a period of sustained prosperity. Successive excavations have revealed a number of large houses, some with painted plaster walls and mosaic floors, as well as evidence for industrial activity, especially metal-working. There were several temples and a theatre, whose excavated remains today form one of the most impressive features of the town. Verulamium's population, according to some authorities, may have reached 15,000 by the end of the first century, rising to perhaps 20,000 in the second century (Frere 1983, 12): more conservatives estimate would be *c*.4,000 and *c*.8,000 (Niblett and Thompson 2005, 154). Some time in the second century a new defensive bank and ditch were constructed, which survive in part as the feature known as the Fosse. Like the earlier defensive ditch, it appears to have run around only three

Figure 17. The walls of Verulamium. Although extensively quarried in medieval times – in part to provide material for the nearby abbey – these are still among the most impressive Roman remains in Hertfordshire.

sides of the town, the marshy valley floor to the north-east presumably providing a suitable defence on that side. By this time the town, with its grid of streets, probably extended over around 100 hectares (Figure 16).

Although much of the north and east of the town was destroyed in a great fire in AD 155, the place recovered once more, and continued to enjoy prosperity throughout the second and into the third century, when it was provided with substantial defensive walls of flint and tile (Niblett 1993, 86–7). These still survive in places, although greatly reduced by medieval quarrying (Figure 17). They embraced a more limited area than the earlier defences, but formed a complete circuit. There are signs, however, that the character of occupation within the area so enclosed was changing, with fewer workshops and more evidence for wealthy houses (Niblett and Thompson 2005, 158). Indeed, it has been pointed out that some of the villas – wealthy rural residences – in the vicinity of the town were abandoned at the start of the second century, perhaps marking the adoption of a fashion for wealthy urban living which continued and intensified thereafter (Niblett and Thompson 2005, 156).

It should be emphasised that occupation was not continuous throughout the area defined by the perimeter defences. On the contrary: numerous excavations have demonstrated that, away from the frontages of the principal roads, there was much open land within the town, some of which comprised paddocks and gardens, while other parts were apparently cultivated as fields or allotments. The area lying between the old perimeter ditch and the late-third-century town walls, in particular, was never very densely occupied (Niblett 1993, 87). To the north of the forum fieldwalking and aerial photography suggest that, although ribbon development extended along the sides of Watling Street, there was little settlement behind the street frontage. Conversely, settlement clearly spilled out *beyond* the town walls, with notable spreads of occupation (of first- to mid-third-century date) along the Silchester Road and large-scale industrial activity outside the south gate. Indeed, this pattern of low density but extensive settlement, conspicuously mixing 'urban' and 'rural' elements, is reminiscent of the character of land use within the late Iron Age *oppidum*. It should also be noted that, like its Iron Age predecessor (and like its medieval successor, St Albans), Verulamium was a site of major ritual significance. The main focus of ceremonial activity appears to have moved from the valley floor to the Folly Lane site on the rising ground to the east of the town, where, as already noted, a Romano-Celtic temple dominating the skyline was erected within the rectangular enclosure, which was linked to the town by a road. Beside this, on the lower slopes to the south-west, a further area of ritual activity associated with a number of deep shafts developed. Two of these shafts contained human skulls, suggesting the presence of the kind of head cult attested from elsewhere in the Celtic world (Niblett 1999, 57–63). A bath house, perhaps of a ritual character, was erected around AD 150 a little further to the south-west. In the second century another road was laid out linking this ceremonial area to one of the principal temples in the Roman town, associated with the theatre (itself probably a primarily religious structure). In Niblett's words, 'It would not be stretching the evidence too far to see the whole of the Folly Lane site, including the lower slopes, as part of a large, ceremonial or religious complex' (Niblett 1999, 99).

Although the Wheelers originally suggested that the town experienced significant decline in the later third century, recent evidence suggests a more complex pattern. There are signs that, in line with wider political and social changes in the empire as a whole, the town became more of an administrative centre and tax collection point, less of a market and place of industrial production. But it seems to have remained prosperous through the fourth century and into the fifth: some of the latest mosaics and wall paintings found anywhere in Britain have been recovered from the centre of the town (Niblett and Thompson 2005, 161–4).

There were a number of other sizeable settlements in Roman Hertfordshire, of the type normally referred to as 'small towns' by archaeologists, meaning towns lacking political status and functions and, to a large extent, the kinds of large public buildings and defences exhibited by Verulamium (Figure 15). The term is in many ways an unsatisfactory one, embracing as it does sites ranging from unplanned industrial hamlets and roadside villages to large settlements containing some public buildings, and exhibiting signs of deliberate planning in their layout. In Hertfordshire, two 'small towns' seem to stand apart from the rest in terms of both size and character: Baldock and Braughing. What is striking is that both, like Verulamium, developed directly from important late Iron Age *oppida*: the three most important Roman towns in the county, in other words, developed directly from the three most important pre-Roman centres. The history of Braughing is perhaps the best understood, thanks to the extensive excavations carried out here in the 1970s by Clive Partridge (1977; 1979; 1981). The settlement declined in importance relative to Verulamium, but its status as a route centre was enhanced by the construction of the Roman road called Ermine Street and the improvement of an existing prehistoric trackway, Stane Street. The former was one of the most important routes in Roman Britain, running from London to Lincoln and York; Stane Street, in contrast, was a road of more local significance leading to Camulodunum (Colchester). The two roads met at a junction a little to the south of the nucleus of the old *oppidum* on Wickham Hill, and other major routes led to the site, including one coming from Baldock. Soon after the Conquest – probably around AD 80 – a grid of streets was laid out on Wickham Hill, and at least one planned street (running parallel to Ermine Street) at the Skeleton Green site. The main area of occupation extended from the River Rib westwards as far as Ermine Street but, as at Verulamium, settlement was not continuous or contemporary throughout this area.

Most of the buildings were of wooden construction, with thatched roofs and plank floors, like those excavated at Skeleton Green, which were erected soon after AD 43. But some were constructed in brick or stone: one, beside the Rib, was a bath house erected in the 70s or 80s which fell out of use in the second century (Burnham and Wacher 1990, 109). It appears too small to have been a public bath and may have been associated with the residence of an official responsible for the administration of a *pagus*, or clan, focused on the town, although it may have had ritual functions. The other was a substantial L-shaped building on Wickham Hill, of uncertain character but possibly a temple, which perhaps replaced the Iron Age religious enclosure at nearby Station Road. Aerial photographs suggest several other masonry structures, including a large house with winged corridors and a substantial double-courtyard building, possibly a market. The presence of these stone buildings indicates that Braughing was a place of some importance, clearly distinguished from neighbouring settlements, although unlike Verulamium it never appears to have been given any kind of defensive circuit. The town presumably functioned as a market, and contained workshops manufacturing a range of goods in iron, bronze and bone. But it may well have had an administrative and social status as the centre for the social group which had occupied the earlier *oppidum* – a *pagus*, or a subdivision of the Catuvellauni, originating perhaps as an independent tribe absorbed into this larger group during the first century AD. The townspeople buried their dead – as was the usual practice – on the outskirts of the settlement, mostly in the area to the west of Ermine Street, although also at Ford Street to the north of the River Quin (Partridge 1981).

At Baldock the main area of occupation, covering more than twenty hectares, lay in the angle formed by the junction of the Icknield Way and the road leading south-eastwards to Braughing. Extensive excavations and geophysical surveys carried out in the 1960s and 70s revealed a complex of rectangular enclosures defined by ditches. These were laid out along lanes which ran back at right angles from the Braughing road, to a large extent perpetuating the road pattern of the earlier *oppidum* (Burnham and Wacher 1990, 281–2). The enclosures contained traces of ovens, pits and wells, but little evidence of buildings, partly because of the extent of later plough damage. Earlier excavations, in the area to the west, revealed traces of two stone structures, although no complete plans could be obtained. Cemeteries were placed at the extremities of the settlement. That to the south-east (Westell 1931) seems to have contained burials dating from the first to the fourth century: 317 cremations and more than 30 inhumations were recovered from an area of *c*.370 square metres. In all, 2,000 graves have been recovered from the area around the town (Niblett 1995b, 53). The town does not seem to have maintained the status it held in pre-Roman times. Like Braughing, it was eclipsed by the success of Verulamium, and seems to have functioned as a small market town and a minor industrial centre (there is evidence for metal-working). But it, too, probably maintained its status as a focus for a local community, a *pagus*, and the temple revealed by aerial photography, but as yet unexcavated, may represent the shrine of this group.

Less fully researched, but apparently of lesser size and status, were the settlements at Ware, Welwyn and around the Cow Roast Inn in Northchurch. All developed, once again, directly from important Iron Age sites, although ones which were clearly of less importance than Baldock or Braughing; the status of settlements in the Roman period thus mirrored, significantly, their relative importance at the end of the Iron Age. That at Ware was located on the north bank of the River Lea, beside Ermine Street, and excavations have revealed evidence for occupation continuing from the mid first until the late fourth centuries AD (Kiln and Partridge 1995, 28–55; Smith 1987, 178). Timber buildings, smithing ovens, ore-roasting hearths and metalled yards were all discovered, together with evidence for bone working and pottery production. The settlement at Welwyn is largely obscured by the buildings of the modern town but again occupied a river crossing, where a minor Roman road forded the Mimram. Traces of ovens, wells and buildings have been located, while – once again – the settlement's periphery was marked by a mixed cremation/inhumation cemetery, at its north-eastern edge (Smith 1987, 232). It is noticeable that a number of particularly wealthy villas, especially those at Dicketts Mead and Lockleys, have been discovered in close proximity. Lastly, the area around the Cow Roast Inn in Northchurch has produced considerable evidence for settlement and industrial activity spanning the period from the first to the fourth century. The main area of settlement extended along both sides of Akeman Street (the Roman road following, roughly, the line of the old A411) for several hundred metres, with side lanes dividing the built-up area into a number of blocks: once again, several villa sites (two at Northchurch, one at Dudswell, possible examples at Berkhamsted and Rails Copse) are known in close proximity (Goodburn 1976; Smith 1987, 235). In addition to these three sites, attention should perhaps be drawn to the extensive areas of pottery kilns (producing 'Hadham Ware') in the area between Little and

Much Hadham: accumulating evidence suggests that this, too, was a major industrial complex, perhaps with Iron Age roots, which included a number of wealthy villas. Although perhaps too diffuse in character to be described as a 'small town', the area was clearly economically important and densely settled. Like the Cow Roast site, it is testimony to the increasing importance of industrial production which, beginning in the late Iron Age, took off in the Roman period, in Hertfordshire as elsewhere in southern England.

Below these 'small towns' in the settlement hierarchy there were a number of other smaller examples, less fully researched and less well understood, which, unlike the places just described, appear to have developed on entirely new sites (Figure 15). Most were small markets or industrial centres lying along major Roman roads. At Cheshunt, Roman material – pottery and building debris – has been found along more than 1.2 kilometres of Ermine Street (Smith 1987, 177; Ely and Edwards 2003). Better known is the site at Brockley Hill, just over the county boundary in Middlesex: this was possibly the site of the Roman posting station *Sulloniaciae*, mentioned in the document known as the Antonine Itinerary. Occupation extends for more than a kilometre along both sides of Watling Street and includes the sites of at least fourteen pottery kilns. Further material, similar in character, has been found on the Hertfordshire side of the county boundary, at Elstree, just over a kilometre to the north: this may represent a separate site, or a continuation of the same area of settlement and industrial activity (Smith 1987, 217). Other settlements of similar general character include that at Bishop's Stortford, just to the east of the point where the Colchester road crosses the River Stort, where ditches, gravel floors, timber slots for buildings and large quantities of pottery and evidence for iron-working have been recorded during building operations and rescue excavations, especially in the Cannons Close area (HER 513).

Although none of these sites appears to have developed from places of Iron Age significance it is nevertheless possible that in some cases their location was influenced by the pre-existing structures of tribal society. Ian Hodder suggested many years ago that although in some ways Iron Age society in south-east England was moving in the direction of a market economy, most forms of exchange were still embedded in social relationships, in structures of kinship and clientage (Hodder 1979). With the incorporation of Britain in the Roman world market exchange increased steadily in importance, but the locations of market activity were still initially determined by social factors:

exchange was more important between, rather than within, communities. Markets thus developed in two main locations: beside Roman forts, where the garrisons constituted a significant body of 'outsiders'; and on the boundaries between the territories of indigenous communities.

In Hertfordshire, as already noted, there is little evidence for early Roman forts. However, it is probable that the Catuvellaunian tribe constituted a loose amalgam of smaller social units – *pagi* – under a paramount chieftain, and there are indications that some of these small towns may have grown up where the boundaries of such groups were crossed by the new Roman military roads. It is notable, for example, that the Brockley Hill site lies on the high clay-covered watershed between the Colne and the Brent (close to what is now the county boundary between Hertfordshire and Middlesex), a likely boundary zone in the late prehistoric period; while the Bishop's Stortford site lies at the point where Stane Street crosses the River Stort, a watercourse which we have already suggested may have constituted an important boundary in prehistoric times. Whereas the major Roman urban centres developed from important Iron Age settlements, in other words, some of the smaller nucleated 'towns' may have grown up on the boundaries between communities.

Certainly, other aspects of Romano-British geography were strongly influenced by pre-existing structures, most notably the pattern of major roads. Some of these, such as Stane Street, were simply tidied-up versions of much older trackways. Two entirely new military routes were laid out across the county, however, soon after the Conquest, running in a series of long, ruler-straight alignments: Watling Street (the modern A5) and Ermine Street. Even these, although entirely new features imposed upon the earlier landscape, were to some extent determined by it. The line of Watling Street was thus decided by the location of the Verlamion *oppidum*: but more striking is the relation of Ermine Street to Braughing. This road enters the county in Cheshunt and runs in a ruler-straight alignment for some twelve kilometres to a point near Hertford Heath. Here it changes direction, adopting a more easterly route, so that it arrives at the *oppidum* at Braughing. Leaving this settlement, it heads roughly north-north-west in a straight line for some 7.5 kilometres until a point in Wyddial (at TL355309) is reached. Here the road returns to something very close to its original alignment, and thus proceeds in the direction of Lincoln. It is almost as if the engineers planned a direct route from London to Lincoln, but added the deviation to Braughing as a kind of afterthought.

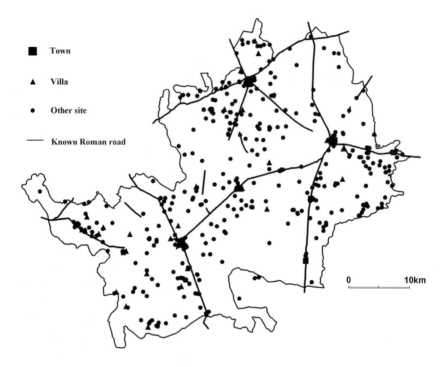

Figure 18. Roman Hertfordshire (source: HER).

Rural settlement in Roman Hertfordshire

Although Hertfordshire has perhaps seen fewer systematic fieldwalking surveys than some neighbouring counties, those that have been carried out, together with the analysis of archaeological material discovered by accident or during watching briefs, and the evidence of excavations and aerial photography, leave no doubt that by the second century settlement was extensive in most parts of the county (Figure 18). The south and west – that is, the Chiltern Dipslope region – is characterised by large Romanised 'villa' establishments, generally concentrated (as we might expect) within the principal river valleys – those of the Gade, Bulbourne, Chess and Ver (Branigan and Niblett 2005). Most, in fact, continued to demonstrate the long-established preference for positions immediately above major valleys, at the junction of the sloping ground with the level, clay-covered plateau. The smaller villas were wealthy Romanised farmsteads, the larger ones were substantial and complex structures, like country houses, which were presumably occupied by members of the Catuvellaunian tribal elite: they stood at 'the apex of the social pyramid in the rural landscape' (Hunn 1994, 44). Most, significantly, seem to have developed directly from Iron Age settlements, although it was not until the last quarter of the first century that Romanised buildings appeared on these sites. A number, including Gorhambury in St Albans and Boxmoor and Gade Park in Hemel Hempstead, have been excavated: others are known in Northchurch, Berkhamsted and King's Langley. Gorhambury was the most luxurious and sophisticated. It was occupied from the first to the mid fourth century, and was a complex and wealthy settlement with farm buildings, barns and granaries as well as bath houses. It developed directly from the enclosed Iron Age settlement whose close relationship with the dyke system of the Verlamion *oppidum* suggests that it was the residence of a figure of some political importance. Jonathan Hunn has tentatively suggested that the villas in the vicinity of Verulamium each had territories of between ten and twenty-five square kilometres, but these figures must be treated with caution because, even assuming that all sites of 'villa' type in the area have indeed been discovered, it remains unclear whether settlements of lesser status – which are also known in some numbers – represent tenanted or dependent farms on villa estates, or smaller but independent properties in their own right (Hunn 1994, 53–4).

These less Romanised – or perhaps more correctly, less wealthy – settlements have not received the same attention from archaeologists. They, too, are often concentrated close to the principal valleys, although they can also be found scattered across the clay-covered interfluves between. Once again, they seem often to have developed directly from late prehistoric settlements. Examples include Breakspeares in St Albans, a site occupied from the second to fourth centuries which was obliterated by the construction of the M1; and that near Beech Tree Cottages in the same parish (Hunn 1994, 44). Wainwright's Ashridge survey showed that the pattern of dispersed upland sites, established by the later Iron Age, was maintained into Roman times apparently with little change (Morris and Wainwright 1995). Many Roman sites on the clay-with-flints plateau may, like their Iron Age predecessors, have been principally engaged in the exploitation of grazing, pannage and woodland, or in iron-smelting.

In the chalky boulder-clay areas of north-eastern Hertfordshire the pattern of Roman settlement displays a number of differences from that of the Chilterns. Here, too, many Iron Age settlements developed directly into 'Roman' ones: and the majority of sites, and the largest and most long-lived, were generally clustered in or beside the major valleys, with smaller and apparently poorer farmsteads scattered more thinly across the interfluves between. But settlements were perhaps more numerous than in the Chilterns, while substantial villas of the Gorhambury type, while by no means absent, were less numerous. Both features perhaps reflect the greater fertility of the boulder-clay soils. Indeed, low-density scatters of Roman pottery in the ploughsoil around these sites indicate that even the interfluve sites were to some extent involved in arable husbandry. The actual density of settlement is difficult to estimate but where the clays are most dissected around one site per square kilometre seems to be about average, as in the area astride the far north-eastern boundary of the county, extending into Essex (Williamson 1986, 124) (although not all such sites need to have been occupied at the same time). Even in the area of the Stevenage–Welwyn Clays, to the west of the main Boulder Clay Plateau – where the clay soils are noticeably more acidic and less fertile in character – Jonathan Hunn's research indicates a density of around one site every two square kilometres. Most are associated with the lighter soils of the major valleys, with fewer on the more acid drift of the upland plateau (Hunn 1996, 52).

Settlement was apparently less intensive on the infertile and intractable London Clay soils of the Southern Uplands. Villa sites are known from the margins of the uplands, in the valleys of the Colne and Lea: they are smaller than those from the Chilterns, but moderately wealthy, especially in the district to the south of Verulamium. Examples include Netherwylde Farm, Moor Park, Park Street, Munden and Hamper Mill in Watford (HER). A number of Roman finds have also been reported from the clay uplands, at locations far from these light valley soils. Many, perhaps most, represent pottery kilns, doubtless utilising the reserves of fuel provided by the extensive woodlands, although some may well have been pastoral establishments. Potteries were also located on lower ground. We even know the name of one: analysis of the *mortaria* produced at Bricket Wood suggests that the name of this industrial complex was *Lugdunum* (Niblett 1995b, 93).

All in all, the available evidence thus suggests that the landscape of Hertfordshire in the Roman period continued to be characterised by a distinction between the light soils of valley, Vale and scarp – on or beside which the principal towns, largest villas and main farms were situated – and the clay-covered interfluves which lay between them. On the fertile chalky boulder clays, farms seem to have been widespread even at a distance from the main valleys and most may have been involved (at least to some extent) in arable production. On the clay-with-flints, however, many interfluve sites were probably involved in grazing and industrial production, while on the poor soils of the Southern Uplands extensive woodlands probably survived, with limited clearance for potteries and, perhaps, specialised grazing farms.

Continuity and change

The essential structures of late Iron Age geography were thus developed, rather than radically transformed, by the Roman Conquest. The locations of major Roman towns, and many rural settlements, seem to have been largely determined by earlier patterns of settlement and earlier systems of territorial organisation. Other aspects of indigenous culture seem to have been perpetuated. Major cult centres at Verulamium, and possibly at Baldock and Braughing, continued to exist: local deities continued to be venerated, although they were often now assimilated into the Roman pantheon and equated with Roman gods. We know, for example, from objects found in a hoard at Barkway in the eighteenth century, that the Catuvellaunian god *Toutatis* was identified with Mars (Niblett 1995b, 98–9). Nevertheless, the extent of cultural continuity should not be exaggerated. New immigrants – administrators, retired soldiers, traders – settled in the county, perhaps in some numbers, and they brought with them new and exotic religions. The Triangular Temple at Verulamium thus appears to have been dedicated to the near eastern goddess Cybele (Wheeler and Wheeler 1936). Christianity had been introduced into the region by the mid third century at the latest, when the first British martyr, Alban, appears to have perished at Verulamium – if later tradition is to be believed (below, pp. 81–2). The sites of two possible churches have been identified at Verulamium, but there is surprisingly little other evidence for the adoption of Christianity in the county, in spite of the fact that it became the official religion of the empire in the early fourth century. Indeed, the pagan temples at Verulamium continued to attract offerings on a large scale until the end of the fourth century, if not beyond. Nevertheless, the main ritual complex at Folly Lane appears to have declined significantly in importance during the later third century, possibly reflecting the success of rival cults, including Christianity.

There were probably also changes in patterns of social organisation during the course of the Roman period. In common with other areas of lowland Britain, it is likely that Hertfordshire experienced a degree of social polarisation. Late Iron Age society had been based on the parallel institutions of tribe, *pagus* and kin on the one hand, and patronage or clientage on the other. Under the impact of Roman law, taxation and a market economy, the importance of the former institutions probably declined, while that of the latter increased. A system in which land was held jointly by kin-groups may have been replaced by one in which much private property existed, often in the form of large estates farmed by tenants and slaves, although this tendency was perhaps more marked in the west of the county than on the fertile boulder clays of the east (Williamson 1988, 80–2). Either way, the leading members of tribal society were integrated into the wider national and international elite of the empire, although the tendency for villas to cluster in the vicinity of the principal urban settlements – especially Verulamium, Braughing, Baldock and Welwyn – suggests a continuing association with particular *pagi* and associated cult centres. Local aristocrats doubtless played their part in the great political dramas of the day. It has been suggested, for example, that the sharp decline in the fortunes of villas in western Hertfordshire in the early third century, revealed by excavation, results from the backing given by their owners to Clodius Albinus in his struggle against Severus, and the subsequent confiscation of their property on the latter's victory (Neal *et al.* 1990, 94–5; Niblett 1995b, 113).

Whatever its cause, the early-third-century decline in the fortunes of the Chiltern villas was not shared by similar establishments elsewhere in the county. There are signs of more widespread difficulties towards the end of the century, but the early fourth century appears to have been a period of prosperity and many villas – including those at Moor Park and Park Street – were rebuilt. This was something of an Indian Summer: the second half of the fourth century, in contrast, saw widespread decline. The Gadebridge villa ceased to operate as a country house and became a simple stock farm in the 360s, while the standard of living at Gorhambury and Dickett Mead declined dramatically (Neal *et al.* 1990). The villa at Lockleys was abandoned altogether around 350 (Rook 1986), and although those at Radwell, Wymondley and Moor Park continued to be occupied until at least the end of the fourth century there is little evidence for occupation on any villa site in the county, except perhaps Park Street to the south of St Albans, much after this. This does not mean that large areas of the county became uninhabited at this time, although the population may well have been falling. But the villa-based rural economy was clearly in decline: this was the start of a period of profound social, economic, cultural and political change. Some time around 410 Britain ceased to be part of the Roman empire. Soon afterwards organised Christianity apparently disappeared from lowland England, together with most of the trappings of Roman civilisation, including writing, and within a century or so both Latin and indigenous British languages had probably ceased to be spoken, at least by the social elite. Roman Britain, in short, became Anglo-Saxon England. What these great changes mean, and how they impacted upon Hertfordshire, are matters to which we must next turn.

Chapter 3
Politics and Territory, 400–1000

Early tribes and territories

Historians and archaeologists continue to debate the nature of the 'end of Roman Britain'. What happened in the fifth and sixth centuries is not only rendered obscure by an absence of contemporary written sources; in addition, there are profound debates over how we should interpret the archaeological evidence. There are, for example, difficulties in distinguishing those changes in material culture which were a consequence of demographic and economic decline from those which reflect new political arrangements or (in particular) changes in ethnicity. Many of the most important visible developments – the disappearance of town life, the end of villas, the collapse of a market economy and the end of coinage – were essentially economic in character, although they had political correlates and consequences. They were manifestations of a profound recession which was as much an outcome as a cause of that great political transformation – the collapse of the Roman empire in the west. But the main arguments among archaeologists concern how we should explain those changes in the archaeological record which are more clearly 'cultural' in character, the most visible of which is the appearance in the fifth and sixth centuries, across much of lowland England, of new forms of cemetery containing cremations in decorated urns or inhumations with grave goods. Both the funerary rites themselves, and the styles of the artefacts associated with them, have close parallels in north Germany and southern Scandinavia. Archaeological and historical evidence thus appear to tell a similar story, for our earliest written sources – most notably, the great historian Bede – recount how lowland Britain was indeed conquered and settled in this period by warlike people from these same areas. North Germany and Scandinavia had always been beyond the Roman world: the inhabitants knew nothing of Christianity and their material culture was, in a whole range of ways, strikingly different from that of people dwelling within the frontiers of the Roman empire.

Almost all archaeologists accept that the new forms of burial – and other changes in material culture – do indeed indicate the arrival in the fifth and sixth centuries of Anglo-Saxon invaders from across the North Sea. Given that we now speak a Germanic language, directly descended from the 'Old English' introduced into the country at this time, it would be hard to deny some kind of influx of new settlers. Debate continues, however, over the scale of that settlement: over whether the newcomers represented a small warrior elite (the numbers of known 'pagan' cemeteries are fairly small, even allowing for some reduction in the size of the indigenous population), or whether the invasion took the form of a fully fledged folk movement, involving the wholesale extermination and replacement of indigenous people (Lucy 2000, 155–73). Some archaeologists suggest that things may be even more complicated than this. They argue that while new people did arrive in Britain at this time, changes in language, dress and beliefs probably had more complex causes and signal a broader shift in patterns of cultural influence. As the Roman empire waned – as the complex economic and administrative system based on the distant Mediterranean collapsed – Britain, and to a lesser extent the other parts of the western Empire, was inexorably drawn into both the economic and the cultural world of the barbarian north. Some of those interred in 'Anglo-Saxon' cemeteries were newcomers: but many, perhaps most, were indigenous people who adopted the new styles and trends because they wished to be accepted into a foreign conquering elite, or simply because, as Rome failed and faded, these were now stylish and fashionable (Hodges 1989).

Whatever happened, it is clear that the territorial integrity of Britain disappeared in the early fifth century, as the Provinces of Britannia disintegrated into a number of distinct polities. Hertfordshire did not exist as an entity until the early tenth century. Before that it was contested ground, divided between the kingdoms of the East Saxons (based on what is now the county of Essex) and Mercia (a large polity extending over much of Midland England). But earlier still, in the fifth and sixth centuries, political entities as large and as centralised as these do not seem to have existed. Instead, according to many scholars, political power was highly fragmented (Bassett

1989). Following the withdrawal of the imperial army in the early fifth century, authority devolved to a large number of relatively small autonomous or semi-autonomous tribal groups, each controlling territories extending over tens or hundreds, rather than thousands, of square kilometres. Some of their names are mentioned in early documents while others are preserved in place-names, most notably some (but by no means all) of those ending with the element *ingas*, meaning 'people of'. Often the first element of such names is a personal name – a war leader, perhaps, or else a real or mythical ancestor of the group: sometimes it is a topographic feature, such as a river.[1] Only gradually did larger political units begin to develop, as small tribes repeatedly conquered and absorbed their neighbours, in what Steven Bassett aptly described as a 'glorious knock-out competition' (Bassett 1989, 26). And it was only in the later sixth and seventh centuries, through a logical continuation of this process, that the larger kingdoms which we meet in the pages of Bede's *Ecclesiastical History* and the *Anglo-Saxon Chronicle*, such as Mercia and Essex, began to emerge, initially perhaps as loose confederations of tribes under a paramount leader. Thereafter the process of rivalry continued, as the main English kingdoms took it in turns to dominate and control, although less commonly to absorb, the others.

One stage in this process is preserved in the Tribal Hidage, a list of the tribute owed to a Mercian overlord (Dumville 1989, 133; Hart 1971; Kirby 1991, 9–12; Davies and Vierck 1974). Scholars still disagree about the precise date of this document, although it was probably drawn up during the reign of King Wulfhere (658–75). It describes the payments due from a range of political entities, assessed in terms of a unit called a hide – hence the document's modern name. These included not only large kingdoms such as Essex or Wessex but also examples of much smaller tribal groups – late survivors of Bassett's 'knock-out competition' – mainly strung around the borders of Mercia and perhaps acting in some sense as buffer states (Yorke 1990, 47). One of these is the *Hicce*, assessed at 300 hides, who seem to have occupied a territory in northern Hertfordshire and south Bedfordshire. The territory or *regio* of the tribe was presumably centred on the modern town of

---

1. The term continued to be used into the late Saxon period for extended kin-groups occupying particular areas of land, or in the sense of 'people living in such-and-such a place'. In addition, while names in which *ingas* is linked with another element, especially the term *tun*, 'farm', can also refer to early tribes, many of these are rather later in date, and seem to employ the term in the sense of 'family' or 'extended family', rather than 'tribe'.

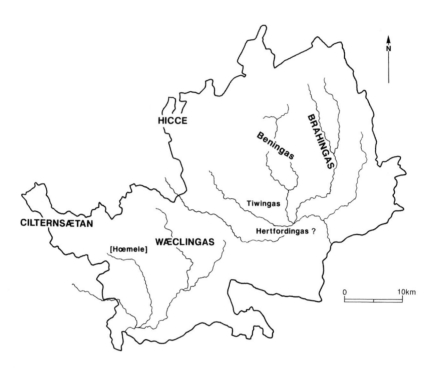

Figure 19. Early Saxon tribes in Hertfordshire.

Hitchin, which preserves its name, but it extended southwards at least as far as Langley, where Hitch Wood is 'the wood belonging to the *Hicce*' (Gover *et al.* 1938, 17). To the north their territory may have extended (as Ian Friel has suggested) as far as that of the *Gifle*, another small tribe listed in the Tribal Hidage, whose name survives in that of the Bedfordshire villages of Northill and Southill (*Nortgiuele* and *Sudgiuele* in Domesday Book). Their territory was probably based on the valley of the River Ivel, which also preserves their name (Friel 1982, 4; Mawer and Stenton 1926, 8, 93, 96).

Another group mentioned in the Tribal Hidage may also have held some land in Hertfordshire: the *Cilternsætan*, the 'dwellers by the Chilterns'. They seem to have occupied a more extensive *regio* than the *Hicce*, to judge from their tribute assessment of 4,000 hides. The majority of their territory probably lay in the main area of the Chiltern Hills and in the clay vale to the north, within the modern counties of Buckinghamshire and Oxfordshire; but it may have extended into what is now Hertfordshire, perhaps bordering the *Hicce* to the west.

Other early tribes in Hertfordshire had been absorbed into larger political units by the time that the Tribal Hidage was drawn up, but we sometimes have hints of their former existence. The most interesting are the *Brahingas*, who have given their name to the modern village of Braughing, first referred to in a charter of the 820s or 30s (Gelling 1979, 81) (Figure 19). The territory of the 'people of Brahha' seems to have been based on the valleys of the Rib and Quin. Another early tribe were the *Wæclingas*, 'the people of Wæcla', who occupied the area around the modern town of St Albans. The Venerable Bede, writing in the early eighth century, knew the town's old Roman name well enough, but also gave its current name as *Wæclingaceaster*, 'the *ceaster* (old Roman fortification) of the Wæclingas' (Colgrave and Mynors 1991, 50). The name was still in use for the town as late as the 990s, when a charter referred to 'Verulamium quod nos vulgariter dicimus Wætlingaceaster' ('Verulamium, which our ignorant call Wætlingcaester') (Crick 2007, 179). This same tribe also, in time, gave its name to the main road leading southwards from Verulamium to London, and northwards as far as Chester: Watling Street.

The *Hicce*, *Brahingas* and *Wæclingas* seem to have been the most important tribes in early Saxon Hertfordshire. Certainly, the territories they controlled, and their central places, evolved into units which were to structure the later administrative framework of the county. But the presence of other groups, probably always to some extent dependent upon or subordinate to these, may also be referred to in place-names. In particular, the village of Bengeo, near Hertford, may take its name from 'the spur of land of the *Beningas*', the 'dwellers on the River Beane'; Benington, some ten kilometres further north up the valley of that river, may likewise be the *tun* or settlement of the *Beningas* (Bailey 1989, 115; Gover *et al.* 1938, 121, 215).[2] Their territory perhaps occupied the whole of the valley of the River Beane, as well as that of its tributary the Old Bourne, with Bengeo representing the southern extremity of their land (Figure 19). Another group may have been centred on Tewin, described as the *terram Tiwingum* in a charter of *c.*945: the 'land of the people of Tiwa', or perhaps 'of the worshippers of the God Tew' (Gover *et al.* 1938, 231). Their territory would have been based on the broad gravel terraces beside the River Mimram, to the west of Hertford. Less certainly, a

---

2. Although it is possible that these names are simply compounds containing the connective *inge*, 'by' or 'at': Bengeo would thus simply be the 'hill spur beside the river Beane'.

few kilometres to the south-east, we have the village of Hertingfordbury, originally 'the defended place of the *Hertfordingas* (the people of Hertford)', which may just possibly suggest a group based on the area around that town and extending along the valley of the River Lea (Gover *et al.* 1938, 227).

Although other tribal groups doubtless existed whose names are completely lost to us, it is nevertheless striking how closely the distribution of those we do know about corresponds with the structures of topography and geography outlined in the opening chapter of this book. The *Hicce* thus occupied the exposures of light chalk soils along and below the escarpment in the far north of the county, while the *Wæclingas* had their heartland on the gravels and well-drained brickearths at the western end of the Vale of St Albans. The broken, dissected terrain around the eastern end of the Vale, where the valleys of the Lea, Mimram, Beane and Rib run through clay-covered uplands, created more splintered pockets of well-drained soil which provided homes for the *Brahingas*, and probably for the *Beningas* and *Tiwingas*, and just possibly for the *Hertfordingas*.

Continuity and survival

Early tribal names like these are unquestionably of Old English form: they were coined by people speaking the precursor of our own language. However, it remains very uncertain whether they indicate that by the sixth century the county's inhabitants were entirely Germanic in culture, and, if so, for how long this had been the case. Indeed, the character of the Roman–Saxon transition continues, as already observed, to be a matter of debate among historians and archaeologists. In the case of Hertfordshire the issue is made particularly intriguing because archaeological evidence for the presence of early Germanic immigrants is almost completely lacking – a situation shared by the neighbouring counties of Middlesex and Essex. In the counties to the north and east – Suffolk, Norfolk, Cambridgeshire and Bedfordshire – large numbers of pagan Saxon burial grounds are known, most strikingly the large cremation cemeteries of the fifth and sixth centuries, which often display a clear association with the main political and military centres of late Roman times. In Hertfordshire large early cemeteries are unknown, and those few burials and cemeteries of probable Saxon date which have been discovered in the county (at Ashwell, St Albans, perhaps Redbourn and Wheathampstead) are all inhumations: a situation mirrored in the adjacent areas of south Buckinghamshire, Essex and Middlesex

(Wingfield 1995). This, and a more general paucity of fifth- and sixth-century Anglo-Saxon artefacts, has led a series of archaeologists and historians – including Sir Mortimer Wheeler, K. Rutherford Davies, Keith Branigan, Warwick Rodwell and Ken Dark – to suggest a measure of Romano-British political and ethnic survival across some, or all, of this area up until the later sixth century – perhaps until the battle of *Biedcanford* (possibly Bedford) in 571 (Branigan 1985, 175–92; Dark 1994, 87–8; Drury and Rodwell 1980, 71; Rutherford Davis 1982; Wheeler 1935, 59–74). A more measured and cautious version of this view has recently been put forward by Baker (2006). Such a sub-Roman territory might have been based on Verulamium, or on London, or on the continuing political integrity of a joint Trinovantian–Catuvellaunian *civitas* (Dark 1994, 87).

As Baker has emphasised, the interpretation of the archaeological evidence for 'continuity' is by no means straightforward (Baker 2006, 251–6). It could be argued that the paucity of early pagan cemeteries in the counties immediately north of the Thames simply reflects a real paucity of people, of any kind, living within this area in the fifth and sixth centuries. It is indeed generally agreed that there was a substantial fall in population in the immediate post-Roman period, so that much land went out of cultivation and settlements disappeared from the more agriculturally marginal areas. Yet it is hard to believe that the entire area of Hertfordshire and adjacent counties, continuously occupied with varying degrees of intensity since early prehistoric times, was now largely abandoned to woodland. It could also be argued that pagan cemeteries exist, or existed, in the district, but have either been destroyed unrecognised in the past or still await discovery. Yet if such cemeteries had once been as common here as in counties such as Norfolk then it is surprising that they have not yet come to light, given the scale of development since the nineteenth century in this urbanised hinterland of London, involving precisely the kinds of activities – the construction of houses, roads and railways, and the extraction of gravel – which have led to their discovery elsewhere.

Nevertheless, it is noteworthy that large-scale 'Celtic survival' is not reflected in other sources of evidence, such as place-names. Indeed, only a handful of names of probable Latin or Celtic origin survive in Hertfordshire (Figure 20). One category has already been discussed – river names. The Brent, Lea and Beane all appear to bear the names of Celtic gods and goddesses, and the names of the Mimram and the Colne may also have a

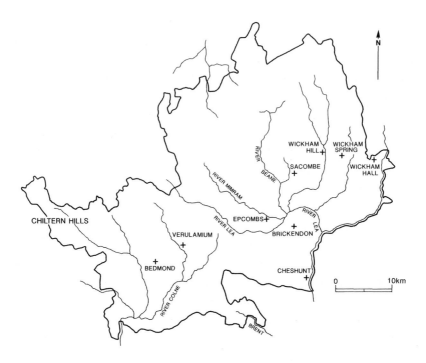

Figure 20. Names of probable pre-Saxon origin in Hertfordshire.

Celtic origin (Davis 1982, 154). The name of the Chiltern Hills (and of the *Cilternsætan*) seems to incorporate the Old British adjective **celto*, 'high' (Gover *et al.* 1938, 7); and the name of the village of Brickendon may, as Rutherford Davis has suggested, include the Celtic element **Brico*, 'hill' (Rutherford Davis 1982, 156). The survival of Celtic names for rivers and other large topographic features is characteristic of other areas of eastern England, including those (such as East Anglia) in which large numbers of early cemeteries are known (Williamson 1993, 54–7). It suggests, perhaps, that the majority only slowly came to adopt the tongue of a dominant minority; and that large topographic features were renamed more slowly than individual settlements and estates.

The name of the River Beane is of particular interest in this context. The oldest recorded version, in the *Anglo-Saxon Chronicle* for 912, is *Bene ficcan*. This may incorporate the Old Welsh word *ficean*, 'little'; but of particular interest is the position of this adjective *after*, rather than *before*, the noun it qualifies – a practice which became normal in Welsh only some time in the later sixth century (Ekwall 1928, 27–8; Gover *et al.* 1938, xv). There has been no modern study of this name, but if the old interpretation is correct it would imply that some form of Welsh was being spoken in east Hertfordshire at a remarkably late date. Moreover, according to Bede, writing in 731, a great synod was held in 679 at 'the place which in the Saxon tongue is called Hatfield' (Colgrave and Mynors 1991, 385), strongly suggesting that there was another name for the place, and that other, non-English languages were still being spoken in the locality. Unfortunately, there are serious doubts over whether the Hatfield in question was, indeed, that in Hertfordshire, or whether Bede was (more probably) referring to Hatfield in Yorkshire.

A handful of other names in Hertfordshire appear to indicate the adoption of Latin terms by English settlers (Figure 20). These include two examples of the term *camp*, derived from the Latin *campus*, 'field' – the parish of Sacombe and Epcombes, a hamlet in Hertingfordbury; two examples of the term *funta*, from the Latin *fons*, a fountain or well – Cheshunt and Bedmond, a hamlet in Abbot's Langley (Chalfont, just across the county boundary in Buckinghamshire, is another probable example); and three possible examples of the term *wicham*, a combination of the Latin *vicus*, 'small settlement', and Old English *ham*, 'village' or 'estate' (Gelling 1978, 80–5). The significance of some of these names will be discussed further: it is sufficient here to say that their paucity suggests the disappearance of Latin as a spoken language at a relatively early date, although once again whether this reflects a massive influx of Saxon settlers and the displacement of the indigenous inhabitants, or a more gradual cultural dominance by an English-speaking elite, remains unclear. It is worth noting, in passing, that the name of one of the most important tribal groups in early Saxon Hertfordshire – the *Hicce* – may itself have originated from a Celtic term for a dry stream bed (Ekwall 1928, 197).

One way of examining developments in the Hertfordshire area in the fifth and sixth centuries is to consider the fate of its principal Roman towns, especially Verulamium, where there have been numerous excavations over the years. Unfortunately, with the end of pottery production and the demise of coinage, post-Roman sequences in the town are hard to date, but a number of finds suggest, in Niblett's words, 'occupation over much of Verulamium continuing into the 5th century' (Niblett 1993, 89). Of particular importance is the accumulating evidence for timber structures cutting into Roman buildings (Hunn 1994, 55; Niblett and Thompson

2005). In the southern corner of Insula XIV, within the town, Sheppard Frere excavated a small corridor house which was built at the end of the fourth century and extensively altered some time later (Niblett and Thompson 2005, 171; Frere 1983, 93–101). Other evidence for probable post-Roman occupation has been recovered from Insulae XIII and XVIII, while Frere's excavations in the 1960s in Insula XXVII, next to the forum, revealed a particularly interesting sequence. A feature interpreted as a corn-drying kiln was inserted into the mosaic floor of a masonry house: the floor had been patched in the late fourth century, and afterwards experienced a fairly extended period of use before a large hall-like building, possibly a barn, was erected on the site. This in turn was cut through by a timber water pipe, apparently bringing water to the centre of the town and thus implying the continued existence of some kind of functioning civic authority. The sequence here is not firmly dated, but must surely extend beyond AD 400, and perhaps well into the fifth century (Frere 1983, 212–24; Niblett and Thompson 2005, 169–72). Post-Roman settlement has also been discovered at a number of places outside the town walls: in Hill Street, *c.*200 metres to the east of the Roman road to Welwyn; and beside the same road, *c.*200 metres further north. The latter site comprised five buildings, one containing two sherds of early Saxon pottery (Niblett 1999, 95–8; Niblett and Thompson 2005, 172–5). A number of chaff-tempered sherds, probably associated, were found nearby; such sherds were also found in the vicinity of the abbey during excavations to the south of the medieval nave (Biddle and Kjolbye-Biddle 1981, 12). Pottery of this kind probably began to be used in the area in the sixth century, although it may have continued in use as late as the eighth century (Niblett and Thompson 2005, 176–7).

In addition to all this, two sub-Roman cemeteries are known from the vicinity of the Roman town. One, at Batchwood, contained at least fifty-six inhumations. They were orientated east–west and lacked grave goods (other than a shale pin and some glass beads), but a post-Roman date was indicated by the fact that they were cut through the rubble of a building demolished in the late fourth century (Frere 1983, 287–8; Hunn 1994, 58). A late Roman cemetery which lay around and beneath the medieval abbey also appears to have continued in use into the fifth century, and, while there is no certain evidence for its use after this, finds of later fifth- and sixth-century metalwork have come from the same general area (Biddle and Kjolbye-Biddle 2001, 60–5). As Niblett has observed, when the evidence for fifth-

and sixth-century occupation is plotted on a map two main foci of settlement are clearly indicated: one in the centre of the town, close to the forum (and thus close to the pre-Roman 'Central Enclosure'); the other in the immediate area of the medieval abbey, on the hill outside the town. Only at the very end of the sixth century, however, is there clear evidence for some kind of Germanic presence in the town, in the form of a small seventh-century inhumation cemetery of normal Saxon kind, discovered just outside the Silchester gate (Ager 1989; Niblett and Thompson 2005, 184–5).

Documentary evidence also implies that the *municipium* retained some importance well beyond AD 410. The *Life* of St Germanus, Bishop of Auxerre, which was composed around 480, describes how the saint came to Britain to fight the Pelagian heresy in 428–9, and while here visited the shrine of Saint Alban, opening the tomb and giving it extra power by donating additional relics which he had brought with him (Levison 1941). Later sources tell us this was at Verulamium, but the writer of the *Vita* is silent on this matter. During his visit Germanus addressed a richly dressed gathering of local people and was involved in repulsing an attack by a party of barbarian raiders. The panic-stricken populace was rallied by the bishop, and prepared an ambush in a valley surrounded by hills. The British, following his instructions, shouted 'alleluia' so loudly that the barbarians fled in terror (Levison 1941; Myres 1960). The story has been taken as evidence that some kind of organised civil life was continuing at Verulamium in the early to mid fifth century, although unfortunately closer reading of the text makes it less clear that the meeting addressed took place here, near Alban's burial place, rather than at London or somewhere else.

Although the *Vita* of Germanus fails to link Alban and Verulamium, the monk and historian Gildas – writing somewhere in Britain around half a century later – specifically describes 'sanctum Albanum Verolamiensem' (Saint Alban of Verulamium) as a 'light in the darkness', and one of the saints whose shrine could no longer be visited by Britons (presumably living in the west of England) because of the presence of barbarian settlers (Winterbottom 1978, 92). Gildas relates the story of Alban's martyrdom in a passage which is probably based on the *Passio Sancti Albani*, written in Auxerre around AD 500 or perhaps earlier (Sharpe 2001). This also formed the basis for the account presented in Bede's *Ecclesiastical History* of 731, although he also supplies a number of other important and independent details (Crick 2007, 6).

Alban was probably martyred in the mid third century. He sheltered a Christian priest fleeing persecution, was converted by him, and offered himself up as a substitute to the Roman authorities. He was martyred on a hill outside the town, God making a spring rise at his feet when, in his passion, he cried out for water. As already noted, St Albans Abbey stands outside the Roman town, on the rising ground above the valley to the east. There are many continental examples of places where major Christian shrines stand in such a relationship to a Roman town, including Tours, Arles, Cologne and Lyon in France, and Bonn in Germany. This is because they occupy the sites of late Roman cemeteries, placed by law and custom beyond town walls: and these contained the burial places of martyrs which came, in late antiquity, to be held in 'special, almost obsessive regard' (Morris 1989, 13). Bede tells us that, some time after Alban's death, 'a church of wonderful workmanship was built, a worthy memorial to his martyrdom. To this day sick people are helped in this place and the working of frequent miracles continues to bring it renown' (Colgrave and Mynors 1991, 35).

Medieval tradition – first recorded in the late eleventh century, when the 'F' version of the *Anglo-Saxon Chronicle* was produced at Canterbury – held that a new church was built to replace this structure in 793 by Offa, king of Mercia. The saint's relics were translated to it, and some kind of religious community was established, or an existing one regularised. There seems little reason to doubt the tradition (Levison 1941, 350; Crick 2007, 16). A third-century martyr's tomb in an extra-mural cemetery may thus have developed, in time, into a major Saxon church and monastery (Levison 1941). Such a development would be unsurprising in Gaul, where Christianity survived the collapse of the Roman empire. It would be more remarkable in Hertfordshire, where the faith – never perhaps deeply entrenched – was supposedly wiped out by pagan invaders. Indeed, there are no other parallels for such a phenomenon in England, where, after the conversion, the principal venerated saints were all early *English* martyrs. Nevertheless the historical evidence appears fairly convincing, and is to some extent backed up by the archaeology. Martin Biddle's excavations on the site of the abbey chapter house in the 1970s revealed a series of ditches of late Roman or early post-Roman date which ran

> precisely at right angles to the axis of the Norman abbey church, and so
> demonstrate that the arrangement of the abbey hill-top has preserved this

alignment since at least as early as the 8th century and possibly since late
Roman or immediate post-Roman times (Biddle and Kjolbye-Biddle 1981, 26)

Subsequent excavations revealed evidence for the late Roman cemetery
beneath the south-western side of the cloisters already described, a cemetery
which might well have included the grave (or supposed grave) of the martyr
(Niblett and Thompson 2005, 145; Biddle and Kjolbye-Biddle 2001).

Yet it is possible that there are deeper, more ancient roots to all this – an
even longer thread of continuity. As Ros Niblett has suggested, the location
of the abbey church – on a hill overlooking the Roman town – mirrors
closely that of the Folly Lane temple a kilometre further to the north-west,
which was abandoned in the course of the third century: and the fact that
Alban, according to tradition, was beheaded may hint that the early church
actively hijacked elements of the older head-cult, and hero-cult, centred on
that shrine (Niblett 1999, 417–18). Either way, the fact that the memory of
Alban was maintained from Roman times into the eighth century strongly
suggests that there was a continuing indigenous population to maintain it. It
does not, certainly, suggest wholesale extermination by invading Saxons.
Attention should also perhaps be drawn to the location of St Michael's
church in St Albans. Although the present structure was built in the late
Saxon period it overlies the forum of the Roman town: an area which itself,
as we have seen, overlay a late Iron Age rectangular enclosure of probable
ritual significance. All in all, it seems likely that Verulamium/St Albans
retained some kind of importance as a central place and cult centre
throughout the post-Roman period: firstly for the tribal territory of the
Wæclingas, and subsequently (as we shall see) for a Mercian royal estate,
before Offa established a monastic community here in 793.

The fate of the Roman town at Braughing is also striking. There can be
little doubt that, just as the *Wæclingas* occupied a territory based on
Verulamium, the *Brahingas* inhabited one based on this large urban site. One
of only three probable Hertfordshire examples of a *wicham* name, Wickham
Hill, lies above and to the south-west of the village of Braughing, and was the
site of the main built-up area of the Roman town. The two largest Roman
settlements in the county thus maintained some kind of significance as central
places well into the early Saxon period and, as we shall see, beyond.

The third of the county's principal Roman towns – that at Baldock –
developed in a rather different way to Verulamium or Braughing. The
principal tribal group in the north of the county, the *Hicce*, seem to have had

their main focus at Hitchin, rather than at Baldock. Indeed, the modern town of Baldock, which overlies the site of the Roman settlement, did not exist in Anglo-Saxon times but was a new creation, a 'planted town', of the twelfth century. Nevertheless, here, too, continuity of a sort can perhaps be discerned. There is some evidence for occupation at Baldock into the fifth century, although its nature is unknown: excavations on the Upper Walls Common site revealed traces of timber buildings, some with sill-beams and some with earth-fast posts, which clearly post-dated the Roman period (Wingfield 1995, 34). The centre of Hitchin lies only seven kilometres away: various finds of Roman material indicate that a number of settlements and cemeteries existed within the area of the town, and while occupation was probably only agricultural in character, it was clearly quite dense (HER 11793, 1418, 6474, 186290, 11793, 187307, etc.). Here, as at St Albans, there are post-Roman cemeteries containing inhumations without grave goods – one at the junction of Bancroft, Brand Street and the High Street (HER 13353) and another on Queens Street. Neither is closely dated, and both could be middle Saxon in date, although in the latter case radiocarbon dating suggests that the burials were made some time between the late Roman and middle Saxon periods (HER 11351). Whatever the precise course of events, Hitchin clearly took over from Baldock as the main centre for a territory based on the area of light soils on and below the Chiltern escarpment of north Hertfordshire, and it is hard to believe that it did so indirectly, or after a lengthy period of dislocation or abandonment.

It is possible that some of the less important 'small towns' of Roman Hertfordshire formed centres for other early tribal territories – for social groups whose existence is hinted at only by place-names, and who may always have been subordinate to, or perhaps formed subdivisions of, the three main tribes. The *Tiwingas*, if they indeed existed, would have been located close to the probable Iron Age *oppidum*, Roman 'small town' and cluster of wealthy villas at Welwyn, to judge from the location of Tewin (see above, p. 75). A group centred on the town of Cheshunt may be another example. As we shall see, an ancient boundary line, preserved in part by a section of the old diocesan boundary, seems to define the edge of a territory based on the Roman roadside settlement here. The first element of Cheshunt's name comes from *ceaster*, the Old English term for a Roman fortification (either a military base or fortified town: the term is ultimately derived from the Latin *castrum*, 'camp'). The second contains the word *funta*, spring, which (as already noted) is a direct loan-word from Latin. No fortification now survives in the built-up parish, but it is possible that the roadside settlement was fortified in some way in late or sub-Roman times, while the survival of a Latin term suggests some degree of continuity, or at least of contact between English and Latin speakers. As we shall see, there are grounds for believing that a number of other social territories in Saxon Hertfordshire had Romano-British origins.

All this raises obvious questions about the origins of the main tribal groups, and of their subordinates or subdivisions, in early Saxon Hertfordshire. It is noteworthy how, when Offa, a king of Essex, granted land in *c.*705 to Waldhere, Bishop of London, at Hemel, in the west of the county, the term used for the district was *pagus*, rather than the more usual *regio* (Gelling 1979, 80). *Pagus* was a Latin word with a variety of meanings, but was still used in the Roman period not simply for an administrative subdivision of a *civitas* but also, as we have seen, for a social subdivision of a tribe, a local kin-group linked by ties of descent. Names like *Brahingas*, 'the people of Brahha', are evidence of comparable Old English social institutions. Were groups like this indeed incomers? Or do we have hints here of the gradual acculturation – the Anglicisation – of existing, long-established communities, *pagi* of the Catuvellauni: and of the resurgence of social forms overshadowed in late Roman times by the growth of a more hierarchical society?

The Roman–Saxon transition in Hertfordshire, as in adjacent areas of Essex and the Chilterns, does appear to have been more delayed, and more gradual, than in many areas of lowland Britain, especially the districts to the north of the Chilterns, where evidence of fifth-century cemeteries is widespread. How we account for this pattern depends, to some extent, on how we envisage the nature of the 'transition' itself. Those who see the changes in material culture as a direct expression of the influx of a new ethnic group would interpret the absence of archaeological evidence for an intrusive Germanic population in essentially historical terms: some kind of post-Roman polity, perhaps based on Verulamium, protected the area from invasion and thus allowed the survival of an 'enclave' in which vestiges of Romano-British life continued into the sixth century. But we perhaps see the issue in a slightly different way if we examine archaeological distributions against the broad sweeps of national topography briefly described in Chapter 1: for by doing this we can see more clearly how the experience of

Hertfordshire and the adjacent areas fits into a wider regional picture.

In East Anglia, the Midlands and north-east England the dominant funerary rite in the fifth and earlier sixth centuries was cremation, with the ashes placed in urns: these were interred in what were often very extensive cemeteries. Inhumation was also practised in these regions, but it only gradually became the most popular method of disposal. While cremation cemeteries are by no means unknown in the south of England, they are rare and generally small in size (Lucy 2000, 140–4). Here inhumation with grave goods was, from the fifth century onwards, the overwhelmingly dominant rite. In addition, while across most of East Anglia, the Midlands and the north-east of England cemeteries – cremation, inhumation, or mixed – are widely scattered, with gaps in their distribution which are usually explicable in terms of high, drift-covered uplands, tracts of heavy, intractable clay, or waterlogged fen, this is less true in the south and south-east. Here many large areas of fertile and relatively easily worked land, as across much of Hertfordshire, have failed to produce any kinds of 'Anglo-Saxon' burials, suggesting that some social groups in the fifth and sixth century may have employed forms of disposal that have left no clear archaeological traces, like many of their predecessors in Roman Britain (Lucy 2000, 140).

Regional differences in burial practice used to be interpreted by archaeologists in terms of the areas settled by the principal Germanic tribes in the fifth and sixth centuries, as famously described by the eighth-century historian Bede:

> The people of Kent and the inhabitants of the Isle of Wight are of Jutish origin, and also those opposite the Isle of Wight, that part of the Kingdom of Wessex which is still today called the nation of the Jutes. From the Saxon country, that is, the district now known as Old Saxony, came the East Saxons, the South Saxons, and the West Saxons. Besides this, from the country of the Angles, that is the land between the kingdoms of the Jutes and the Saxons, which is called *Angulus*, came the East Angles, the Middle Angles, the Mercians, and all the Northumbrian race ... as well as the other Anglian tribes ... (Colgrave and Mynors 1991, 51)

Cremation cemeteries were thus concentrated within, although not entirely restricted to, those areas which Bede believed had been settled by people coming from Angeln – East Anglia, Mercia and Northumbria. This same general pattern, moreover, is reflected, albeit more weakly, in the distribution of certain kinds of artefact, especially those related to forms of dress, in the fifth and sixth centuries. So-called 'Anglian' material, largely restricted to East Anglia, the Midlands and the north-east, is typified by the artefacts known as 'wrist clasps' and by particular styles of brooch – those classified by archaeologists as 'equal armed', 'cruciform' and 'annular', together with most of the 'square-headed' variety. In 'Saxon' areas, in contrast – essentially, the south of England – wrist clasps are largely absent and different forms of brooch predominate – a particular kind of square-headed ('Group VIII'), quoit and radiate-headed (Hills 1998, 184; Parker Pearson *et al.* 1993, 34–6; Hines 1984). In fact, it has long been recognised that 'Saxon' material occurs widely in 'Anglian' areas, although the inverse is rather less true: but the patterns are intriguing nevertheless.

Modern archaeologists, for the most part, do not accept the neat ethnic labels or the simplicity of Bede's account which was, after all, written more than two centuries after the *Adventus Saxonum*. The modern orthodoxy is that the Germanic settlers were, in fact, culturally diverse and ethnically mixed. In the words of Sam Lucy:

> The immediate post-Roman period in Britain, and indeed in the whole of
> Europe, was a time when identities were in an extreme state of flux .. when
> charismatic leaders could gather strong bands of followers around them and
> gain control of often extensive tracts of territory ... (Lucy 2000, 4).

In the process of migration people from a wide area of northern Germany and southern Scandinavia might become incorporated within the same war band. Nevertheless, the material culture of the period does display, at least to a degree, the kind of geographical patterning outlined above, and this requires some form of explanation – not least, in the present context, to elucidate the early development of Hertfordshire itself. The evidence certainly indicates regional variations in culture, affecting such matters as styles of dress, in the fifth and sixth centuries:

> In East Anglia, the East Midlands and Yorkshire, women wore cruciform and
> annular brooches, and fastened their sleeves with metal clasps. In southern
> England, in Sussex, Wessex and Essex, they preferred round brooches and did
> not use clasps (Hills 1998, 184).

The significance of these patterns becomes rather clearer when we consider them against the configuration of drainage basins and watersheds in southern

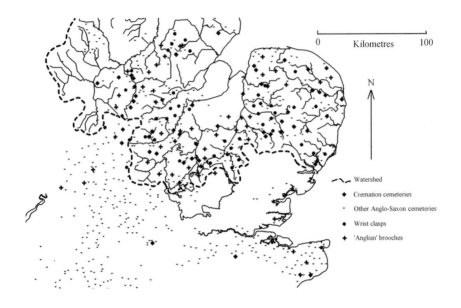

Figure 21. The location of Hertfordshire in relation to the distribution of 'Anglian' artefacts, cremation cemeteries and the boundaries of the 'North Sea Province'.

and eastern England, which was briefly discussed in Chapter 1. As suggested there, patterns of topography – the contrast between 'river' and 'wold' – might structure not only local patterns of identity and allegiance, but also much wider ones. Not only individual river valleys, but also entire regional catchments, might approximate to social or cultural territories. As already suggested, situations in which contact and communication between individuals and groups of people was easy and regular tended to engender if not a measure of social or political identity then at least some sharing of beliefs, language and fashions. Where contact was restricted, in contrast – for topographic or other reasons – there was more divergence in development. In the immediate post-Roman period, however, we have another factor to bear in mind. This was a time when England was, perhaps more than at any other period, subject to the movement of people, artefacts and ideas coming from foreign lands – from Ireland, Scotland and, above all, the European mainland. Where the principal English rivers entered the sea – that is, in which direction they and their catchments faced – is thus also a matter of some importance. The three great 'provinces' briefly described in Chapter 1 – facing the North Sea, the Irish Sea and the Channel and the Thames estuary respectively – may thus have been more important in structuring patterns of contact in the immediate post-Roman period than at any time before or since.

'Anglian' England – with its cremation cemeteries and distinctive artefacts – clearly corresponds with the 'North Sea Province' (Figure 21). Its distinctive character must in part reflect the fact that it faces out across the North Sea to regions which had never been within the Roman *limes*. But this pattern of cultural influences did not necessarily operate over a short period of time, or even solely in one direction. As Catherine Hills has noted:

> People did not get into their boats and sail to England, never to return. The communities on both sides of the North Sea remained in contact. The connections between them could have owed as much to the exchange of ideas and goods through trade, religion and political relationships as to migration. (Hills 1998, 183)

'Saxon' England, in contrast – essentially, what I have defined here as the 'English Channel Province' – faces France and the southern parts of the Low Countries, lands which had formed parts of the Roman Empire. The absence of large cremation cemeteries from this region probably indicates that it was less subject to major cultural influences from 'barbarian' lands, and perhaps less affected by 'barbarian' immigration in the immediate post-Roman period. Indeed, as a number of scholars have argued, the appearance in this region in the fifth century of cemeteries containing inhumations with grave goods may have been the consequence of indigenous developments within late Roman society, rather than representing, in any simple and straightforward way, the signature of 'invaders'. In Hills' words:

> Late Roman burials were mostly unfurnished inhumations, but the later fourth century saw the appearance in Britain and northern Gaul of inhumations accompanied by weapons and belt fittings. Although these have often been interpreted as the burials of Germanic mercenary soldiers, there is not really any reason to see them purely in ethnic terms, although it does seem to have been a fashion prevalent among a military elite, which included men of Germanic origins. These burials may have contributed to the development of the rite [i.e. inhumation burial with grave goods] seen throughout western Europe and southern Britain between the fifth and seventh centuries. (Hills 1998, 184)

The marked paucity of any obviously pagan Saxon burials from many areas of southern England should be read in a similar way, as evidence for the perpetuation of essentially Romano-British forms of funerary practice well into the sixth century. The south did, of course, eventually become 'Anglo-Saxon' in cultural and, in particular, in linguistic terms. But the character of the transition was evidently different from that in the 'North Sea Province', and extended over a longer period of time.

With the exception of rivers like the Hiz and the Ivel, in the far north of the county, all of Hertfordshire's rivers drain south, into the Thames. The county, south of the watershed running along the Chilterns, lies firmly within the catchment of the Thames – within the Channel Province. Moreover, that section of the boundary between the two 'provinces' which passes through Hertfordshire – along the crest of the Chiltern Hills and the 'East Anglian Heights' – follows an interfluve which is at that point wider and higher than it is to the east or west, where the watershed follows rather lower hills, and is often hardly discernible as a topographic feature. In Hertfordshire – or at least, in the majority of the county, lying south of the watershed – connections with the south should thus have been particularly strong in the immediate post-Roman period, and those with the Midlands and the east correspondingly weak. It is in this context that we should see the paucity of pagan cemeteries, especially early cremation cemeteries, in the county, and in the areas lying immediately to the south, east and west – in Essex, Middlesex and the Chilterns.

Debate about these matters will doubtless continue. What does seem likely is that by the end of the sixth century the county was divided between a number of distinct tribal groups whose territories were based – like the main arable areas of earlier periods – on the principal exposures of light, well-drained soil. The most important of these territories, and some of their subdivisions, seem to have been focused on sites of Roman importance, and the groups themselves may have developed, more or less directly, from subdivisions of the Catuvellauni, albeit dominated by a new Germanic elite and gradually coming to adopt the latter's language and culture. Although much about the immediate post-Roman period remains completely obscure, the available evidence clearly suggests at least a measure of continuity of political and perhaps social structures from the fourth century into the seventh century and beyond.

Mercia and Essex

In the course of the sixth and early seventh centuries larger political units – kingdoms – gradually emerged in lowland England through the conquest, absorption and amalgamation of smaller tribal entities; the political history of middle Saxon England is that of the wars and conquests between these various fledgling states. Different kingdoms in turn came to dominate England – Northumbria in the seventh century, Mercia in the eighth, and Wessex in the late ninth and tenth, leading ultimately to the unification of England. For much of this period Hertfordshire was divided territory, lying between the kingdoms of Mercia and Essex, and its development in middle Saxon times cannot be understood without a brief review of the history of these polities.

Mercia first appears on the historical stage with the great victories of its king, Penda, in the middle decades of the seventh century (Yorke 1990, 102–3). By the end of that century we can see it more clearly as a large and powerful kingdom embracing much of the Midlands and centred on the Trent basin. As already noted, the Tribal Hidage shows it surrounded by a number of small polities, of whom the *Cilternsætan* and *Hicce* are examples, which never attained the size or permanence of Essex, Wessex and the rest. Other sources make it clear that most of these were effectively 'buffer states' which, while retaining a measure of autonomy, were firmly under Mercian control (Yorke 1990, 106). Some were ruled by members of the Mercian royal family or their close relatives; others by leaders tied to them by patronage or obligation; while, in others, Mercian kings possessed extensive estates or patronised religious houses.

The eighth century was the century of the Mercians. Under Æthelbald (716–57) and Offa (757–96) they came to dominate all the other kingdoms of southern England (Yorke 1990, 111–17). The 'buffer states' were systematically absorbed. They ceased to be described as kingdoms or peoples, and became instead Mercian *ealdormanries*. Even the large kingdom of Kent was, by the end of Offa's reign, ruled directly from Mercia. Although native dynasties continued in East Anglia, Essex, Northumbria and Wessex, these too were now effectively satellite provinces. Military conquest brought other forms of wealth. Control of the Kentish ports, and of London – seized from the East Saxons – presumably allowed the Mercian kings to grow rich on the tolls from trade. And yet, in the unstable and shifting kaleidoscope of Anglo-Saxon power politics, the ascendancy of Mercia was temporary. Offa died in 796 and was succeeded by his son Egfrith; but he too died after a mere 141 days (Yorke 1990, 117). His successor, a distant cousin called Cenwulf, continued Offa's policies with some success; but on his death in 821 a series of kings was championed by rival noble families, and succeeded each other with some rapidity. Two of the subject kingdoms – East Anglia and Wessex – began to shake off the yoke of Mercian domination. The West Saxons had the greatest success. King Egberht, who came to the throne in 802, annexed Kent, Essex, Surrey and the lands of the South Saxons, and even attempted to rule Mercia directly, after driving King Wiglaf into exile in 829. Wiglaf returned to power the following year, but the annexations of southern England – including, crucially (as we shall see), Essex – proved permanent.

Yet it was not the West Saxons, but foreign invaders – the Vikings – who finally destroyed Mercia. Scandinavian raiders first attacked England in 792, when the monastery of Lindisfarne in Northumbria was sacked. Two generations of seasonal raiding followed before, in 865, the 'great army' arrived with permanent conquest in mind. Northumbria and East Anglia were soon overrun by the invaders, whose attention then turned to Mercia, the Viking forces wintering in Nottingham in 868, London in 872 and Lindsey in 873. The Mercian king Burhred was exiled in 874, and the Vikings seized eastern Mercia, although they allowed one Ceolwulf II to remain, more or less as a client king, as ruler of the western part of the kingdom (Yorke 1990, 123).

Ceolwulf was succeeded after five years by Æthelred, who in 886/7 married Æthelflaed, the daughter of King Alfred of Wessex. After this the western portion of Mercia was dependent upon, although not yet completely annexed by, Wessex, while the eastern half remained Danish territory, settled to varying degrees by members of the Danish army and possibly by peasants migrating from the Scandinavian homelands. In contemporary charters and other documents Æthelred is not styled 'king' of the Mercians, but rather *dux* ('leader'), Procurator, or *ealdorman*. Following his death in 911 his widow, Æthelflaed, co-operated with Alfred's successor, her brother Edward the Elder, in the re-conquest of those areas of Mercia settled by the Danes. But Mercia never regained its independence. Æthelflaed died in 918, and from *c.*920 Mercia was effectively absorbed into the West Saxon state.

Essex, the kingdom of the East Saxons, was always a more obscure polity than Mercia. Its origins are unclear, and the earliest king of whom we have any information is Sledd, whose son Sæbert converted to Christianity and founded the bishopric of the East Saxons in 604 (Yorke 1990, 46–7). The core of the kingdom was always the modern county of Essex, but it embraced much adjacent territory, including eastern Hertfordshire, a fact still remembered in the thirteenth century when William of Malmesbury wrote that 'half of Hertfordshire' once lay within the kingdom (Giles 1866, 93). Essex also controlled, at various times, much of Middlesex, London and Surrey (Yorke 1990, 49). It was London, rather than Colchester, which became the seat of the bishop of the East Saxons. Middlesex means 'Middle Saxons' but, in spite of the similarity of its name to that of Essex, this area does not ever seem to have formed a separate kingdom. The Middle Saxons are first mentioned in a document of the late eighth century recording a grant of land in 704 (Kirby 1991, 7): so far as the evidence goes, they were a loose confederation of peoples in the area around London, conquered at an early date (probably before the late sixth century) by the East Saxons.

In spite of such early successes Essex never gained the power and prominence of East Anglia, Kent or Mercia (Yorke 1990, 46–56). Indeed, for most of its history the kingdom was dominated by one neighbour after another, and at times by kingdoms still further afield, Wessex or Northumbria. For much of the seventh century Kentish influence was most strongly felt. Sæbert's conversion to Christianity was made under the aegis of his uncle, King Æthelberht of Kent, and it was he rather than Sæbert who founded and endowed the cathedral of St Paul's in London. Following Sæbert's death a pagan reaction set in under his three sons – possibly in opposition to Kentish influence – but under Sigiberht 'Sanctus' Christianity was restored in 653, this time under Northumbrian aegis. Yet once again pagan reaction followed, and Sigiberht was murdered. His joint successors, Swithelm and Swithfrith, appear to have restored Christianity once more; and they and their joint successors, Sæbbi and Sigehere, seem to have fallen, by turns, under the domination of Kent and Mercia (Yorke 1990, 48). The entire kingdom probably passed under the control of Caedwalla of Wessex during his brief overlordship of southern England in the 680s. Under Æthelred of Mercia, Mercian dominance was restored. Æthelred, Offa and their successors granted land in Middlesex without any reference to East Saxon rulers, and London fell completely under Mercian control: both Æthelbald and Offa had mints there. Nevertheless, there is no evidence that the main core of the kingdom itself was absorbed into Mercia, and East Saxon kings continued to grant land here without reference to their Mercian overlords.

By a strange turn of fate it was not Mercia but the expanding kingdom of Wessex which finally brought about the demise of Essex as an independent polity. Following King Egberht's great victory over the Mercians at *Ellendun* (Wroughton in Wiltshire) he sent his son Æthelwulf, in 825, to the kingdom of Kent in order to eject its Mercian underking Baldred; and in the words of the *Anglo-Saxon Chronicle*, 'the inhabitants of Kent turned to him, and the Surrey men and the South Saxons and the East Saxons' (Swanton 1996, 61). Although, as we have seen, the West Saxon conquest of Mercia was short-lived, the annexation of these southern dependencies proved more permanent. The East Saxons are heard of no more as an independent people: their territory henceforth formed part of Wessex.

No apology is made for this brief digression into the political history of middle Saxon England, for much about the early development of the Hertfordshire area can be understood only within this wider context. For much of the seventh and early eighth centuries the county was probably debatable ground – in part because of its proximity to London, already a place of key economic importance, but largely because of its position at the margins of two political and perhaps cultural blocks. Mercia and its satellite 'buffer states' – all part of the 'Anglian' cultural zone – lay to the north-west of the Chiltern watershed: the East Saxons and the subject Middle Saxons lay to the south and east. But that watershed is not a very significant topographic feature and the political units which developed in the course of the middle Saxon period did not have boundaries which slavishly followed those of earlier cultural zones. When a frontier eventually became fixed – probably in the early eighth century – it followed a rather different line. As late as 705, as we have seen, the East Saxon King Offa was able to grant land as far west as the *pagus* of *Hæmel*. But, for the most part, the centre and west of Hertfordshire was firmly in Mercian hands, while only the far east was East Saxon territory.

In the north-west of the county the *Hicce* seem to have been fully absorbed into the Mercian kingdom in the course of the seventh or eighth centuries. Perhaps – following common Mercian policy – this was achieved through the establishment of dynastic connections, by the marriage of some member of the Mercian royal family to one of the tribal elite. It is noticeable that prominent Mercian names crop up as place-name elements here. The name of the village of Ickleford, three kilometres to the north of Hitchin, means 'ford of *Icel*', a name shared by a number of early Mercian kings (Gover *et al.* 1938, 12). Nearby are the parishes of Great and Little Offley, *Offanlege* in a tenth-century will – 'Offa's clearing' (Gover *et al.* 1938, 19;

Crick 2007, 146). Matthew Paris, writing in the thirteenth century, actually recorded a tradition that Offa established a vill here, at which he later died (Luard 1872, 363). None of this evidence amounts to much, but it is just possible that some dim memory of the district's close connection with the Mercian royal house is preserved here. The influence of Mercian kings was also often strengthened on the frontiers of their kingdom through the foundation and endowment of monasteries. Offa thus established communities at Bath and at Cookham in Berkshire, both close to the southern borders of his kingdom, and it is in this context that we should see the probable establishment of St Albans Abbey in 793 (Crick 2007, 16).

The core of East Saxon territory was in the far east of the county, in the valleys of the Rivers Ash, Rib, Quin, Stort and lower Lea. The name of Sawbridgeworth, *Sabrigeworth*, may preserve the name of King Sæbert; while the name of Sacombe, whose second element we have already discussed, may incorporate in its first the name *Swæfa*, a shortened form of Swæfred, the name of a king who ruled Essex in the early eighth century (Gover *et al.* 1938, 137, 193–4). As East Saxon power waned that of Mercia grew, and by the second half of the eighth century (as we have seen) Mercian kings were granting land in Hertfordshire and Middlesex without any reference to East Saxon rulers. Nevertheless, East Saxon influence remained strong in this part of Hertfordshire. As late as 825 ten hides of land at Braughing were leased by Bishop Ceolberht of London and the community of St Paul's to Sigric, 'minister' of Wiglaf, king of Mercia (Gelling 1979, 81–2). One of the witnesses was 'Sigric rex Orientalum Saxonum' – probably Sigered, last king of the East Saxons (Gelling 1979, 82).

Although the area controlled by the two kingdoms doubtless fluctuated, their spheres of influence at one point in time may be preserved, in part, by the configuration of ecclesiastical territories. It is now widely accepted by historians that the pattern of ecclesiastical administration in early medieval England – the system of dioceses – often reflected patterns of political power (Winchester 1990, 69–71). The first bishops were established by tribal kings as each kingdom was converted; and the jurisdiction of the former was thus conterminous with the political territory of the latter – although in debatable border territory like Hertfordshire, ecclesiastical boundaries, like political ones, may not have become fixed before the eighth century.

In medieval times the west and centre of Hertfordshire lay within the Diocese of Lincoln (except for the area around St Albans, which formed an

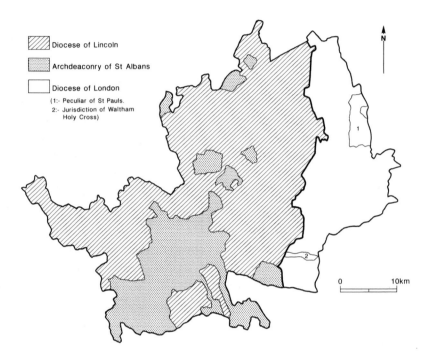

Figure 22. Hertfordshire: medieval ecclesiastical organisation.

independent archdeaconry). But east Hertfordshire, like Essex and Middlesex, lay in the Diocese of London (Figure 22). The latter, as we have seen, was established in 604 as the see of the East Saxons; but the Lincoln diocese has a more complex history. Originally, after conversion, a single diocese had served both the Mercians and the various 'buffer states' – the *Hwicce, Hicce, Giffle* and the rest (Winchester 1990, 71). The original seat of the bishop is unknown. What is certain is that in 669 it was transferred to Lichfield, and under Bishop Seaxwulf (675–91) the diocese was divided. The new dioceses – of Hereford, Worcester, Leicester and Lindsey – reflected the various tribal subdivisions of the Mercian kingdom, while Lichfield continued to serve the core of Mercian territory.

Leicester seems to have been created to serve southern Mercia and the various small tribes to the south and east – the groups sometimes called the Middle Angles, and including the *Hicce* and the *Cilternsætan* (Hart 1977, 49). The see survived in this form until the Danish invasions, when Dorchester – nine miles south of Oxford, on the southern edges of Mercia –

became the seat for a new see created by amalgamating Lindsey and Leicester. This arrangement continued, in spite of Dorchester's somewhat asymmetrical position within the diocese, until after the Norman Conquest, when in 1072 Bishop Remigius finally moved the seat to Lincoln (Ollard *et al.* 1948, 339). It is noteworthy that St Albans Abbey continued to have close contacts with Dorchester throughout the later Saxon period. In Crick's words, 'every bishop of Dorchester to hold office between Æthelred's death and the Norman Conquest can be connected with St Albans in some way'. It was the bishop of Dorchester who appears to have acted as the diocesan of St Albans – that is, the bishop responsible for the external affairs of the community – rather than the bishop of London, who was geographically much closer (Crick 2007, 26).

Originally, therefore, the west of Hertfordshire lay in the see of Leicester, corresponding with the territory of the *Hicce* and other 'Middle Anglian' groups dominated or conquered by Mercia; while the east of the county lay within the Diocese of London, and was East Saxon territory. The actual line taken by the boundary between the two dioceses is thus of some interest. In some places its course appears arbitrary and late, kinking uneasily, for example, around the contorted boundary between the parishes of Braughing and Westmill. The disruptions caused by the Viking invasions of the ninth century and the eventual conquest of the whole region by the West Saxons doubtless led to much alteration and readjustment. Nevertheless, two sections in particular look ancient and may preserve the course of an early frontier between Mercia and Essex.

One begins *c.*500 metres to the north of Mentley Lane (at TL368249) as the parish boundary between Braughing and Munden and runs south for some two kilometres in a fairly straight line (Figures 23 and 24). It then turns through some 20° (at a point some 400 metres to the east of Hatchett Farm: TL365220) and follows another relatively straight course for just over two kilometres as far as the Roman road which leads south-west from Braughing (Lowgate Lane). This line – nearly six kilometres in all – also forms, for all its length, the boundary between the Hundreds of Braughing and Broadwater. The two straight sections were clearly laid out through relatively open countryside: typically for an ancient boundary, few if any modern field boundaries continue across it, while local roads and lanes regularly change direction, or kink noticeably, as they reach it.

A second stretch of ancient-looking boundary can be found in the far

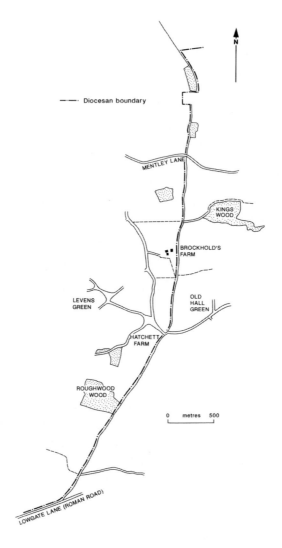

Figure 23. The boundary between the medieval Dioceses of Lincoln and London in the area to the east of Braughing.

south-east of the county, forming the western boundary of the parishes of Cheshunt, Wormley, Broxbourne and a small section of the western boundary of Hoddesdon, and terminating at the Roman road Ermine Street, near Highfield Wood (TL347086). For much of its length this also forms, once again, a hundred boundary. This section adopts a more sinuous course than that discussed above but it is, once again, a prominent feature of the

Figure 24. A section of the boundary between the medieval Dioceses of Lincoln and London in Little Munden, which may preserve the line of an ancient frontier between the kingdoms of Essex and Mercia.

landscape, seldom crossed by field boundaries, and at which tracks and roads change direction or 'kink' markedly. The line continues as a major landscape feature (a woodland boundary) far beyond the point where the diocesan boundary now leaves it to turn northwards and follow the line of Ermine Street. This it does for a kilometre before veering to the west, forming the boundary between Little Amwell and Hertford All Saints. It continues around the western side of Ware and Thundridge, arriving in time at Lowgate Lane, and thus at the first section of boundary described above.

If the diocesan boundary does indeed preserve, in part, the division between the two kingdoms, then some intriguing possibilities present themselves. If, as suggested earlier, polities such as Essex and Mercia were constructed out of smaller tribal 'building blocks', consolidated through a prolonged period of war and conquest, then it follows that the various sections of frontier eventually established between them must often have had an earlier existence, as the boundaries of these smaller, archaic entities. The straight sections of the diocesan boundary which form the division between Standon, Braughing and Westmill to the east, and Sacombe and the Mundens to the west, roughly follow the watershed between the River Rib and the Old Bourne and Beane; and thus, presumably, the line of the boundary between the *Brahingas* and the *Beningas*. The *Brahingas* were thus incorporated into the territory of the East Saxons, while the *Beningas* – perhaps always a group subordinate to the *Hicce* – were absorbed into Mercia. Significantly, that part of east Hertfordshire which lay within the Diocese of London was always known as the Deanery of Braughing. In a similar way, it is probable that to the south of the River Lea the long, curving boundary of the diocese, forming the western edge of the parishes of Cheshunt, Wormley, and Broxbourne, has fossilised the bounds of a territory based on the Roman settlement at Cheshunt, which was likewise absorbed at an early date into the kingdom of Essex.

But the course of the diocesan boundary has other implications. Although in detail its line around Hertford may well be the consequence of later adjustment, it is nevertheless noteworthy that the site of the town lies on, or very close, to it. Most scholars now doubt whether the place called 'Heorutford' by Bede, where the first synod of the English church met in 673, can be identified with Hertford (Hartford in Huntingdonshire is probably a more plausible candidate), but this nevertheless remains possible. In the 670s the East Saxons were, like much of southern England, dominated by the kingdom of Kent under King Hlothere. Indeed, in 675 Abbot Eorcenwald of Chertsey, probably a relation of Hlothere, was consecrated bishop of London by Archbishop Theodore (Higham 1995, 122). Hlothere's hegemony was being challenged by the South Saxons, who were allied with Mercia; Hlothere himself was closely connected with the Northumbrians, whose king, Ecgfrith, acted in person as Archbishop Theodore's protector at the 'Heorutford' synod. Hertford, on the frontier between two kingdoms and two rival alliances, would be an obvious place to hold the synod. Similar considerations might explain why the next synod, that of 679, met at Hatfield, a mere nine kilometres to the west of the boundary line – assuming that the Hatfield referred to by Bede was indeed the Hertfordshire one, rather than that in Yorkshire (Higham 1995, 117).

Either way, Hertfordshire occupied disputed ground, border territory, during much of the Saxon period, with the west and centre becoming Mercian territory and the east forming part of the kingdom of the East Saxons. These early kingdoms were controlled from major estate centres which, in the case of Mercia especially, were often defended sites, or *burhs*, and it has long been suggested that one of these was located at St Albans. According to a story which has been repeated on many occasions – and which has its origins in antiquarian writings of the nineteenth century, and especially in the researches of R. Grove Lowe (Page 1905–6, 151) – the main focus of occupation in the area shifted, probably in the eighth century, from Verulamium eastwards across the river Ver. The new site was called Kingsbury, 'the king's fort'. It supposedly occupied some eleven hectares on the low plateau to the north-east of what is now Fishpool Street, and was defended by ramparts which can still allegedly be recognised in places. There is no doubt that some kind of royal site existed at St Albans – the *Gesta Abbatum*, recounting its supposed purchase by Abbot Wulsin in the tenth century, describes it as a *municipium* (Riley 1867, 23). But Isobel Thompson has recently cast doubt upon whether it was located in this precise place. The 'defences' comprise two or three short sections of relatively minor bank, ditch and escarpment, undated and not obviously defensive in character. There is no evidence that they ever formed a continuous circuit. More importantly, a number of archaeological interventions in the area have failed to uncover any evidence for middle or later Saxon occupation, although numerous finds of Roman date have been made, including part of a cemetery, together with some evidence for occupation in the immediate post-Roman period (the site off the Welwyn Road, already discussed: above, p. 80). In Thompson's words, 'the plateau may look like an obvious site for a defended position, but to date there is no positive indication of its existence' (Niblett and Thompson 2005, 182). This area has been identified as 'Kingsbury' on maps only since the late nineteenth century, in part perhaps because of antiquarian speculations. Before this, the name appears to have been used for the area at the north-east end of St Michael's Street, by the river crossing, where the abbey mill stood (Niblett and Thompson 2005, 183). Earlier still, in medieval times, St Michael's church in the centre of Verulamium was usually described as *ecclesia Sancti Michaelis de Kyngesbiri* – suggesting, as Thompson persuasively argues, that the *burh* was actually located within the Roman town itself, perhaps utilising part of the ruined walls as a defence. As already noted, there is good evidence for continuing settlement from the area of the forum – around St Michael's – into the sixth and seventh centuries, as well as from the area around the abbey; and both sites have produced evidence for middle and later Saxon occupation, including (in the case of the forum area) a coin of the Mercian king Burgred (853–74) (Niblett and Thompson 2005, 186).

Another *burh*, probably a more conventional middle Saxon defended site, may have existed at Hitchin. The hamlet of Bearton Green, a little to the north-west of the town, takes its name from the Old English *Byrhtun*, 'farm belonging to the *burh*' (Gover *et al.* 1938, 9). In 2004 a large ditch orientated roughly north-north-east–south-south-west was discovered in the middle of the town, in the area between Bucklersbury and Paynes Park. In places it was up to 4.25 metres wide and 2.4 metres deep, and it had steeply sloping sides, features suggesting a defensive function. It contained small amounts of prehistoric and Roman material, but later Saxon artefacts were found in the upper fills, suggesting that it was originally cut in the middle Saxon period (Howlett 2008, 192; HER 1225284). This may well have formed part of the defences of the *burh* of Hitchin, which would thus have occupied the area to the west of the river, embracing the church and the area of the present marketplace. If the Mercian kings maintained a *burh* at St Albans it would not be surprising to find one here. It is possible that, like the *burh* at Hertford (below, p. 108), both *burhs* were established during the Danish wars and the subsequent re-conquest of the area in the ninth and early tenth centuries. But the lack of any documentary references to either of them in this context, and their close association with the two main centres of Mercian power in Hertfordshire, strongly suggests a middle Saxon date. Attention should perhaps also be drawn in this context to the enigmatic banks and ditches which surround Gatesbury Wood, to the south-east of the Roman town of Braughing. As discussed above, recent work has cast doubt on whether these are, in reality, anything other than medieval woodbanks, but this may be a mistake – some at least of the earthworks here appear to be pre-medieval, and probably prehistoric. The name attached to the earthwork – 'Gaeta's *burh*' – may hint that the site was re-used in some way in the post-Roman period, although it lies over a kilometre to the south of probable minster site within the present village.

The coming of the Danes

It was the political events of the early tenth century which led to the creation of Hertfordshire: but, once again, these cannot be understood without discussing briefly their wider context – the invasion of eastern England by Viking armies in the second half of the ninth century, and its re-conquest by West Saxon kings in the course of the tenth. In 879, according to the *Anglo-Saxon Chronicle*, the Viking 'host' moved from Cirencester 'into East Anglia, and settled that land, and shared it out' (Swanton 1996, 77). The following year they occupied Northumbria and around the same time seized the eastern half of Mercia, leaving the puppet Ceolwulf to rule the west of that kingdom (Yorke 1990, 123). The conquest of eastern England was thus complete, and only Wessex remained as an intact, independent English kingdom. Its people had resisted Viking incursions vigorously, first under King Æthelred and subsequently under King Alfred; and the Danish army under Guthrum was roundly defeated by them at the battle of Edington and a treaty made – the treaty of Wedmore – in 878. There were further clashes between the West Saxons and the Danes in the 880s, and in 892 another large army arrived from Scandinavia, established bases in the Danish-settled east of England, and – combining with Danes already settled here – raided widely across the country by land and sea for the next four years. Only in 896 was peace finally restored as the army split up, many of its men returning to East Anglia and Northumbria or going on to further adventures in Normandy.

The fate of Hertfordshire during these years appears, on the face of it, fairly straightforward. The text survives of a treaty made between Alfred and Guthrum which divided England into two spheres of influence, West Saxon to the west and Danish (the 'Danelaw') to the east. The boundary between the two leaders and their peoples was to run along the Thames to its confluence with the River Lea; thence to the source of that river (near Leagrave, in Bedfordshire); from there in a straight line to Bedford; and finally along the River Ouse to its junction with Watling Street (at Stony Stratford in Buckinghamshire) (Stenton 1971, 260–1). The traditional reading of this treaty suggests that the northern and eastern portions of Hertfordshire lay clearly within the Danelaw, with the southern and western parts (i.e. to the south of the Lea) within West Saxon territory. Although the precise context of the treaty has been debated by historians, most agree that it was drawn up some time between 886 and 890 (Stenton 1971, 260–1; Davis 1982).

The conventional interpretation of this document has, however, been questioned by the historian David Dumville, who has argued forcibly that it was not made in the 880s at all, but rather in 878 – implying that it in fact represents the treaty drawn up at Wedmore, following the battle of Edington (Dumville 1992, 14–15). At this time the Danes had occupied East Anglia and also eastern Mercia, of which west Hertfordshire formed a part. Essex, however – which had been conquered by the West Saxons in the 820s – still remained largely in Alfred's hands (Dumville 1992, 8–9). Danish armies were certainly operating in Essex in the 870s but the entries in the *Anglo-Saxon Chronicle* show them always in the east of that county, not in the centre or west. In Dumville's words, 'When they wanted a safe base for their women or chattels, Essex was not their choice but East Anglia. All these facts suggest that … Essex was territory that was being debated' (Dumville 1992, 9). Distant from the main centres of West Saxon power, and exposed to a long sea coast, it must have been hard territory to defend; yet the *Anglo-Saxon Chronicle*, our main source for the political history of this period, gives no indication that Essex was actually overrun and occupied by the Danes in the way that East Anglia certainly was. Indeed, one entry for 896 – looking back to events earlier in the late 880s and 90s – records the valiant deaths of 'many of the king's best thanes', including Brihtwulf, ealdorman of Essex (Swanton 1996, 90). It is also noteworthy that in 903, when Æthelwold (Alfred's nephew) was unsuccessful candidate for the West Saxon succession, he fled to Northumbria and then, with a Viking force, attacked Essex. The implication is that the area was not under Danish control at this time, and that he was seizing, symbolically, an outlying portion of the West Saxon kingdom (Dumville 1992, 10). It is possible that the political situation to some extent mirrored patterns of economic and cultural contact: Danish influence and settlement was essentially confined to the 'North Sea Province' (above, p. 19), and Essex lay outside this.

If these arguments are correct, they demand a radical reappraisal of the treaty made between Guthrum and Alfred, and in particular of the meaning of the boundary which it established between them: a reappraisal which has implications for the early development of Hertfordshire. In 878, as Dumville suggests, the land to the east of the stated line must have been under Alfred's control; it was the land to the *west* which was held by Guthrum. The conventional interpretation, in other words, is back to front: eastern Mercia had fallen to the Danes, but Essex was still English. The fact that the boundary established by the treaty ran some way to the west of what I have suggested may have been the earlier frontier between Mercia and Essex perhaps indicates that the English had been successful in recovering some territory from the Danes – presumably through the conquest of Hitchin and its dependencies – thus occupying the wedge of land between the River Lea (the lines of the frontier established by the treaty) and the old frontier (represented by the diocesan boundary).

Far from establishing a long-lived territorial dispensation, the arrangements stated in the treaty probably survived for only a few years. Alfred occupied London in 886 and granted control of it – and of the

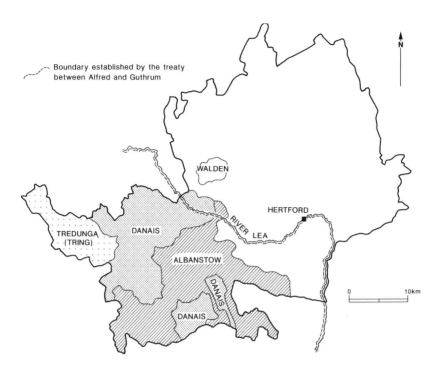

Figure 25. Hertfordshire in the Viking period: the Alfred–Guthrum frontier, the hundreds of west Hertfordshire and the location of Walden (see text).

adjacent areas of south-eastern Mercia, which he had also seized – to his son-in-law Æthelred, king of Mercia. Interestingly, it would seem that Æthelred's control extended over a slightly wider area than that recently re-conquered from the Danes, to judge from a charter of 888 by which, styling himself *procurator* of the kingdom of the Mercians, he granted fifteen *manentes* at *Waledene* – St Paul's Walden in Hertfordshire, north-east of the River Lea and thus, according to Dumville's reinterpretation of the treaty, within the English sphere of influence established in 878 (Birch 1885, 194–5). It is thus probable that Alfred also ceded to Æthelred territory centred on Hitchin which had, at the time of the treaty with Guthrum, been under West Saxon control, but which had traditionally formed part of the Mercian kingdom.

Dumville's reinterpretation of the Alfred–Guthrum treaty is persuasive, although not without problems. In particular, while it is easy to see how the southern section of the treaty boundary, passing along the River Lea, could represent a slightly expanded frontier of the old East Saxon kingdom, the northern stretch – along the Ouse as far as Watling Street – would embrace an extended salient, running between Danish East Anglia to the east and Danish Mercia to the west. Indeed, Dumville's ideas have been challenged (Keynes 1998, 31–4): but the Hertfordshire evidence provides some powerful support for them.

Following the West Saxon re-conquest of eastern England in the early tenth century Hertfordshire, like other areas in southern England, was divided into a number of administrative areas called hundreds. The western side of the county was, by the time of Domesday, divided between the Hundreds of Dacorum and Albanstow, later called Cashio (Figure 25). The two were interdigitated in a complex way, in that while, for the most part, Dacorum covered the north-west of the county, and Albanstow the south-west, isolated sections of the former existed as islands within the latter – all or part of the vills of Bushey, Aldenham, Shenley, Napsbury, *Titeberst* and North Mimms. To add to the confusion, St Paul's Walden formed an isolated island of Albanstow between Broadwater and Hitchin Hundreds. Other such isolated islands were established in the east of the county in the century or so after the making of Domesday. All the vills in Albanstow/Cashio Hundred contained substantial holdings of the Abbey of St Albans, suggesting that, almost certainly, Dacorum and Albanstow were once one unit, Albanstow having been carved out of Dacorum some time in the eleventh century in order to provide a single jurisdiction for the abbot of St Albans, who then proceeded to add to it most of the abbey's more distant holdings.

The name Dacorum means 'hundred of the Dacians', the latter a word used erroneously in the Middle Ages for the Danes because of a legend that certain tribes from Dacia had, in the remote past, migrated to Denmark (Gover *et al.* 1938, xviii–xix, 25–6). In Domesday the hundred is actually referred to as *Danais* or *Daneys*, the Danish hundred. Almost the whole of its area lay to the south and west of the River Lea, causing the authors of the EPNS volume for Hertfordshire in 1938 some confusion about the presence on the 'wrong' side of the frontier of 'this most remarkable name' (Gover *et al.* 1938, xviii). Dumville's reinterpretation of the treaty offers, of course, a convincing explanation; conversely, it is difficult to understand the name if Dumville's interpretation is not accepted.

At the time of Domesday a substantial part of Dacorum actually comprised another hundred, which disappeared completely soon after the Conquest: one which embraced the vills of Aldbury, Berkhamsted, Little Gaddesden, Hemel Hempstead, King's Langley, Puttenham, part of Redbourn, Shenley and Wiggington. This was called Tring Hundred (*Tredunga, Tredunge, Treunge* in Domesday). It is just possible, as the authors of the EPNS volume tentatively suggested, that its name derives from the Old Norse *þriðjungr*, 'third part' – the term which has given us the three 'Ridings' of Yorkshire (Gover *et al.* 1938, 25–6).

Even if this latter argument is discarded – and it is certainly hard to see how an administrative division would have given its name to a place, the vill (later town) of Tring – the name of Dacorum certainly supports Dumville's reinterpretation of political history in the 870s and 880s, and suggests that, for a short time, the southern and western areas of Hertfordshire, like much of eastern Mercia, were under Danish domination. Nevertheless, I do not mean to suggest that there was any significant Danish settlement in any part of the county. Unlike Norfolk, Suffolk or the counties of north-eastern England, there are virtually no place-names in Hertfordshire which indicate Danish influence. We must envisage the Danish presence as essentially transient, with the indigenous inhabitants living for a short time under the rule of, and paying tribute or taxes to, a Danish elite, just as they had formerly done to a Mercian one. It is true that late Saxon documents reveal that many local people bore, by the eleventh century, Scandinavian names: men such as Wulf, who held land at Aston and at Oxwick (in Codicote), and who drew up his will some time in the 1030s or 40s. Most of the beneficiaries of the will also have Scandinavian names (Crick 2007, 198–204). But this reflects not so much large-scale immigration in the ninth century as the cultural dominance of Scandinavia across the whole of England in the eleventh, associated with the reign of the Scandinavian king Cnut and his son, Harthacnut.

The origins of Hertfordshire

As already noted, following the death of Alfred in 899 his son, Edward the Elder, worked with Æthelred and subsequently Æthelflaed, 'Lady of the Mercians', to conquer the areas of eastern England occupied by the Danes, thereby in time creating a single unified English state. By 918 the West Saxons had largely achieved this aim: the whole of England south of the Humber was under English rule. According to the conventional view,

Æthelflaed's principal contribution to the re-conquest was to fortify the frontier of English Mercia and harry the Danes in the east, while Edward advanced northwards into Essex and Hertfordshire, and later into Cambridgeshire and Huntingdonshire (Stenton 1971, 319–63). It was during these campaigns, in 912, that Edward built the first *burh*, or fort, at Hertford, erecting another, as we shall see, in the following year. But in the light of the arguments advanced above it is, perhaps, necessary to re-examine the context of these events: for if eastern Hertfordshire had never fallen under Danish control, and if the Danish occupation of the south-west of the county was essentially short-lived (ending with Alfred's seizure of London in 886 and the granting of these lands to Æthelred), then what precisely was Edward doing building a *burh* here, some way from Danish territory, in 912?

We need to remember here that the simple story, of a gradual triumph of Christian England over pagan Danes, probably conceals more complex patterns of alliance and affiliation in the ninth and tenth centuries. The *Anglo-Saxon Chronicle* hints at some of these complexities, although generally trying hard to suppress them; and, as we have seen, no less a person than King Alfred's nephew Æthelwold was, when disappointed over the succession in 903, prepared to flee to Viking Northumbria, return with a fleet to attack Essex and then – in alliance with the East Anglian Danes – harry Mercia and Wessex.

The relevant *Chronicle* entry for 912 simply notes that 'around Martinmass ... King Edward ordered to be built the more northerly stronghold at Hertford, between the Maran and the Beane and the Lea' (Swanton 1996, 97). There is no mention of Danes here, and, as we have seen, Æthelred of Mercia was granting land not far away, in Walden, in 888. The previous entry in the *Chronicle* may hint at an alternative explanation for the construction of the fort, however: 'Æthelred, ealdorman in Mercia, departed, and King Edward succeeded to London and to Oxford *and to all the lands which belonged thereto*' (my italics) (Swanton 1996, 97).

In other words, Edward, a West Saxon king, was laying claim to his brother-in-law's lands in Mercia, or at least to those in south-eastern Mercia, including west Hertfordshire. This move might not have been welcomed by all members of the Mercian nobility, not least by those who might themselves have had a claim to the Mercian throne. Edward, as we have seen, allowed his sister to rule the bulk of English Mercia, but in 911 the seizure of so much Mercian territory might have appeared as a blatant piece of West

Saxon aggression. Given that other parts of eastern Mercia were still under Danish domination at this time, Edward may also have feared Danish intervention in any resulting dispute. The construction of the fort at Hertford – on the probable eastern boundary of Æthelred's lands – may have had as much to do with West Saxon domination of eastern Mercia as with any systematic counter-offensive against the Danes. It is noteworthy, although probably coincidental, that the site chosen for the *burh* lay close to what had, prior to the Danish invasions, apparently been the *frontier* between two kingdoms, Mercia and Essex, marked by the diocesan boundary. It is just possible that Edward was involved in a deliberate attempt to disrupt old patterns of loyalty and allegiance, creating a new territory and a new administrative centre that cut across an ancient social and political division. By intention, or otherwise, the new shire was focused on a town built on one of the ancient fault-lines of Anglo-Saxon England.

Essex, as we have seen, had probably remained largely under English control throughout the late ninth century, although there is evidence that the northern parts may have been annexed by the East Anglian Danes, and the whole area remained vulnerable to attack – as the expedition of Æthelwold in 903 vividly demonstrated. The construction of the fort at Hertford was followed, in 913, by activity in Essex: Edward went with a force to Maldon, erected a fortification at Witham and received the submission of 'a good number of people who were earlier under the control of Danish men', who were presumably living in north Essex, on the borders of Danish East Anglia. In the same year the *Chronicle* recorded how 'some of his reinforcements made the stronghold at Hertford on the south side of the Lea' (Swanton 1996, 97).

Double strongholds, on opposing sides of rivers, were a common feature of the period: Edward thus constructed *burhs* 'on each side of the river' at Buckingham in 914; added a *burh* on the south side of the river to the existing fort on the north side at Bedford in 915; and in 920 built two *burhs* at Nottingham (Swanton 1996, 100, 104). Such an arrangement made it easier to control the movement of ships along the river. The precise site of neither of the Hertford *burhs* is known for certain. As noted above, the *Anglo-Saxon Chronicle* locates the first 'between the Maran, the Beane, and the Lea' (Swanton 1996, 97). This is something of a topographic puzzle, for today the Maran, or Mimram, joins the Lea around 600 metres above Hertford Castle; the Lea is joined by the Beane another kilometre downstream; the phrase 'between' the three rivers thus makes little sense. Sal

Garfi has, however, plausibly suggested that in the early tenth century the Mimram followed the course of what is now no more than a minor ditch which passes just to the north of St Andrew's church and the present car park in St Andrew Street, joining the Lea just to the west of the castle mount. The *Chronicle* description would thus indicate a northern *burh* immediately to the north of this point, and Garfi has used the pattern of roads and boundaries to reconstruct its layout, suggesting that it occupied an irregular rectangle in the Old Cross–St Andrew Street–Cowbridge area (Garfi 1995, 124–6). Using similar techniques, Garfi suggested that the southern *burh* was in the area to the south-east, located west/north-west of the castle, in and around Maidenhead and Bull Plain (Garfi 1995, 126–7): in 1973 what was probably the eastern defensive ditch was discovered during excavations in the Railway Street/Bircherly Green area, and further sections were discovered in subsequent excavations, together with evidence for intensive late Saxon occupation in the area to the west, inside the *burh* (Borrill 1981; Partridge 2008, 145). The layout of streets and properties suggests that the interior of the southern *burh* was laid out on planned, regular lines (Partridge 2008, 145). No such regularity can be discerned in the area of the northern *burh*, which may have been an essentially military enclosure, remaining empty of properties until encroached upon by the expansion of the medieval town.

We do not know for certain that the shire of Hertford came into existence at the time that the *burhs* were constructed, but this is highly probable: the former was the territory which provided the resources to maintain, and garrison, the latter. Shires and *burhs* seem to have been interconnected instruments of West Saxon expansion. Certainly, by the second half of the tenth century, at the latest, England had been divided into shires, for their universality is assumed in the laws of Edgar (959–75); and as their subdivisions, hundreds, are referred to in a law of Edmund (939–46), they were presumably in existence in the first half of the century (Jewell 1972, 45, 48). If Hertfordshire was not created in 912 or 913, it must have come into existence very soon afterwards. Nevertheless, it must be said that the earliest reference to the shire by name comes almost a century later, in the 'E' version of the *Anglo-Saxon Chronicle*, which records how in 1011 the Danes – in a second wave of invasions – overran the shire of *Heorotford* (Swanton 1996, 141). This version of the *Chronicle* was itself written down only in the twelfth century (between 1121 and 1154), by monks at Peterborough, and although this particular section may well incorporate earlier material there can be no certainty about this. Indeed, the earliest *certain* use of the shire's name comes from a charter of the late 1050s or early 1060s (Gover *et al.* 1938, 1).

Whenever they were first created, shires were a fundamental tool of the late Saxon state, with administrative, judicial and military functions. The main tax – the *geld* – was collected through them and their subdivisions; and they probably formed the basis for organising the militia, or *fyrd*. Tenth-century laws make it clear that each shire had a court, which met twice a year, presided over by the bishop and an official called an *ealdorman*. This arrangement changed in the course of the eleventh century, however, as larger units were created – groups of shires – under the authority of an earl: ealdormen disappeared but a new official emerged, a shire reeve or sheriff, who was responsible (under the earl) for the running of each shire (Jewell 1972, 44–6).

In Mercia and adjoining regions shires were new creations: they did not develop directly from earlier territories. Nevertheless, sections of their boundaries sometimes followed existing lines in the landscape – the boundaries of earlier administrative units and estates – and, partly for this reason, partly for reasons of administrative convenience, in many places county boundaries correspond with major topographic features such as major watercourses and prominent watersheds. In the case of Hertfordshire this is only really true of the eastern boundary, which follows the River Lea and then the Stort as far as Stortford, and then the watershed between the Rivers Ash and Stort. Much of the southern boundary, similarly, runs across the high London Clay uplands, although it does not usually follow the precise line of the watershed here but instead passes along minor watercourses, valleys and ridges: part of its course here may have been defined at a relatively late date, for this was a sparsely settled and well-wooded district in early medieval times, and it is noteworthy that this is the only area in which parishes sharing the same name are sundered by the county boundary. Until boundary changes in 1974, South Mimms lay in Middlesex and North Mimms in Hertfordshire, while East and Chipping Barnet lay in Hertfordshire and Friern Barnet in Middlesex.

It is the northern and western boundaries of the county, however, which appear most arbitrary, and here we might suspect that there was more disruption of earlier territorial arrangements. There are signs, as we shall see, that an early estate based on Hitchin was sundered by the county boundary,

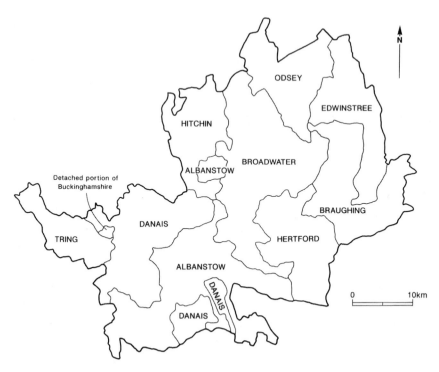

Figure 26. Hertfordshire: Domesday hundreds.

while in the far north the Hertfordshire hundred of Odsey takes its name from a place in the adjoining county of Cambridgeshire, suggesting that there was some readjustment of the boundary here after its initial creation. It is noteworthy in this context that the northern boundary passes through, or along, a large number of prehistoric monuments, as if its creators were attempting to fix a new and unfamiliar line in the landscape by reference to particularly long-established features. Thus Ravensborough Castle, Wilbury Hill, the probable long barrow at Pegsdon and a number of sections of what may or may not be the Icknield Way all fall on its line. The western boundary of the county, running somewhat erratically along the Chiltern dipslope, is the most curious. Sometimes it follows prominent topographic features – the River Chess, the imposing dry valley of Flaunden Bottom. But elsewhere it seems to take a quite arbitrary line, or to follow features such as minor lanes which, by implication, were already present in the landscape.

I have already noted that Hertfordshire, like other southern shires, was divided into units called hundreds. Like shires, these seem to have developed in the tenth century. They are first referred to by name in a law of Edmund (939–46), although the main legislation concerning them dates to the time of Edgar (959–75) (Jewell 1972, 47). The origins and early development of Hertfordshire's hundreds remains poorly understood. Whenever they first came into existence, they had clearly undergone a number of changes before we first encounter them in the pages of Domesday Book – as the case of Dacorum and Albanstow, described above, makes clear.

At the time of Domesday there were nine hundreds in the county: Albanstow, Braughing, Broadwater, Danais, Edwinstree, Hertford, Hitchin (actually, a half hundred), Odsey and Tring (Figure 26). With the exception of Danais, or Dacorum, all have names which refer to the place where their courts met. This was either an important settlement – the centre of a large royal or ecclesiastical estate – or else some customary, open-air meeting place. Braughing, Hitchin, Hertford, Albanstow and possibly Tring fall into the first category; Edwinstree, Broadwater and probably Odsey into the second. Edwinstree means, literally, 'Edwine's tree': the traditional meeting place of that hundred may have been close to a crossing of the River Ash in Furneux Pelham where there is a field called Meeting Field, which may account for the alternative name for the hundred, Eddiford, which appears in a subsidy roll from the reign of Henry VI. Broadwater Hundred met at the place called Broadwater in the parish of Knebworth (Gover *et al.* 1938, 117, 69). Odsey is a more puzzling case, for its name, as noted above, seems to refer to a place which today lies just outside the county: Odsey Grange and manor lie within the parish of Guilden Morden, in the Armingford Hundred of south Cambridgeshire. Although in the sixteenth century the lands of that manor extended over the county boundary into Hertfordshire it nevertheless seems strange that the hundred should derive its name from (and presumably meet at) an obscure place in a neighbouring county. It is possible that the northern part of Odsey Hundred originally lay in Cambridgeshire, with Odsey itself forming the meeting place for a large hundred originally embracing Armingford as well. It is noteworthy that this part of Odsey Hundred comprises one of Hertfordshire's anomalous 'salients', with the parishes of Ashwell, Bygrave, Caldecote, Radwell and Hinxworth extending beyond the natural topographic boundary of the Chiltern watershed and out onto the Midland plain. Some readjustment of the county boundary, after its initial creation but before the time of Domesday, may be indicated.

The Domesday hundreds thus appear to be artificial and comparatively recent creations. Nevertheless, patterns of administrative and fiscal organisation seldom develop out of nothing, and in other parts of England these units often appear to have been built out of earlier entities – ancient folk-territories and estates. There is little hard evidence of this in Hertfordshire, except perhaps in the east, where hundred boundaries do display some relationship with topography. The parallel with the boundary of the county itself is noteworthy, perhaps hinting that earlier administrative arrangements were badly disrupted in the west by Danish conquest, so that territorial boundaries were created on more of a blank slate, although the disruption caused to existing structures of administration by the aggrandising efforts of St Albans Abbey and the creation of Albanstow were doubtless also a factor here. The boundary between Braughing Hundred and Broadwater follows the watershed between the Rib and the Beane – the old diocesan boundary already discussed – while that between Braughing and Edwinstree follows closely the watersheds between the Rib and the Ash and the Ash and the Stort. Braughing Hundred, in fact, was probably constructed out of three earlier land units based on Braughing, Ware and Stortford. The curious 'peninsula' of Edwinstree Hundred, which separates the eastern portion of Braughing from the western, seems, similarly, to correspond with an ancient territory based on Much or Little Hadham. Parts of the south-western boundary of Hertford Hundred, likewise, appear to be of some antiquity, preserving in part the bounds of an ancient territory based on Cheshunt. Consideration of these issues, however, brings us to patterns of early tenurial and economic organisation – to the early evolution of territories, estates and manors – and it is to these matters that we must now turn.

Chapter 4
Early Territorial Organisation

Great estates

We have, in the previous chapter, followed the political development of the area now occupied by Hertfordshire from the end of the Roman period to the time of the Norman Conquest. We have seen how, in the fifth and sixth centuries, the area was apparently divided between a number of distinct tribal groups; and how in time these were absorbed into larger kingdoms, with the East Saxons coming to control the east of the county and Mercia the centre and west. Brief occupation of the Mercian district by the Danes in the late ninth century was followed by West Saxon conquest and, as England emerged as a unified state, Hertfordshire itself came into existence as an administrative entity.

It is against this general background that we can now begin to examine the development of territorial organisation, landscape and settlement during the Anglo-Saxon period. In this endeavour we are seriously hampered by the exceedingly meagre archaeological evidence for early and middle Saxon settlement in the county. Only a handful of settlement sites from these periods are known from Hertfordshire, most notably those at Foxholes Farm, near Hertford Heath; Blackhorse Farm in Baldock; Broadwater, near Stevenage; Pirton; Mill Road in Hertford; Old Parkbury and Bricket Wood, near St Albans; various sites in and around that town; The Grove, to the north of Watford; and Ware (HER; Wingfield 1995). This paucity of evidence should not be taken at face value. Across much of England settlements from these periods have left meagre surface traces, as the sand- and chaff-tempered wares produced in the Hertfordshire area during the early and middle Saxon periods are much less durable than the pottery of

Roman or medieval date. It is also much less visible both to archaeologists carrying out field surveys and workmen involved in excavating building trenches or quarrying sand or gravel. Nevertheless, there can be little doubt that here – as elsewhere in England – the population fell dramatically at the end of the Roman period, and much marginal land was abandoned. The *Hicce*, *Brahingas* and *Wæclingas* lived in a much less crowded and perhaps more egalitarian world than their Romano-British predecessors, and the territories they occupied were exploited at lower levels of intensity.

The middle Saxon period – that is, the period between *c.* AD 600 and 850 – is characterised throughout England by two interrelated developments. Population began to grow again, and settlement and cultivation to expand; and more stratified forms of social organisation gradually developed (Hodges 1989). As centralised kingdoms such as Essex and Mercia emerged, so too did the systems of territorial organisation necessary to sustain elites of warriors bound to the service of their kings. According to many scholars, in middle Saxon times England was divided into much larger territorial units than those which we encounter in the pages of Domesday Book. Instead of relatively small vills and manors, the countryside was partitioned into more extensive territories, to which historians sometimes give the name 'multiple estate' (Jones 1971; 1979; Faith 1997). These, in Sawyer's words, each contained 'the varied resources needed to sustain life' (Sawyer 1979, 7). They often embraced a number of economically specialised sub-units – farms or hamlets which, as well as providing sustenance for their inhabitants, also supplied a particular good or service to the estate centre, or *caput*. Some of these units, usually located near the centre of the estate, were primarily arable in character, while others, in more marginal locations, were essentially pastoral, or involved in the production of wood and timber. According to this model, such large estates were originally royal – the patrimony of tribal kings – although they might be granted out for periods of time as the endowment for a warrior in the king's retinue. Gradually, however, they became permanently alienated, as noble families or monastic institutions gained full rights of ownership over them; and, once alienated, especially into secular hands, they tended to fragment as they were divided by inheritance or portions were sold or granted away. Even when they remained in royal hands portions often became detached as lesser men gained proprietorial rights over them, either by grant or by usurpation. However it occurred, the underlying causes of the fission of large estates were increasing population and the development of more complex forms of social and economic organisation – the emergence of larger kingdoms, and (ultimately) the development in late Saxon times of a market economy, which rendered redundant the complicated forms of redistributive exchange which such territories represented.

By 1066 the fission of secular estates was far advanced, especially in the more densely settled areas of England, and a pattern of smaller economic and administrative units – manors and vills – had emerged. Nevertheless, hints of the earlier existence of such territories can often be detected in the archaic dues and duties owed by one place to another, and in the evidence of place-names. Moreover, long after outlying portions had been alienated, some administrative or jurisdictional authority over a portion of their inhabitants might be retained, especially when the estate core had remained in royal hands; and we sometimes find that ancient estate centres became the meeting place for hundreds and gave their names to them (Williamson 1993, 94–100). In short, a range of clues can be used, with varying degrees of confidence, to reconstruct patterns of middle Saxon territorial organisation.

So far as the evidence goes, large middle Saxon estates often evolved from earlier folk-territories. Once a small tribe had been absorbed (by conquest or otherwise) into a neighbouring polity – when, for example, the *Brahingas* were absorbed into the kingdom of the East Saxons – their territory, or ancient subdivisions of it, would become part of the royal patrimony which could be conveniently granted to a warrior. In Chapter 2 I suggested that the main tribal groups in early Saxon Hertfordshire, and possibly some of their principal subdivisions, had as their 'central places' sites of Roman importance. Some of these social groups may even have developed ultimately from subdivisions of the Catuvellauni. In some places, therefore – and Braughing may well be one of them – we can perhaps see a continuous thread of development, from Catuvellaunian *pagus* to early tribal territory to middle Saxon 'multiple estate'. Such continuity of territorial organisation was, of course, strongly influenced and encouraged by patterns of topography, by the enduring contrast between river and wold – that is, by the distribution (on the one hand) of light scarp and valley soils and (on the other) of clay-covered 'uplands'. Nevertheless, there are dangers in seeing the Anglo-Saxon age as a period of solid territorial stability. It is clear that this period saw the creation of new large estates and the fragmentation of old ones; and it is quite likely that the outer limits of territories could fluctuate over time, as settlements and districts were added or subtracted from them by royal fiat or, later, by purchase and inheritance.

It is also important to emphasise (for it is not always sufficiently emphasised in books like this) that the reconstruction of such early estates is to a large extent based on speculation. The earliest actual evidence for the configuration of estates and properties in the county – the earliest descriptions of their boundaries – in fact dates only from the later tenth and eleventh centuries, by which time 'multiple estates' had largely fragmented and the patterns of territorial organisation familiar from Domesday had already emerged. This evidence comes in the form of the boundary clauses to *charters*, documents by which land was donated (usually to monastic institutions), or ownership of it confirmed, usually by the king. In a world that lacked maps, describing the bounds of a property was the only way in which it could be located on the ground and its extent defined. As we shall see, many of the marker points described in boundary clauses (and not all charters, it must be emphasised, have such a clause) are now hard to identify, and in most cases the extent and configuration of the estates so described can only be imperfectly and approximately established: in some cases, indeed, they cannot really be reconstructed at all. But charters, and their boundary clauses, can sometimes be used (in combination with other evidence) not only to reconstruct contemporary patterns of landholding, but also to suggest more ancient systems of territorial organisation. Hertfordshire has a number of such charters, and the evidence they provide not only for the study of territorial organisation but also – because of the range of topographic features described in the boundary clauses – for reconstructing the character of the late Saxon landscape is invaluable.

The progressive fission of secular units in the course of the Saxon period was mirrored in the development of ecclesiastical territories (Blair 1985; 1988; Morris 1989, 93–139). In the first two or three centuries following the Conversion relatively few churches existed and each thus served an extensive area, usually with a team of priests. These churches were called *minsters* and their territories *parochiae*. As the population grew, and as large estates fragmented into smaller units, the new proprietors – local lords – erected new churches, which became parish churches: sometimes this was done with permission, sometimes not (Morris 1989, 140–67; Blair 2005). These churches were intended to serve the owner and his family, and also the spiritual needs of the inhabitants of his estate. In the more densely settled areas of England this process was well advanced by the time of Domesday (although less so than the fission of secular territories). But, once again, the pattern of minster territories can often be reconstructed through the residual obligations owed by 'daughter' to 'mother' churches. Particular kinds of dedication, and particular features of construction and location, can also provide hints about the early status of individual churches.

The developmental paths of secular and ecclesiastical territories were linked in a number of ways. The early minsters were, not surprisingly, often located close to or at the centres of large estates: *parochiae* and estate were originally, in many cases, the same. Identifying the sites of minsters can thus help us identify early estate centres, and vice versa. Moreover, because the pattern of medieval parishes often 'ghosted' that of earlier estates – as local thegns built churches in later Saxon times to serve their estates, and endowed them with land and tithes from their own lands – the arrangement of parish boundaries can also, on occasions, suggest that several contiguous parishes originated through the fission of one larger, earlier territory. However, extreme caution needs to be exercised here, especially when interpreting the *detailed* course of parish boundaries: the bounds of the estates described in many Hertfordshire charters seem to be only loosely related to medieval parish boundaries, suggesting a measure of realignment and adjustment in the early Middle Ages, or after.

Hitchin

Hitchin is perhaps the clearest example of a large estate and minster territory that we have in Hertfordshire. We saw in the previous chapter how that town derives its name from the *Hicce*, a tribe mentioned in the Tribal Hidage whose *regio* extended over a large area of north Hertfordshire and south Bedfordshire. It seems reasonable to suppose that the area later occupied by the town formed, in some sense, the central place or main settlement for this group or its leaders. After the tribe was absorbed into Mercia, some time in the seventh or early eighth century, Hitchin retained its importance as an administrative centre (the names of some Mercian kings may be preserved in local place-names) and its importance as a royal centre seems to have been maintained even following West Saxon conquest. In her will, probably drawn up in the 980s, one Æthelgifu – a noblewoman with estates scattered across Bedfordshire, Northamptonshire, Cambridgeshire and Hertfordshire – described how she had defended her claims to the estates left to her by her

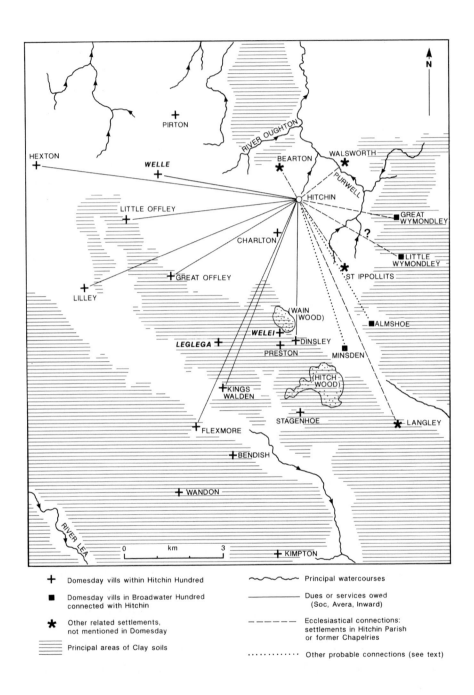

Figure 27. The Hitchin estate.

husband against those of his kin with a great oath taken at Hitchin (Crick 2007, 151). But it is Domesday which first fully alerts us to Hitchin's importance as the centre of a great royal estate, as Ian Friel ably demonstrated (Friel 1982). By this time, the town had given its name to the Hundred (or Half-hundred) of Hitchin. This suggests that the vill was still in royal hands when the hundredal system was established early in the previous century – large royal manors were commonly the meeting places for hundredal courts. In 1066, according to Domesday Book, it was held by Earl Harold, but this may have been a recent alienation from the Crown.

Domesday tells us that the following places were included within the hundred: the vill of *Welei* or *Wilei*, which comprised part of the later parish of Preston; Pirton; Hexton; Westoning, in Bedfordshire; *Flesmere* (Flexmore) and *Leglega* (now Ley Green), comprising the northern section of the parish of King's Walden; King's Walden itself; Charlton, now a hamlet within the parish of Hitchin; Dinsley, now Temple Dinsley in Preston; Lilley; Great and Little Offley; *Welle*, now represented by Wellbury House in Offley; Kimpton; Stagenhoe; and Wandon and Bendish, now hamlets in King's Walden and St Paul's Walden respectively. Domesday also states that by 1086 Hitchin had again become a royal manor, in King William's hands, and that it was the head of a group of manors in north Hertfordshire which are described as 'lying in' Hitchin, or as having been 'attached to' or 'placed in' that manor. These include many, but not all, of the places in Hitchin Hundred (Pirton, Bendish, Lilley, *Leglega*, Stagenhoe, Flexmore and Kimpton were excluded), together with Wymondley and Minsden in the adjacent hundred of Broadwater. Some of these places – Walden, Dinsley, Offley, and *Welle* and *Wilei* – had, according to Domesday, become attached to Hitchin only since the Conquest. But most already 'lay' there under Harold – they were manors held by him, and administered from Hitchin. Hexton and Wymondley had recently been associated with Hitchin, by Harold himself, but others were probably anciently connected (Figure 27). Walden is interesting in this respect. At the time of Domesday it was divided between two manors, one held by the king but formerly by an undertenant of Harold (King's Walden), the other by the Abbey of St Albans (St Pauls Walden). We know, however, when the abbey received this property for, as already noted, it was granted it in 888, by a charter which still survives (Crick 2007, no. 6). The donor was Æthelred, husband of Alfred's daughter Æthelflaed. Described in the document as 'Procurator of the realm of the Mercians', he was in fact son and heir to Ceolwulf, who had been king of an independent kingdom. Walden was evidently royal Mercian property at the time and so, by implication, was Hitchin itself.

With only six exceptions (Kimpton, Lilley, Bendish, Stagenhoe, Hexton and Pirton) all the places in Hitchin Hundred which were not in Harold's hands in 1066 were held by his 'men'. But more interesting is the fact that many of these places displayed more archaic forms of connection with Hitchin. Domesday tells us that at Charlton, Offley, Walden, Hexton and *Wilei* the *soc*, or jurisdiction, over the inhabitants lay in Hitchin. In addition, most of the vills mentioned above contained at least one estate held by individuals described as *sokemen*. They sometimes seem to have held land jointly, presumably as a kin-group, like the five sokemen who were still holding Great Offley in 1086 (Figure 27).

In other counties, where individuals of this class were more numerous, they appear to represent relatively prosperous peasant landowners who owed traditional duties of a non-servile nature to some ancient estate centre, even though in some cases they lived in a place which had become tenurially separated from it. Often these obligations had become limited to money payments, and the duty to attend court and to submit to the jurisdiction of the lord of the ancient estate. But sometimes a range of practical services was still demanded, and in the case of Hitchin, Domesday tells us that these were duties called *avera* and *inward* – 'cartage' and 'escort' – one or both of which was still owed by the sokemen of Offley, *Wilei*, Flexmore, Lilley, Walden and Dinsley. While sokemen (and occasionally free men) owed similar obligations elsewhere in the county, the places where their obligations were to be carried out is generally unspecified and their vills cannot thus be connected with any estate centre; in most of the cases described above, however, it was explicitly at Hitchin that obligations were owed.

The parish of Hitchin itself contains four subsidiary hamlets which were – to judge from their names, which are of Old English type – almost certainly in existence at the time of Domesday, although they are not mentioned by it. They are Walsworth, Bearton Green, Preston and Langley, the latter including within its boundaries the Domesday manor of Minsden. Hitchin and Langley together almost surround the parish of Ippollitts, or St Ippollitts, which was originally a chapelry of Hitchin (Page 1912, 3, 27–8). It was probably coincident with the Domesday vill of *Almshou*, whose name survives in those of Almshoe Bury and Little Almshoe within the parish. Like Minsden,

Almshou lay in Broadwater Hundred at the time of Domesday, and formed part of the holding of the Bishop of Bayeux: but the topographical evidence and ecclesiastical connection strongly suggests that it was once a part of Hitchin. The parish church of Great Wymondley was originally a chapel of Hitchin (Page 1912, 186), perhaps indicating that, in spite of Domesday's statement that Wymondley had only been 'added' to Hitchin by Harold, it actually had more ancient connections with that place. It is tempting to suggest on topographic grounds that Letchworth and Willian, to the north of the Wymondleys, were also once part of the estate, but there is no real evidence for this. Norton, too, is interesting in this respect, as it was clearly once the 'North *tun*' of somewhere, and the only place of obvious importance lying vaguely to its south is Hitchin. If it was indeed once part of Hitchin, it had evidently been severed from it by 1007, when its possession by St Albans Abbey was confirmed by King Æthelred (Crick 2007, no. 12). The bounds described in the charter appear, more or less, to be those of the present parish of Norton. The same charter confirmed the abbey's possession of an estate in a place called *Rodanhangron*, which they no longer owned by 1066. Its location is unknown (it does not appear in documents after Domesday) but it perhaps lay immediately to the west of Norton.

It is noteworthy that Domesday Book describes how the Bedfordshire vill of Westoning 'lay in' Hitchin Hundred, while the nearby vills of Poleshanger and Meppershall, while not explicitly described as lying there, were listed in the Hertfordshire rather than in the Bedfordshire section of the Survey. Later documents show that detached portions of Shillington parish also lay in Hitchin Hundred. These connections may have been comparatively recent, as Domesday itself tells us that Westoning's obligations 'lay in' Bedfordshire before 1066, but they could be ancient, dating back to the time before the creation of the county boundary, and ultimately to the *regio* of the *Hicce*, as Ian Friel has suggested (Friel 1982, 10–12). Either way, we have here clear traces of an early royal estate, with a central core of *inland* (on the lighter soils near Hitchin itself) occupied by peasant cultivators and an outer penumbra of *warland* (comprising settlements on the higher and more distant land) in which the dues owed by the inhabitants were less onerous.

The names of some of the places within this ancient territory may throw light on its character and organisation. The hamlet of Bearton Green, as we have already noted, was the 'tun belonging to the *burh*'. The name of another hamlet within the parish – Charlton, the settlement of the *ceorls*, or

free peasants – seems to be an intentional contrast with Walsworth, earlier
the *Weala tun*, the settlement of the serfs or Britons (Gover *et al*. 1938,
9–10). Pirton was the *tun* where the pears grew, Bendish the enclosure where
beans were cultivated, Lilley the clearing where flax was grown (Gover *et al*.
1938, 18, 21, 116; Friel 1982, 14). Whether these names record, dimly, a
measure of early economic specialisation within the estate remains unclear.

We would expect a place of this importance to have had a minster and,
sure enough, the will of Æthelgifu, drawn up in the 980s, included a bequest
to a minster community here (Crick 2007, no. 7). Domesday also informs us
that there was a minster at Hitchin, describing how two of the five hides at
which the vill was assessed 'lie in the *minster* (*monasterium*) of this estate'.
Even without the explicit use of this term, this extraordinary large glebe
would have signalled the church's superior status. Nevertheless, just as
outlying portions of the estate had, to varying degrees, become detached
from the centre by this time, so too had the minster's territory experienced a
degree of fission. Domesday records priests at King's Walden, Great Offley
and Minsden, presumably indicating the presence of parish churches there.
The name of Preston, a substantial village which always remained a hamlet
of Hitchin – 'the priests' *tun*' – suggests that it was originally the portion of
the estate reserved for the sustenance of the minster priests. The parish
church of Hitchin today carries no clue of any early importance – it is a large,
prosperous structure 'evidently representing the commercial wealth of a late
medieval town' (Pevsner and Cherry 1977, 197). In other words, any
evidence of an early significance has been erased by systematic subsequent
rebuilding. Its original dedication, however – to St Andrew (Doggett 1988,
24) – is a common one for early minsters.

Hitchin's importance in the religious hierarchy can be traced both
forwards and backwards in time. By 1291, when the *Taxatio Ecclesiastica*
was drawn up, Hitchin had become the head of, and had given its name to,
a rural deanery. And in the south of the parish of Ippollitts (and thus within
the old parish of Hitchin), just to the north of the modern village of Preston,
lies Wain Wood, and the probable site of the lost Domesday vill of *Wilei*. The
earliest forms of the first of these names are *Wayndene* and *Weyngdene*,
possibly from *weohingadene*, 'valley of the worshippers at the shrine' – the
shrine itself perhaps being referred to in the name *Wilei*, from *weoh/wig*,
leah, 'the grove where (heathen) worship takes place' (Gover *et al*. 1938,
14–15) (although it should be noted that there are alternative interpretations

of both names: Gelling 1975). Sperberry Hill, from the OE meaning 'hill of speech' and probably the earliest meeting place of the Hundred of Hitchin, lies 200 metres to the south of St Ippollitts church and two kilometres to the north-east of Wain Wood.

As already noted, there is good evidence that Hitchin was a defended Mercian *burh*, and traces of a substantial ditch have been found in the area between Bucklersbury and Paynes Park (HER 125284). Other possible evidence of early and middle Saxon occupation in the town is patchy, but includes another ditch running to the south of the church (HER 13615); an undated cemetery containing inhumations without grave goods at the junction of Bancroft, Brand Street and the High Street (HER 13353); and another cemetery of similar character with six burials on Queens Street. In this last case, radiocarbon dating suggests that the burials were late Roman or middle Saxon in date (HER 11351). If the latter, they presumably pre-dated the establishment of the minster and its graveyard.

Early territorial organisation: the north and east

No other early estate in Hertfordshire can be reconstructed with such clarity and conviction as Hitchin. The fact that it remained in royal hands into the tenth century, if not beyond, ensured that traces of its archaic structure still remained in place at the time of Domesday, although as early as 888, as we have seen, St Paul's Walden was a separate property, while by the 980s part of Offley was bequeathed in the will of Æthelgifu (Crick 2007, no. 7). For the most part, early estates fragmented more completely, and at an earlier date. Moreover, as already noted, their identification is made more problematic by the fact that large tenurial units could be created anew in the course of the later Saxon period, reassembled in new configurations by large landowners through purchase or inheritance. Æthelgifu's will of *c*.980 thus describes a property comprising holdings so far-flung that they cannot originally have all belonged to a compact estate: Westwick in St Albans, Oakhurst in Aldenham, Gaddesden, Standon, Munden and Offley, together with swine pastures at Tewin (as well as estates in Northamptonshire and Bedfordshire). Yet elements of the old system clearly remained in place at this time, for the terms of the will made provision for the regular payment of unspecified 'food-rents' to the minster at Hitchin; payments of 'malt, meal, and fish' to the minsters at Braughing and Welwyn; and payments of malt, meal, honey, wethers, lambs, bullocks, cheeses and wine to the Abbey of St

Albans. Indeed, some elements of this archaic form of economic organisation persisted far into the Middle Ages, especially in the case of monastic houses. Even in the thirteenth century the tenants of Therfield had to supply a 'farm' including flour, meal, malt, peas, cheese, bacon, honey, butter, eggs, hens, geese, sheep, lamb and beef to their lords, the monks of Ramsey Abbey in Cambridgeshire, as well as undertaking carrying services to Cambridge, Ware and London (Page 1912, 279). Archaic renders made by one place to another are not in themselves evidence for the layout of middle Saxon estates, and fission could clearly be followed by reassembly as much as by the development of smaller estates or manors.

Dissolution of early estates seems to have progressed fastest, and farthest, in the more densely settled areas of the county, principally the north and east, and it is here that early patterns of territorial organisation are hardest – but not impossible – to detect. Braughing is the most obvious candidate. We have seen how the *Brahingas* were apparently a tribal group who occupied a territory based on the Roman town (and earlier *oppidum*) at Braughing. They were dominated at an early date by, and eventually absorbed into, the kingdom of the East Saxons. In a direct parallel with Hitchin, however, Braughing maintained an administrative importance into the later Saxon period, providing the meeting place for and giving its name to the hundred in which it lay (Short 1988). As in the case of Hitchin, this strongly suggests that the estate remained in royal hands as late as the tenth century. The 'core' of Braughing itself may have been retained even later, for Domesday tells us that the two thanes who held this manor before the Conquest could not sell their lands 'because they always lay in the alms [lands] in the time of King Edward and of all his predecessors'. Nevertheless, the territory seems to have largely fragmented quite early, and its bounds are harder to detect than those of Hitchin. In 825 Ceolberht, bishop of London, leased ten hides of land in Braughing to Sigeric, minister of Wiglaf, king of Mercia, which he was to hold on condition that it passed to his kin or, if he had none, to the church of St Andrew (Gelling 1979, 81–2). Standon, which seems to have formed part of the estate, had become an independent entity by c.980, for it is another of the places mentioned in the will of Æthelgifu, and may indeed have been one of her residences (Crick 2007, no. 7; Whitelock 1968, 34); it may possibly be referred to in an even earlier charter, of c.851, although this is less certain (Gelling 1979, 82).

The centre of the Roman town, on the significantly named Wickham Hill, lies in the south-western corner of Braughing parish, and the boundary

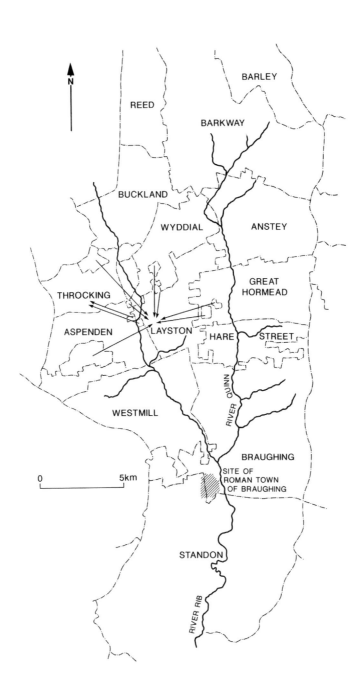

Figure 28. The Braughing estate (after Short 1988).

between Braughing and Standon runs right across it. The configuration of parish boundaries suggests that both had formed one territory, which – to judge from the complex and contorted nature of Braughing's northern boundary – may also have included Westmill and Little Hormead. Great and Little Hormead were clearly originally one vill for, in addition to their shared name, a detached parcel of Great Hormead lay within Little Hormead, and a detached parcel of Little Hormead lay within that; so the estate may have included both these parishes. As David Short cogently argued in his pioneering article (Short 1988), the same logic strongly suggests that Layston, Aspenden, Throcking and Wyddial were also once part of the same territory (Figure 28). All have complex, intricate boundaries obviously established at a relatively late date, for they kink around individual fields and former open-field furlongs. The probable outer boundaries of the estate do not have this kind of intricate irregularity, especially that to the east, which forms for much of its length the boundary between Braughing and Edwinstree Hundreds (Short 1988, 8–10). What Short did not perhaps emphasise enough was the way in which the 'outer' boundaries correspond, for the most part, with major topographic features – the watershed between the Rib and the Beane to the west, and that between the Rib and the Ash, and between the Quin and the Ash, to the east. He suggested that, to the north, the estate originally extended as far as the county boundary with Cambridgeshire, here marked by the line of the supposed Icknield Way, and would have thus embraced Reed, Barkway and Barley (Short 1988, 8–10). More probably the high watershed of the East Anglian heights was originally, in the middle Saxon period, wooded ground, intercommoned by communities living on both sides of the escarpment: Barley is the 'clearing with the burial mound'; the name Reed means simply 'rough ground' (Gover *et al.* 1938, 161, 172). There may have been no defined boundary here.

Once again, early secular importance was mirrored in ecclesiastical arrangements. Like Hitchin, Braughing was the site of a minster: the will of Æthelgifu left the reversion of half her estate at Munden, food-rents while one Ælfwold held it and cattle from Standon to a minster at Braughing. The charter drawn up in the 820s or 30s by which the Bishop of London leased land to one Sigeric, minister to the king of Mercia, indicates that, as at Hitchin, the church was originally dedicated to St Andrew. It is perhaps unsurprising to learn from the 1291 *Taxatio Ecclesiastica* that Braughing was the head of a rural deanery (Astle *et al.* 1802).

Æthelgifu left the other half of the Munden estate to a minster at Welwyn (Crick 2007, no. 7). Originally Munden seems to have formed part of a larger territory based on Benington, which occupied the valley of the River Beane and that of its tributary, the Old Bourne. The boundary dividing Great Munden from Braughing and Standon is clearly an ancient one for (as noted) it corresponds to that between the Dioceses of Lincoln and London and therefore, presumably, at some stage formed the frontier between Mercia and Essex. Southwards, the diocesan boundary continues without interruption as the parish boundary between Standon (to the east) and Sacombe (to the west). Great Munden and Little Munden have a complex and convoluted boundary (more so before 1888, when a detached portion of Little Munden was added to Great) (Page 1912, 124) and this, together with their shared name, suggests that they were once one territory. Within these parishes lies the small settlement of Libury, a separate vill called *Stuterhela* in Domesday. There were sokemen here in 1066, men of Ælmer of Benington, and others were recorded at Sacombe. Ælmer was a great landowner with wide estates, but his principal residence was at Benington and it is likely that these sokemen were anciently attached to this place.

The late-eleventh-century *History* of Croyland Abbey, written by the monk Ingulphe, describes how King Bertulfe of Mercia held a great council at a place called 'Benningdon' in 850, at which the monk Askill, sent by Abbot Siward, bemoaned the disastrous effects that Viking raids were having upon the abbey's estates (Riley 1908, 24). The eighteenth-century historian Chauncy believed that this was a reference to Benington but, unfortunately, Benson in Oxfordshire, known to be an important royal vill, is a more likely candidate (Chauncy 1700, II, 75).

It is possible that, just as the neighbouring estate of Braughing seems to have developed from the tribal territory of the *Brahingas*, the Benington estate also had an earlier existence, as the land of the *Beningas*, the 'dwellers on the river Beane': Benington is the '*tun* of the Beningas'. I suggested earlier that the territory of this group – whose existence is indicated, it must be said, by no more than place-name evidence – may have extended as far south as Bengeo, 'the spur of land of the *Beningas*'. Either way, the estate presumably embraced Watton-at-Stone – the parish boundary between Benington and Watton was convoluted and in medieval times the manors of Wood Hall and Crowborough here were both held by the lords of Benington, while, significantly, the advowson (the right to appoint to the living) passed with

Figure 29. The rare Anglo-Saxon rood in Walkern church suggests that it may have been an early minster associated with an estate centre at nearby Benington.

the former manor, rather than with the manor of Watton itself, from at least 1304 (Page 1912, 164). Topography dictates that Stapleford, lying between Watton and Bengeo, must also have been a part of this ancient land unit. To the north of Watton, the complex boundary with Aston similarly suggests that it was part of the estate. It is tempting to suggest that this was a case where minster site and estate centre were distinct, albeit lying in close proximity; and that Walkern – immediately to the north-west of Benington – was the site of the minster, for the church here contains fragments of a substantial late Saxon building, together with a rare example of a carved Saxon rood (Smith 1973, 30–4) (Figure 29). Once again, it is unclear precisely how far north the estate extended, but Weston (the west *tun*), Ardeley, Cottered, Rushden and perhaps Luffenhall in Clothall and Wallington may have taken its territory as far as the high watershed running along the East Anglian Heights where, again, there may have been tracts of intercommoned woodland.

To the west the bounds of the Benington estate are also unclear, once again probably because an extensive area of intercommoned woodland, pasture and swine-pasture once existed here, embracing the parishes of Langley (the 'long clearing'), Gravely (the 'clearing in the thicket'), Great and Little Wymondley ('Wilmund's clearing') and Stevenage ('the place at the strong oak') (Gover *et al.* 1938, 17, 125, 148, 137–8). The fact that this wooded tract was once shared between a number of far-flung communities is indicated by the complex pattern of parish boundaries and manorial connections in the area. Until boundary changes in 1907 the parish of Letchworth in the far north of Hertfordshire had a small detached portion eleven kilometres to the south, on the southern edge of the parish of Stevenage (sandwiched between Stevenage and Knebworth) (Page 1912, 118) (Figure 30). This contained only one settlement, Burleigh Farm, first mentioned in 1180 (Gover *et al.* 1938, 131) (Figure 31). Its name means 'clearing of the *burh*', perhaps a reference to Hitchin, of which Letchworth may once have formed a part. Langley – which was formerly part of Hitchin parish – lay only a kilometre to the north-west, and, as we have seen, the name of the *Hicce* is preserved in the name of Hitch Wood, in what is now Langley parish (Page 1912, 186; Gover *et al.* 1938, 17). The estates to the south and east of this wooded district also had rights or property here. Benington probably had connections with the Stevenage area, for the Domesday manor of Box, which had land in both Benington and Walkern,

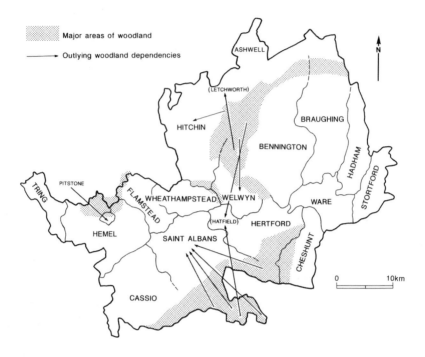

Figure 30. Hertfordshire: a provisional map of middle Saxon territorial organisation.

also had possessions in Stevenage. So too, perhaps, did an estate centred on Welwyn, some nine kilometres to the south in the valley of the Mimram, for Domesday tells us that a hide and a half of land at Chells in Stevenage, *Escelueia*, held by one Alwin in 1066, 'lay in Welwyn', and he could not sell it outside that manor.

There are some signs that estates even further afield acquired shares in the woods of this area. Graveley, which lies immediately to the north of Stevenage, is an intriguing and perplexing case. The parish contains two medieval churches: one, St Mary's, is the parish church; the other served the hamlet of Chesfield or Chisfield ('Cifel's clearing'), already a distinct settlement at the time of Domesday (the place does not appear as a separate vill in the survey but the *Inquisitio Eliensis*, a draft of the returns that relate to the Abbey of Ely's holdings, refers to 'Geoffrey of Chesfield' as one of the representatives for the Hertfordshire hundreds where Ely had possessions). Unusually, the advowson of Graveley was not held with the main manor of the parish, but was from at least 1225 attached to the small manor of

Figure 31. Burleigh Farm, Langley, near Stevenage, was once a detached portion of Letchworth parish, some eleven kilometres to the north. It originated in Saxon times as an isolated ranch, exploiting the extensive tracts of woodland that then existed in the area. It still appears to stand in a clearing – the area remains fairly well-wooded.

Simondshyde in Hatfield, some seventeen kilometres to the south (Page 1912, 90). The church at Chesfield was dedicated to St Etheldreda, and this also suggests a connection with Hatfield, which was granted in *c*.970 to the Abbey of Ely in Cambridgeshire. Etheldreda was the founder and patron saint of Ely, and the dedication was a common one for churches erected on abbey properties. The only other Hertfordshire examples are in Hatfield itself and (until the seventeenth century, when its dedication was changed) at Totteridge, another Ely property (Figure 30).

What is particularly striking about this tract of formerly wooded territory is that it corresponds closely with aspects of natural topography. Not only does it occupy a particularly wide interfluve between the Rivers Beane and Mimram (albeit one crossed from north to south by the low ground of the Hitchin Gap). It also corresponds, fairly closely, with the district of decalcified and poorly draining soils defined in the first chapter as the Stevenage–Welwyn Clays. The locality is still noticeably well-wooded compared with the areas further to the east. The village of Langley, almost surrounded by woods, seems both on the ground and on the map to deserve its name, 'the long clearing'. Burleigh Farm, to the south-east, still seems like an island of cleared ground in a sea of woodland (Figure 31).

To the south of these woodlands, an early estate seems to have occupied the central section of the Mimram valley. It was apparently based on Welwyn, a settlement located on well-drained soils beside the river at the point where it is crossed by the Roman road running from Verulamium/St Albans to Braughing. Æthelgifu left the reversion of half an estate at Munden, and food-rents from that place, to the minster here in the 980s (Crick 2007, no. 7). The present church actually overlies the Roman road. It was largely rebuilt in the late nineteenth and twentieth centuries, but it is known that the west tower, which fell down in 1634, stood on the north side of the building, suggesting that it may have survived from an earlier structure occupying a slightly different position. This may explain why, over the years, a number of burials have been discovered in the area to the north of the church, beyond the confines of the present churchyard. All lacked grave goods, and were thus presumably Christian. Of particular note is the fact that five such burials, discovered beneath The Grange in 1986, yielded radiocarbon dates which centred on AD 670, suggesting that the minster was already of considerable antiquity when Æthelgifu drew up her will (HER 4327; 10902). As at Braughing, we have hints of long-term continuity, for, as we have seen, there was a significant Iron Age settlement here, probably of *oppidum* type, which was succeeded by a Roman 'small town'. Several important late Iron Age burials and a number of wealthy villas are also known from the immediate area. The Iron Age and Roman settlement was centred slightly to the east of the medieval village but evidently extended beneath it: indeed, numerous Roman finds have come from the churchyard itself, presumably from dwellings located beside the Roman road.

As we have also seen, Welwyn *may* have become the focus for a tribal group called the *Tiwingas* in the immediate post-Roman period, and this in turn may have developed into a large estate centred on Welwyn and embracing – to judge from the configuration of parish boundaries – a number of the adjacent parishes. Digswell was clearly cut out of Welwyn at a relatively late date, for both of its separate sections were almost surrounded by that parish. The name of Codicote, 'Culþhere's cottages' (Gover *et al.* 1938, 109), indicates a dependent status, and it is hard to think what place it might have been dependent upon other than its immediate neighbour, Welwyn, to the east. If this was the case, then the layout of parishes makes it almost inescapable that the two Ayots also formed parts of this territory. Tewin and Datchworth may also have been components. The territory thus tentatively described had clearly fragmented by the later tenth century, for Æthelgifu's various bequests in her will of *c*.980 included 'the land at Tewin as swine-pasture' (Crick 2007, no. 7), but some parts of the estate may have survived as royal property into the eleventh century. A charter of 1002 records that King Æthelred granted five hides at Codicote to one Ælfhelm, his minister or close servant, in return for 152 gold mancuses (he in turn granting it to St Albans Abbey, whose property it then remained) (Crick 2007, no. 10). In addition, in the second quarter of the century the neighbouring estate of Oxwick, probably located somewhere within Codicote parish, was also bequeathed to the monks by one Ulf (Crick 2007, no. 10). In Crick's words, 'If he, like Ælfhelm, was a royal servant, as seems probable, the combined estate may once have belonged to the royal fisc' (Crick 2007, 178). Lastly, in 1066 one of the largest manors in Welwyn itself was still held by a priest 'in alms from the King'; 'It lies in the lands of the church of this estate'. To the north-east the estate presumably ran up to the boundary with the Benington estate, while to the north it would have extended up to the extensive tracts of woodland in the area around Stevenage and Langley where, as has already been noted, the manor of Chells in Stevenage apparently formed an outlying dependency of Welwyn. To the east, it was probably bounded by a territory based on Hertford.

Whether or not the great synod of 673 really took place in Hertford, the name of the adjacent parish of Hertingfordbury – the 'defended place of the people of Hertford' (Gover *et al.* 1938, 227) – suggests some early importance. Curiously, Æthelgifu's will left bequests to a minster community at Hertingfordbury, not Hertford: once again, it is possible that minster and estate centre were on different, but neighbouring, sites. The hide of land still attached to the church here at the time of Domesday seems to confirm its status as a minster; half the tithes from the church were being paid to St Albans Abbey by the late eleventh century (Riley 1867, 56). There is clearly a complicated and probably irrecoverable story here, but there is enough detail to perhaps suggest that the Edwardian *burh* was established at or near a place of earlier importance. Apart from the borough itself, which was in the hands of the king, Domesday shows that the only manor in Bayford, immediately to the south-west and on the far side of the River Lea, was also royal. To the west of Bayford lies Little Berkhamsted and, to the west of this, Essendon. All had parish boundaries running at right angles to the Lea, southwards onto the London Clay uplands. Essendon does not appear in Domesday, later sources making it clear that at this time it formed part of Bayford. As Little Berkhamsted lay between the two, it seems inescapable that all three places once formed a single royal property. Domesday makes it clear that by 1066 Little Berkhamsted was divided between the holdings of Saemer the Priest, 'a widow, Leofeva', and Wulfric Warden. But it helpfully adds: 'These were of the almslands of King Edward, and of all the Kings his predecessors, as the Shire testifies': that is, they were ancient Crown land. To the east of Bayford, Brickendon may once – to judge from the pattern of boundaries – have formed part of this royal property, but if so must have become separated by the later tenth century, when Ælfhelm Pogan bequeathed an estate here to Waltham Abbey, who still owned it at the time of Domesday. It became a 'liberty' some time between 1174 and 1184, when Henry II granted the monks (who had replaced the canons) freedom from geld and toll, and various measures of legal independence. But the place had no church, forming as it did part of the parish of Hertford St Mary. Little Amwell, to the south-east, was also held by Waltham, and also became a liberty, but cannot be clearly identified in Domesday (which gives information only about a single 'Amwell'). It too formed part of Hertford St Mary, unlike Great Amwell to the east. In spite of their shared name the two were sundered by the diocesan boundary, Great Amwell forming part of the Diocese of London but St Mary lying within the Diocese of Lincoln, subsequently St Albans (Page 1912, 418).

In short, there are grounds for suggesting that a major estate may once have existed around the confluence of the Lea, Mimram and Beane, centred on Hertford and including Hertingfordbury, Essendon, Little Berkhamsted, Bayford, Brickendon, and perhaps Little Amwell. While it is possible that this was formed when the *burh* at Hertford was established in the early tenth century, it may well be older. Whether the 'heath-covered open land' of Hatfield, lying immediately to the west and south-west, was also once a part of this territory is uncertain. If so, it had been severed by *c.*970, when it was given *to* King Edgar by one Oedmaer, so that it could be granted as *bocland* to the Abbey of Ely (Page 1912, 91). Archaeological evidence for early–middle Saxon occupation within the town of Hertford remains meagre, being restricted to a probable early or middle Saxon sunken-featured building discovered in 2005 at the former council depot in Mill Road (TL329129: HER 13123). But given the remarkable lack of sites of this period known from Hertfordshire, such evidence may be significant.

Moving now to the eastern edges of the county, the Braughing estate appears to have been bounded to the east by a continuous boundary, a prominent landscape feature which still runs along the watershed between the Rivers Quin and Ash. This line is followed by parish boundaries, and for much of its length by the boundary between the Hundreds of Braughing and Edwinstree (Figure 30). To the east lies the narrow valley of the River Ash, and to the east of this another long, fairly continuous series of parish boundaries runs along the watershed between the Ash and the Stort. The long, thin area so defined, essentially the valley of the Ash, contains the medieval parishes of Much and Little Hadham, Albury, and Furneux, Brent and Stocking Pelham, with Meesden at the extreme north. The configuration of parish boundaries suggests that this once formed a single territory. Its centre may well have been Hadham, the only place in this part of the county which appears in the documentary record before the eleventh century. In fact, it appears twice. In a charter drawn up some time between 946 and 975 King Edgar allowed Æthelflaed, widow of his father Edmund, to give land at Hadham to St Paul's in London; and by her will, probably dating to 975, she left what was probably other land in Hadham to Ealdorman Brihnoth and his sister for their lives, with subsequent reversion to St Paul's (Gelling 1979). Æthelflaed of Damerham, as she is normally known, was Edmund's second wife and the daughter of Ælfgar, a man who was almost certainly the ealdorman of Essex. Her sister Ælflaed was married to Brihtnoth, who succeeded as ealdorman, and whose death fighting the Danes is celebrated in the great Old English poem *The Battle of Maldon*. Æthelflæd thus came from noble East Saxon stock, and her possession of estates here is yet another reminder of the fact that this part of the county once lay within the East Saxon kingdom. As the ealdormen of the various English regions were sometimes descended from the royal families that had formerly ruled them as independent kingdoms, it is possible that Hadham had once been demesne of the East Saxon kings.

Although we might expect the estate centre to lie at Much Hadham, it may have been at Little Hadham, near to where (as at Welwyn) a Roman road crossed a significant river, in this case the Ash. The two Hadhams are not clearly differentiated in Domesday, when most of the land here was held, like much of that in neighbouring townships, by the bishop of London, whose seat was St Paul's Cathedral. Perhaps the name Hadham – 'the heath estate', an early form of place-name – replaced some kind of tribal name of *ingas* type at a very early date. The area is one of intense Roman activity: it is the site of a major pottery industry and has a number of wealthy villas. It is also noteworthy that a possible example of a *Wicham* name – Wickham Well or Spring – lies on the parish boundary between Much and Little Hadham (TL417214: Gelling 1978, 74; Rodwell 1975, 98). What is striking is that this lies only *c.*300 metres to the south-west of the curious enclosure, a putative Iron Age hillfort, in Caley Wood. Even more curiously, quantities of late Roman pottery have reputedly been found in the ditch of this enclosure, which itself lies some 2.5 kilometres to the south-west of Little Hadham church.

This estate's eastern edge, as already noted, was defined by another prominent watershed line, forming in part the county boundary with Essex, and in part, once again, the boundary between Edwinstree and Braughing Hundreds. Beyond this boundary lay a territory which was probably based on Bishop's Stortford. The configuration of parish boundaries certainly suggests that Thorley, the 'thorn clearing', immediately to the south, was severed from Stortford at a relatively late date. But Thorley also had connections with the large parish of Sawbridgeworth to *its* south: the manor of Thorley Hall thus had strips in some of the common fields of that vill, 'an additional argument in favour of the intimate connection between the two parishes' (Page 1912, 374). Thorley, Sawbridgeworth and Bishop's Stortford parishes very probably once formed a single large territory, which originally extended still further south, for a detached portion of Sawbridgeworth lies within the parish of Gilston, while – compounding parochial confusion – a detached parcel of Gilston lay within this! Stortford lies on well-drained soils beside the Stort near to the point, once again, where that river is crossed by a Roman road, that leading from Braughing to Colchester. It is noteworthy that Stortford was the site of a Roman 'small town' (Smith 1987, 162), although this lay, unlike the later medieval town, on the east bank of the river, beneath what is now the Cannons Close estate (TL493221: HER 513). Only settlements of more rural character have been recorded from the west bank, although some of these were certainly occupied into the fourth century (Rye Street: TL489221: HER 12051). The Domesday manor of Wickham Hall, another example of a *Wicham* name, lies just over a kilometre to the north-west.

To the west of this estate and to the south of Braughing, the configuration of parish boundaries suggests a territory embracing Ware, Thundridge (which was originally its chapelry (Page 1912, 379)), Stanstead Abbots, Widford, Hunsdon and, on its eastern edge, Eastwick, 'the East Farm' (Gover *et al.* 1938, 191). Ware was almost certainly the estate centre, and at the time of Domesday was still a particularly large and important manor. Once again, Ware stands at a point where a major Roman road (Ermine Street) crosses a river (the Lea); and, as at Welwyn and Braughing, the medieval settlement is associated with a Roman 'small town' – an industrial and commercial centre with Iron Age origins, covering some two hectares either side of Ermine Street to the north of the river (centred TL352144: HER 6521). Material of late-fourth- and possible fifth-century date has been found in a number of places in and around the town, and there have been some early Anglo-Saxon finds in the town centre, sometimes in direct association with evidence of Romano-British occupation, as at Place House (TL356144: HER 9378). More importantly, excavations on the Ware Library site in 1983 revealed evidence of post-holes and, possibly, floors associated both with Roman artefacts and with chaff-tempered pottery of sixth- to eighth-century date. In addition, limited excavations carried out in 1987 in the area between 65 and 83 High Street revealed traces of riverside structures of Saxon date, while further finds of grass-tempered pottery were made during excavations carried out along both sides of Baldock Street (Kiln and Partridge 1995, 72, 142–3: HER 356143; 356245).

Lastly, in the far north of the county, there are faint indications of a territory based on what is now the large village – but was in early medieval times the small town – of Ashwell. The importance of the place in the long-term history of this far northern 'salient' of the county – and, indeed, in that of the lands lying immediately to the south – is clearly indicated by the way that the local roads converge on it. Bygrave and Newnham, for example, lie two kilometres apart but there is no road directly connecting them: access is via Ashwell, a round trip of six kilometres. With a recorded population of eighty-three and an assessment of eight and a half hides, it was the largest vill by far in the 'salient' in 1086, and the biggest in Odsey Hundred. One of the manors in the nearby vill of Hinxworth had been a berewick of Ashwell before the Conquest: the configuration of parish boundaries may imply that Bygrave, and the diminutive vills of Radwell, Newnham and Caldecote, had also once been dependencies (Short 2008, 163). The name of Newnham, the 'new estate', suggests it was created by being carved out of some older territory.

As will be described later, by the time of Domesday Ashwell was one of only a handful of boroughs in the county. This was associated with the main manor, the property of Westminster Abbey. A charter purporting to record the donation of the manor by King Edward shortly before the Conquest – along with grants or confirmations of much other property – is generally regarded as a forgery, but it may well preserve a genuine tradition that the manor remained as royal demesne into the eleventh century (Gelling 1979). There was certainly a minster here in the later tenth century, for Æthelgifu bequeathed twenty sheep to it in her will of *c*.980, again suggesting a place of some importance (Crick 2007, no. 7). As suggested above (p. 113), this territory may well have extended across the county boundary into Cambridgeshire and formed the basis for the somewhat anomalous Odsey Hundred. Large numbers of Romano-British finds and sites are known from Ashwell parish (HER 415, 425, 1178, 1681, 2841, 2973, 4449, 10414, 11379, 13371, 13707), including at least two villas, a ritual feasting site at Bluegates Farm, and a cemetery at Slip End. At least two Roman occupation sites appear to underlie the modern village itself. All this suggests some continuation of the place's importance in the Iron Age, attested by the 'hillfort' at Arbury Banks, which overlooks the village. The importance of the area in the immediate post-Roman period may be signalled by the sub-Roman burial reportedly discovered in the Slip End cemetery (Wingfield 1995, 34), by evidence of early Saxon settlement 1.5 kilometres to the east of the village, and by various finds of early Saxon pottery and metalwork within the parish. Saxon as well as Roman material has been discovered within Arbury Banks itself (perhaps paralleling the finds of late Roman pottery reportedly made in the Caley Wood earthwork). Once again, a possible middle Saxon estate centre may have developed within an area of much more ancient significance.

The above account is, of necessity, incomplete and speculative. Other large estates may have existed in northern and eastern Hertfordshire in the middle Saxon period, and the bounds of those tentatively outlined above may well have changed over time. Nevertheless, it seems likely that this extensive area was, in this period, divided up into eight or nine large territories based on the modern towns or villages of Hitchin, Braughing, Welwyn, Ashwell and – less certainly – Benington, Hadham, Stortford, Hertford and Ware. All were places located within major river valleys, often near the points where the rivers were crossed by Roman roads. In most cases we have some evidence suggesting that these estates developed from early Saxon tribal territories, Romano-British 'small towns', or both. Imperfect though the evidence unquestionably is, we have hints here, if nothing more, of long-term territorial continuity.

Early territorial organisation: the Chiltern Dipslope

The west of the county, the dipslope of the Chiltern Hills, presents a very different picture. Here a number of large estates seem to have survived intact, or virtually so, at the time of the Domesday Survey. In part this was probably a consequence of the fact that, as Domesday shows, the area was more sparsely settled than the east of the county. The clay-with-flints soils which cover the uplands between the major valleys are less fertile than those formed on the chalky boulder clays, and the uplands themselves are more extensive than in the east, while reliable supplies of running water are available only in the principal valleys. On the main area of the Chiltern Dipslope, to the south and west of the River Lea, Domesday records a mere thirteen vills within an area of over 350 square kilometres: Berkhamsted, Cashio, Flamstead, Gaddesden (Great and Little are not explicitly distinguished by the survey), Hemel Hempstead, Redbourn, Rickmansworth, St Albans, Wheathampstead, Windridge, Hanstead, Langley (King's and Abbot's) and Sandridge. Almost all were based on settlements within the major river valleys: those of the Ver, Lea, Colne, Gade and Bulbourne. Conversely, a number of places which were, later in the Middle Ages, to become independent parishes are not mentioned by the Survey. These include the villages of Sarratt, Northchurch, Flaunden, Bovingdon and Harpenden. As we shall see, most of these places *were* apparently in existence by the time of the Norman Conquest, but Domesday ignores them because they still formed part of some larger estate.

By the time of Domesday large areas on the Chiltern Dipslope, and in the Vale of St Albans, were occupied by estates belonging to St Albans Abbey: Cashio, Rickmansworth, Hanstead, Windridge, Sandridge, Langley and Redbourn. The abbey had further holdings on the heavy London Clay uplands to the south of the Vale – in Shenley and *Titeberst* (Theobald Street in Aldenham) – while later sources show that it also held other properties here, probably at the time of the Conquest still tracts of appurtenant woodland, including what were to become the parishes of Ridge and Elstree

(Page 1908, 349, 387). The early history of the Abbey's lands in this district, and especially in the immediate vicinity of St Albans itself, is particularly obscure, in spite of the fact that the acquisition of much of the abbey's property in the district is recorded in a collection of charters, which has recently been edited and published by Julia Crick (Crick 2007).

Any attempt to unravel this complex story must begin with a short account of the history of the abbey itself. Matthew Paris's account of the thirteenth century, in the earlier sections of the *Gesta Abbatum*, describes the generous privileges granted at the abbey's foundation, but is largely mythical (Niblett and Thompson 2005, 360). William of Malmesbury, writing a little earlier and with less of an axe to grind (Matthew Paris was a monk at St Albans) presents a more muted account, describing how Offa ordered the relics of Saint Alban – hitherto 'obscurely buried' – to be taken up and placed in a magnificent shrine, which was itself placed within 'a church of most beautiful workmanship', and a group of monks assembled to tend it (Giles 1866, 78). In reality, the early history of the abbey is very poorly documented, and even its foundation by Offa is only attested in sources from the late eleventh and twelfth centuries (Crick 2007, 14–18). An absence of historical evidence in part reflects the abbey's relative obscurity in pre-Conquest times; it does not seem to have benefited from much royal interest in the centuries after its initial foundation, and it does not seem to have been a place of particular importance in ninth- or tenth-century England – no royal gatherings are known to have taken place there, and few writers refer to it, although the cult of Alban himself was widely celebrated (Crick 2007, 9–11).

This changed in the later tenth century, however. Following the establishment of a unified English state, King Edgar and his successors regularised old monasteries, established many new ones and generously endowed them, in part reflecting a fashionable enthusiasm for monastic reform which was sweeping across Europe at this time, but also as part of an attempt to centralise political power within the new English kingdom. The *Vita Oswaldi*, written in *c*.1005, names St Albans as one of three sites offered to Oswald (later Bishop of Worcester) at which to establish reformed monasteries, presumably around *c*.980. A later *Vita* (written by one Eadmer) describes how Oswald appointed one Ælfric as abbot after the existing community here had been expelled (Whitelock 1968, 69–70). Ælfric, unlike earlier abbots, appears to have enjoyed close relationships with the court, which brought particular royal favour to the abbey. He gave up the abbacy around 995 when he became archbishop of Canterbury, and was succeeded by his brother, Leofric (Crick 2007, 18–20). The Biddles' excavations at St Albans revealed that major changes were made to the abbey following its refoundation. In particular, a substantial covered way over six metres wide was constructed leading southwards from the nave for some thirty-eight metres – 'a processional way linking two parts of the pre-Norman ecclesiastical complex' (Biddle and Kjolbye-Biddle 2001, 66–9). This has parallels at Aachen and elsewhere, where similar corridors connected a church basilica and a monastic basilica. In addition, fragments of window glass and of polychrome glazed floor tiles have been recovered from the graves in the adjacent cemetery, indicating the presence of a sophisticated church. In Crick's words, 'the relaunching of the cult of St Alban and the refurbishing of the community's endowment and traditions sponsored by Ælfric and Leofric found material expression in the construction of a high-status church and associated monastic complex' (Crick 2007, 24).

The refoundation was followed by a wave of donations of estates, not only by the Crown but also by local nobles, which are detailed in a remarkable series of charters. But, in addition, some of these record – or purport to record – much earlier acquisitions. One, supposedly dating from the time of the original foundation of 793, records a grant by Offa and his son Ecgfrith of thirty-four *mansiones* at *Caegsho* (Cashio), six at *Heanhamstede* (Hanstead), and a further ten at Stanmore in Middlesex. The charter is unquestionably a post-Conquest forgery and unlikely to be based on a genuine original. The same is true of another, purporting to date from 796, recording a royal grant of Pinesfield (in Rickmansworth) to the abbey (Birch 1885, 373–5; Keynes 1993, 265–8; Crick 2007). In the words of Simon Keynes, 'it is obvious that the diplomas of Offa and Ecgfrith cannot be authentic in their received form. The diplomas are integral to the abbey's conception of its early history and endowment; but they fail the most elementary of tests' (Keynes 1993, 273).

Cashio was a large estate, rated at thirty-four hides in the supposed charter of 793. It eventually – in the post-Conquest period – gave its name to what had formerly been Albanstow Hundred. The location of Cashiobury and Cashio Bridge, and the absence of Watford from the Domesday record, indicate that Cashio embraced the area of Watford, and was perhaps based around the confluence of the Colne and the Gade, probably including the northern parts of what is now Rickmansworth parish (Longman 1976). But it extended some way beyond this area, westward into Sarratt, to judge from the bounds included in the charter. These are of particular interest. Although they are post-Conquest in their present form, they exhibit a number of unusual features which suggest that they may well be based on earlier material, presumably dating to the time (whenever that was) that the estate was first handed to the abbey. In particular, they make sense only if we assume that they run in an *anticlockwise* rather than a clockwise direction, an almost unique circumstance: the charter clauses attached to pre-Conquest charters almost always run the other way. We can say this with some confidence because, although few of the boundary markers can now be identified, the line described *ends* at the River Chess, having a little earlier 'come to the boundary between Hylamstede [presumably Hemel Hempstead] and Cassio' (Crick 2007, 118). As the Chess lies to the west of Cashio and Hemel to the north this would be topographically impossible if the boundary description ran in the usual direction. But there is another peculiar feature. The bounds are clearly not those of the whole of the estate. Instead, they are specifically 'the bounds between Langley and Cashio', that is, the northern boundary only. The later southern boundary of the parish of King's Langley runs – first with Watford to the south, and then with Sarratt – westwards up to a 'T-junction' with the boundary of Bovingdon – which was, until recent times, part of the parish of Hemel Hempstead. The charter boundary evidently did the same (it 'comes to the boundary between Hylamstede and Cashio'). The boundary described in the charter then evidently turned south, now apparently following close to the later parochial boundary between Bovingdon and Sarratt, and thus indicating that the latter formed part of Cashio at this time.

The fact that only part of the boundary of the estate is described strongly implies that the grantor, whoever he or she was, was dividing a much larger pre-existing territory which originally embraced both Langley and Cashio, and was fixing the new bounds accordingly. Although the layout of parish boundaries must, for reasons already explained, be treated with some caution as evidence for early territorial organisation, it is easy to see from their configuration how the two Langleys and Watford/Sarratt might once have formed a single unit. Either way, Cashio was a very large estate, one of the most extensive of the Abbey's holdings and one of its earliest acquisitions. But it was topographically and historically quite distinct from St Albans itself.

The character of Hanstead in this regard is less clear. This was, initially at least, a rather smaller territory adjoining Cashio directly to the north-east. It was presumably based on what was later Hanstead House, on the west bank of the River Colne but close to that river's confluence with the Ver (Figure 32). This place, and some at least of what had once been its territory, eventually came to lie in St Stephen's, one of the subsidiary rural parishes of St Albans. But it may not originally have been closely associated with St Albans, lying as it does nearly six kilometres to the south of the abbey, and on the southern margins of St Stephen's. It was perhaps always more closely connected with Cashio. Not only (if we give any credence to the charter) was it granted to the abbey at the same time as that estate, but it may subsequently have received much of Cashio's territory, for administrative and fiscal purposes. The charter assigns thirty-four hides to Cashio and six to Hanstead, a total of forty. By 1066, to judge from Domesday, they were each rated at twenty hides.

As already noted, the estate of Pinesfield was also claimed as part of the abbey's early, Offan endowment (Crick 2007, 4). Its name is preserved in those of Pinesfield Farm and Pinesfield Hall, in the south-east of Rickmansworth parish. The charter gives the bounds of the estate, but they are again hard to reconstruct in detail, appearing to describe, with their references to 'the boundary enclosure of the Chalfont people', the Colne and the Chess, a territory embracing only that part of Rickmansworth lying to the west of the former river and to the south-west of the latter (including modern Chorleywood).

Medieval monks, while keen to emphasise the antiquity of their foundations and privileges, often misunderstood the character of early monasticism. Middle Saxon monasteries did not generally hold vast estates, and were often simply communities attached to minsters associated with important royal vills: and St Albans certainly appears to have been one of the latter. As we have seen, there are good grounds for believing that Verulamium and its immediate hinterland became in the immediate post-Roman period the tribal territory of the group called the *Waeclingas*; and also that this subsequently developed into an important Mercian estate with a *burh* – Kingsbury – at its heart. This estate did not only comprise the present town of St Albans, but also the adjacent rural parishes of St Peter's, St Michael's and St Stephen's. According to the *Gesta Abbatum*, these three churches were originally established by Abbot Wulfsin in the mid tenth

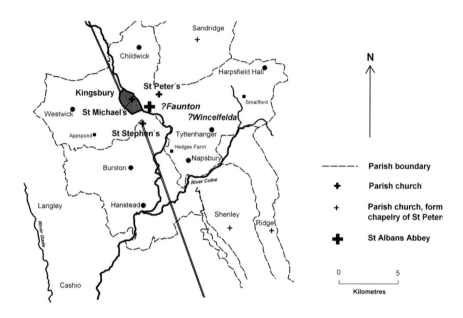

Figure 32. The St Albans area, showing places referred to in the discussion of early estates.

century (Riley 1867, 22) to serve the people dwelling in the area around St Albans, but, as Jonathan Hunn has pointed out, the site of St Michael's was not acquired by the abbey until the end of the tenth century and it is likely that all, in fact, were established around 1000 (Hunn 1994, 70). Both St Michael's and St Stephen's certainly contain late Saxon fabric and their almost identical plans suggests that they were built at the same time. The bounds of the three parishes fan out from St Albans itself, almost like the spokes of a wheel, indicating that they once formed one territory (Figure 32). In the Middle Ages the parish of St Peter's also originally included, to the north, what is now Sandridge (which continued to be a chapelry until the fourteenth century) and, on the clay soils to the south, the parishes of Ridge and Northaw.

In the tenth and eleventh centuries the monks of St Albans were evidently keen to emphasise the antiquity of their lands and privileges – common practice on the part of ecclesiastical houses. Indeed, they not only claimed that the monastery had received much of its property at its original foundation in the late eighth century, but also extensive liberties from royal dues and from control by the bishop. Nevertheless, we must not be too sceptical: Cashio, Hanstead and Pinesfield may not have been given to the community by Offa, but they were all probably acquired some time before the abbey's refoundation of the late tenth century. A charter of 957, concerning land in north Middlesex granted to Westminster Abbey, refers to its boundary with property belonging to the monks of St Albans. This was probably Stanmore, which was also supposedly part of Offa's original endowment of 793 (Gelling 1979, no. 220). The charter survives only as an eleventh-century copy, but 'its authenticity has generally been accepted, and its diplomatic is consistent with a mid-tenth-century date' (Crick 2007, 84). If Stanmore in Middlesex had been acquired by the middle of the tenth century there is no reason to suppose that the same was not also true of Cashio, Hanstead and Pinesfield in Hertfordshire. All may well have been the property of the abbey as early as the ninth century, before the Danish incursions: although probably not, as claimed, in the late eighth. But it is noteworthy that all three lay at some distance from the abbey itself, beyond the bounds of the royal estate, and largely within an area which Domesday suggests was still well-wooded and sparsely populated.

Whatever the date at which these 'core' properties were given to the abbey, the bulk of its lands were clearly acquired much later, like those of most other great monastic houses – during the time of monastic reform in the tenth and eleventh centuries. Many lay elsewhere in the county, at some distance from the area of south-west Hertfordshire that is our present concern. They include a number of places already mentioned in this chapter – Norton and Rodhanger near Stevenage, purchased for the community by Ælfric himself after he had retired from his role as abbot; Codicote and Oxwick, donated and bequeathed in 1002 and the 1030s/40s respectively; and lands at Barley, Flamstead, Gaddesden, King's Walden and Studham, this last just over the county boundary in Bedfordshire (Crick 2007, nos 6, 7, 10, 11, 12, 15, 17). The community was also given property further afield in Buckinghamshire, Northamptonshire and London. Before returning to some of these places, however, we must first consider the community's acquisitions in the immediate vicinity of St Albans itself.

In 996 – if the charters surviving as later copies can be believed – King Æthelred granted the abbey four *mansae* at Burston (in St Stephen's) and four at *Wincelfelda* (lost, somewhere in St Albans); together with nine *hagae* or house plots in *Væcliga caester* (St Albans itself) and land at Westwick (in St Michael's parish) (Crick 2007, no. 9). An estate associated with the old *burh* of Kingsbury and a block of attached woodland in the far south of the

county were granted by Æthelred in 1005; while in the 1040s the lost
þwangtune – 'Faunton' – was given by the nobleman Æthelwine Niger
(together with land at Redbourn and Langley) (Crick 2007, nos 14 and 14a).

It is striking that none of these estates appears by name in Domesday
Book. Conversely, many of the local St Albans manors which *are* recorded in
Domesday are not represented among the properties for which there are
extant charters. St Albans itself, an estate of ten hides in Domesday, is
mentioned only in the context of the nine house plots in the town which were
granted to the abbey in 996; Rickmansworth, Sandridge, Shenley, Napsbury
and *Titeberst* in Aldenham are all completely missing from the charters. All
this suggests (like the adjustment of hidage assessments between Cashio and
Hanstead) some reorganisation of properties in the St Albans area, or at least
of their taxation assessments, in the course of the eleventh century. But it also
raises difficult questions concerning which of the 'charter' estates were
combined to create which of the estates listed in Domesday.

Somewhat surprisingly, the problem is not much helped by the fact that
many (Winchfield, Pinesfeld, Oxhey/Batchworth, Kingsbury and Burston)
include quite detailed boundary clauses which should allow us to relate the
extent, or at least the location, of the estates in question to that of the manors
described in Domesday. In most cases the boundary markers are obscure, so
reconstruction of their bounds is very problematic. We can say with some
confidence that Oxhey and Batchworth (granted in 1007 but with no hidation
assessment given) were combined with the five hides at Pinesfield to create the
fifteen hides of Rickmansworth. Oxhey later formed part of the parish of
Watford, but it lay to the south of the Colne and this association may
represent a relatively recent, post-Conquest development. But the estates
nearer St Albans itself constitute a more intractable problem. Winchfield,
Burston and Kingsbury, together with the estates of Westwick and Faunton,
for which we do not have boundary clauses, are all assumed to lie within St
Albans and its associated parishes: the names of both Burston and Westwick
are preserved in those of later manorial 'halls' in the area (within the parishes
of St Stephen and St Michael respectively). But the charter bounds are, in all
cases, particularly obscure and the area covered by the estates in question
uncertain.

The bounds for Winchfield are perhaps easiest to interpret, at least in
broad terms (Crick 2007, no. 9). The boundary begins by running from the
'rough tumulus' to 'Tidda's spring', and then 'along the boundary to the

boundary with Faunton'. It then passed 'along the boundary to the Therfield people's boundary. Then there east along the boundary to the Harpsfield people.' The name of the latter group is preserved in that of Harspfield Hall, destroyed in the twentieth century by the construction of Hatfield aerodrome: this provides one important reference point. After this, the boundary ran to 'Wulfsige's burial-place', 'along the brook in front of Bryni's tumulus' to Bryni's tumulus itself, then to the 'deep ford' and finally back to the 'rough tumulus'. As charter bounds run in a clockwise direction, the brook can only have been the stream to the south-west of Harpsfield Hall which still runs south from Beech Farm and through the hamlet of Smallford to the River Colne. The 'deep ford' referred to in the charter was presumably across the river, a few hundred metres to the south of the hamlet, and may well have been so named to distinguish it from the nearby 'small ford' which crossed the tributary stream. All this indicates, pretty clearly, that the Winchfield estate lay to the east of St Albans and north of the Colne, and presumably occupied much of the central section of what became St Peter's parish. Given that bounds run clockwise, this also suggests that the estate at Faunton lay immediately to the west of this, presumably between Winchfield and St Albans itself (Figure 32).

The location of the Kingsbury estate is much harder to determine, not least because we can by no means be sure that the area of Kingsbury – referred to in the charter as the 'old fort' – was itself included within it. Like the grant of the detached section of woodland in the Barnet area which was made at the same time (below, p. 158), the estate is explicitly described as being 'attached to' the old fortification, a form of words which may well imply that the *burh* itself – the old Roman town – did not lie within it. The boundary markers are mostly obscure, but the third clause refers to a spot called *Apps Mere*, the 'aspen pond'. There is still a place called Appspond in St Stephen's parish, a few kilometres to the south-west of St Albans, which can possibly, but by no means certainly, be identified with a place called *Apesmere* mentioned in a document of 1309 (Gover *et al.* 1938, 90). This suggests that Kingsbury's land lay in this general area, in St Stephen's parish, and to the west of the River Ver. However, this was crowded territory in terms of known pre-Conquest estates (Figure 32). Westwick Farm, presumably marking the focus of Westwick (granted to the abbey in *c.*980 and 996), lay little more than a kilometre to the north-west; Burston Farm, similarly marking the centre of the Burston estate (also granted in 996), lay only two kilometres to the south-east; while the focus of Hanstead lay less than two kilometres to the south of this. Moreover, there are two other points mentioned on the boundary which seem to suggest that the estate lay on the *eastern* side of the Ver. Shortly after leaving *Apps Mere* the boundary comes to 'the valley of the Shenley people': Shenley lies to the south-east of St Peter's parish, beyond the Colne. North of the Colne lies Napsbury, *Absa* in Domesday and *Apsa* in other early documents – 'at the aspen tree'. Later, shortly before returning to *Apps Mere*, the boundary runs from a ford – which must certainly be over the Ver – to a place called 'Hacc's Acre' or 'Hedges Acre'. Hedges Farm stands immediately above a fording place on the Ver, to the east of the river, in St Peter's (TL156047) – a kilometre or so north-west of Napsbury. All this may suggest that in reality the land attached to Kingsbury lay in what is now London Colney in St Peter's, perhaps extending south into Shenley and *Titeburst*, which, as already noted, do not appear among the estates granted by charter, but were in part the property of the abbey at the time of Domesday. It may also have included land in Ridge, not mentioned by name in Domesday but the property of St Albans by the thirteenth century.

The bounds of Burston are also hard to follow. Burston Hall, as already noted, lay in St Stephen's, to the west of the Ver. But the particularly opaque boundary clause may indicate that its land extended east of that river and to the south of the Colne, for here too we have a reference to 'Shenley valley'. It is thus possible that some of the missing Domesday properties of the abbey, in Shenley, *Titeberst* and Ridge, were also included within the bounds of this estate, although they may in part have formed outlying areas of woodland appurtenant to these and other territories in the immediate area of St Albans. In a similar way, the charter estate at Westwick may have included much of Sandridge parish, to the north of St Albans.

We can thus, very tentatively, reconstruct the territorial history of St Albans in the following way. At some early date the monastic community, which was located close to the centre of a major Mercian estate, was given lands lying some distance to the west – the largely wooded tracts of Cashio (perhaps severed for the purpose from a large estate including Langley), Hanstead and Pinesfield, together with woodland at Stanmore. This donation appears to have been received before the refoundation of *c*.970, and possibly before the Danish occupation of Mercia in the late ninth century. The more fertile and cultivated land around St Albans itself, in contrast – and in the associated parishes of St Stephen's, St Peter's and St Michael's – continued into the tenth century in secular hands, partly as a major royal estate, partly perhaps as land in other hands, possibly acquired during the disruptions of the Danish incursions. Following the re-conquest of the area from the Danes, English kings granted successive portions of St Albans to the abbey, ending with the alienation of the *burh* itself, and its associated lands, in 1005. Other portions, in the hands of noble landowners – Faunton, and parts of Westwick – were also donated to the abbey in the century after refoundation. The community thus came to own the whole of the original estate, including areas of attached woodland on the clay uplands to the south of the Vale. This, it must be admitted, is not an entirely satisfactory account: more detailed work by local historians and others may well refine or refute it.

We may leave St Albans, with some relief, and turn to less complex matters of tenurial organisation. To the west of the old royal estate of *Wæclingacaester* lay a territory based on the upper Gade valley. As early as 705 Offa, king of the East Saxons, granted land in the *pagus* of *Hæmele* to Wealdhere, bishop of London. The name is borne by the modern town of Hemel Hempstead, and this may have been its centre. Until 1841 Hemel was a huge parish, covering some 12,440 acres and embracing a vast tract of land on the clay-with-flints uplands between the Gade and the Chess: but in that year Bovingdon and Flaunden were severed from it, becoming separate parishes (Page 1908, 216). To judge from the configuration of parish boundaries, a territory based on the town may originally have included the two Gaddesdens, to the north, although at least part of this area had become a separate entity by *c.*980, when Æthelgifu granted land here to St Albans Abbey (the boundary clause is discussed below, p. 172). However, it is possible that this large tract was originally part of a still more extensive land unit, for no Anglo-Saxon finds are known from the area around Hemel Hempstead and the town's church – although large – contains no obviously early fabric and has no evidence of minster status. Instead, Hemel and its dependencies may once have formed only the southern and eastern portion of *Hæmele*, which was in fact based on Berkhamsted.

Figure 33. Anglo-Saxon masonry, including Roman brick, in the south and west walls of St Mary's, Northchurch, indicates that this was once a substantial minster associated with a major estate centre.

The origins and development of Berkhamsted have been discussed at length in an important article by Doggett and Hunn (1985). Its original focus was not modern Berkhamsted itself, but rather Northchurch, some two kilometres to the west. Northchurch was originally known as North Berkhamsted or Berkhamsted St Mary: the modern name first appears in documents only in the fourteenth century (Gover *et al.* 1938, 48). The parish church of Northchurch, St Mary's, incorporates fragments of a large Anglo-Saxon building, surely a minster: the southern and western walls of the nave are both largely of Anglo-Saxon date, constructed of flints with blocks of limestone and clunch together with a number of Roman tiles (Smith 1973, 17–19; Sherwood 2008, 228–9) (Figure 33). The focus of Berkhamsted presumably moved to the present site following the construction of the castle there soon after the Norman Conquest, and the creation of a borough beside it (Doggett and Hunn 1985, 22), although some settlement already existed in this area, to judge from the finds of early or middle Saxon pottery (and some late Saxon) from Chesham Road, in the heart of the old town

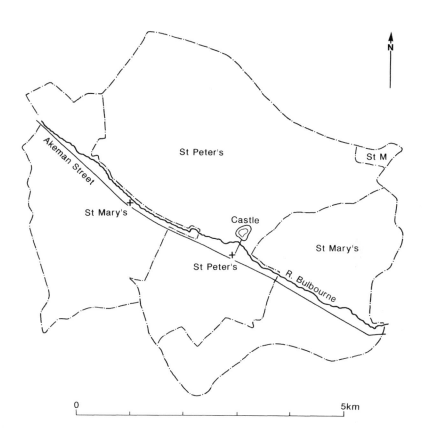

Figure 34. The parochial organisation of Berkhamsted (after Doggett and Hunn 1985).

(HER 10725). The old parish of Berkhamsted was divided, probably first in the late eleventh or twelfth century, between St Mary's and a church originally dedicated to St James, later to St Peter. The new parish occupied the centre of the old parish, leaving the latter divided into three separate portions (Figure 34)[3]

The higher ground to the north of Berkhamsted, on the high Chiltern ridge, was probably always shared territory: an extensive area of intercommoned woodland and wood-pasture exploited not only by communities dwelling in the valleys of the Gade and Bulbourne but also by people living north of the

---

3. Doggett and Hunn suggest that St James was on a different site, near the position of the present Post Office, but this seems to make little sense in terms of the topography of the town, for it would place it at the western extremity of the borough, and some distance from the castle.

escarpment, in what is now Buckinghamshire. Extensive woods and commons survived here into the modern period: indeed, this is still one of the wildest areas of the county, much of it carefully managed by the National Trust. The wood called The Frith – literally, 'the wood' – to the north of Berkhamstead was said to contain over 763 acres as late as 1357 (Page 1908, 162). The inhabitants of the town could exploit the herbage for grazing, except during the pannage season, which ran from the feast of St Michael to that of St Martin. As late as the reign of Edward VI it was said that 2,000 individuals claimed common rights here: not only people dwelling in Berkhamsted, Northchurch, Nettleden and Gaddesden, but also in the outlying parts of Hemel Hempstead as far away as Bovingdon and Flaunden, as well as in settlements lying to the north of the hills, Pitstone and Cheddington (Page 1908, 162). The existence of such tracts of valuable swine-pasture and woodland here in Saxon times doubtless explains the curious case of Nettleden, a parish created (and transferred to Hertfordshire) only in 1895. Formerly it had been an outlying section – a separate chapelry – of the parish of Pitstone, and an isolated portion of the parish of Ivinghoe: an island of Buckinghamshire surrounded on all sides by the Hertfordshire parishes of Berkhamsted, Great Gaddesden, Little Gaddesden and Northchurch.

While the lower section of the Ver valley was occupied by an estate based on St Albans, the upper Ver seems always to have formed a separate territory focused on the village of Redbourn. This seems to have included the adjoining parish of Flamstead, and also therefore Markyate, which formed a part of Flamstead until 1897 (Page 1908, 193). Flamstead and Redbourn were clearly separate places by the eleventh century. One hide at Flamstead was granted to St Albans by King Æthelred in 1005, and the charter describes the boundary of the estate (Crick 2007, 11). It ran from the 'sedge meadow' via *Idene* to 'woodman's gate'. As the first of these places is presumably on the flood plain of the Ver, and the last also features as a marker in the boundary clause of the Gaddesden charter, somewhere to the north of Holtsmere End (perhaps near Stag End), the *Idene* – a valley of some kind – is presumably the dry valley which runs to the south of Flamstead village and which contains Trowley Bottom Farm. From 'woodman's gate' the boundary ran via the 'three boundaries' and the 'heap of wood' to *mearcleagete*, 'the gate at the boundary clearing'. The latter place is clearly Markyate. From here the boundary ran via 'boar seat' to 'Pyppa's Gate', which may well have been near the hamlet of Pepsal End

('Pyppe's Hill'), before proceeding to *Hearpedene*. This name is an early form of Harpenden, the neighbouring parish, but was here used as a topographic term – for the dry valley in which that place lies – rather than for a settlement. From here, the boundary ran via 'Pobbas' tract of marsh grass' back to the 'sedge meadows'. The bounds define, broadly but not exactly, the medieval parish of Flamstead before the creation of the new parish of Markyate in the nineteenth century. They exclude Redbourn, which the abbey also received some forty years later, as part of Æthelwine Niger's donations. Yet, in spite of the fact that they were thus clearly separate places by the early eleventh century, there are good reasons for believing that Redbourn and Flamstead once formed a single territory.

Firstly, the church of Flamstead remained a chapel of Redbourn until it was promoted to parochial status in the early twelfth century (Page 1908, 195): this does not prove that the two were also one *secular* territory, but it does strongly suggest it. Secondly, a wide projection of Flamstead parish extends a long way to the south of the village, almost as far as the parish church of Redbourn and the adjacent Iron Age earthwork, the Aubreys. And it is near here, rather than within the village of Flamstead, that the main manorial site of the vill is located – at Flamstead Bury. Thirdly, attention should be drawn to the name of Flamstead – 'place of refuge' (Gover *et al.* 1938, 32). This makes little obvious sense unless it is a reference to the Aubreys hillfort, and perhaps to its re-use as a local stronghold in the post-Roman period. None of these pieces of evidence prove that Redbourn and Flamstead were once one, but they certainly suggest it. There are other signs of Redbourn's early importance. Roger Wendover recorded how, in June 1178, monks from St Albans – following instructions received in a vision from St Amphibalus, the priest who had converted Alban – opened barrows on Redbourn Common and discovered what sound like Anglo-Saxon inhumation burials, one of which was furnished with spear and knife. The site probably lay around 600 metres to the north-west of the church. As with several of the probable estate centres discussed so far, Redbourn lay close to the place where a Roman road (Watling Street) crossed a significant river (the Ver).

Eastwards, across the watershed into the valley of the Lea, the next early estate was clearly based on Wheathampstead. This place was granted to Westminster Abbey by Edward the Confessor in *c.*1060, and had formerly, by implication, been royal demesne. The charter has a detailed boundary clause

Figure 35. Wheathampstead appears to have been one of the principal Middle Saxon estate centres in west Hertfordshire and its church, which contains Saxon fabric and sits within a particularly spacious churchyard, was probably a minster.

which shows that the estate included all, or almost all, of what later became the parish of Harpenden, but which remained as a chapelry of Wheathampstead until the middle of the nineteenth century. The estate shared a common boundary with Flamstead, and some of the points listed in the boundary clauses at the ends of their respective charters are the same (Rumble 1977; Munby 1973, 3–9). The configuration of parish boundaries suggests that the long north-eastern projection of Sandridge parish – the portion later comprising the manor of Brides Hall – was also part of the estate, a conjecture supported by Ian Freeman's detailed study of the surviving remains of the estate's boundary. The northern section of this still comprises, for much of its length, a great double bank with hedgerows containing nine or ten shrub species per thirty-metre stretch (Freeman 1977, 18–19). The size and antiquity of the original boundary is also indicated by the way that 'every road or lane that crosses the hedge-line is deflected from its own line to follow the line of the hedge for at least a few yards' (Freeman 1977, 19).

St Helen's, the parish church of Wheathampstead, is very probably an early minster. It stands in a particularly large churchyard, the southern and western walls of the south transept are almost certainly of pre-Conquest date (Figure 35: Smith 1973, 34), and foundations of a former apsidal end to the chancel, probably contemporary with the southern and western walls of the south transept, were uncovered during renovations in the 1860s (HER 2877). Excavations carried out by Saunders and Havercroft in 1979 revealed a number of burials beneath an old ground surface sealed by the fourteenth-century nave wall. Some of these were 'distinguished by a distinctive burial rite, having the head packed round with large flints' (Saunders and Havercroft 1982b, 108). Such 'flint pillows' are known from a number of places in England and are associated with burials of middle Saxon date. An earlier Saxon importance is suggested by the richly furnished inhumation burial, or burials, discovered on the north side of the Lea (near the former railway station) in 1885 (TL180145: HER 1637). The name of Wheathampstead, like Hanstead, Flamstead and Berkhamsted, features the suffix *-stead* or *-hamstead*, meaning 'place' or 'estate', clearly a favoured name for the principal settlements in this district.

In the north and east of Hertfordshire, as we have seen, a number of Saxon estate centres seem to relate closely to sites of Roman importance, principally the 'small towns'. On the Chiltern Dipslope there are several similar associations. Apart from the obvious case of St Albans itself, attention might be drawn to Berkhamsted/Hemel, for what was probably the original focus of that estate, at Northchurch, lies only two kilometres from the centre of the Iron Age iron-working site and Romano-British 'small town' at the Cow Roast Inn. A significant concentration of Roman finds has come from Wheathampstead: several Roman buildings underlie parts of the village, including one with mosaic pavements (HER 1597, 12652). We should not make too much of such locational coincidences, but it is possible that some of the early medieval land units in the area had, once again, much more ancient origins.

Early territorial organisation: the Southern Uplands

The region of heavy infertile clays and acid gravels in the far south of the county was much less attractive to early settlement than any of the districts so far discussed. It is flanked by areas of more amenable soils derived from exposures of chalk, Eocene deposits or glacial sands (in the Vale of St Albans and the Colne valley to the north-west and west, and in the Lea valley to the east and north) but the distance between these ribbons of more attractive land is considerable. Domesday mentions a number of vills in the area, some of which have already been discussed in relation to the territorial development of Hertford and St Albans – they formed parts of these probable estates – and in addition it is likely that Cheshunt formed a separate land unit based on the Lea valley, which embraced Broxbourne, Wormley and Hoddesdon (and which may have developed from a tribal territory based on a Roman 'small town' (above, p. 62–3)). Most Domesday vills in the district are located around the margins of the clay uplands. Several are represented today by settlements located on the floors of the Lea or Colne valleys, usually close to (within *c.*500 metres of) the river: Broxbourne, Amwell, Hoddesdon, Cheshunt, Napsbury and, probably, Bushey (the Domesday focus of which seems to have been at Bushey Hall, beside the Colne, rather than at the present village site). Others, such as North Mimms, Aldenham, Essendon and Wormley, are located at the upper edge of these valleys, near to the junction of the light valley soils with the London Clay; while yet others are located beside the lower reaches of tributary valleys – Brickendon, Bayford, Little Berkhamsted and Shenley. Only one of the vills mentioned by Domesday – *Titeberst*, the modern Theobald Street in Borehamwood – is situated more than a kilometre from light, well-drained soils. With this single exception, the Domesday map of the uplands is a blank. A number of places in this district which had, by the later Middle Ages, grown into sizeable communities, often separate vills and parishes, simply do not appear: Borehamwood, Northaw, Elstree, Ridge, Chipping and East Barnet, Totteridge, Monken Hadley and Arkley. Many are first mentioned in documents as late as the thirteenth century; Arkeley, for instance, makes its first appearance in 1248 (Gover *et al.* 1938). We have, however, one pre-Conquest documentary source relating to this area. When King Æthelred gave Kingsbury to the monks of St Albans in 1005 the grant included an area of attached woodland, the bounds of which include references to the *hæð leah*, the 'heath clearing' – that is, (Monken) Hadley – and, once again, to a boundary with the 'Shenley people'. In an important analysis of the charter bounds, Taylor showed that they embraced an extensive area of land in what is now Middlesex, stretching from Edmonton in the east to Totteridge in the west and northwards to Monken Hadley, thus embracing most of Barnet (Taylor 1995; Taylor 2008, 256–8; Crick 2007,

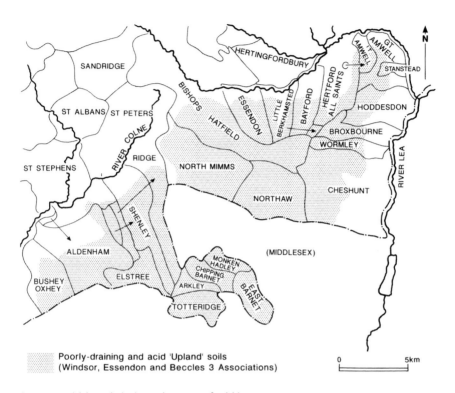

Figure 36. Parish boundaries in south-east Hertfordshire.

188–9). Significantly, almost all of the 'upland' vills have names associated with woodland or its clearance: Borehamwood is the 'wood by the hill homestead'; Northaw, the 'northern woodland enclosure'; Hadley, the 'heath clearing'; Barnet, the 'place cleared by burning' (Gover *et al.* 1938, 74, 113, 75, 70). The meaning of Arkley is uncertain but clearly incorporates the element *leah*, 'clearing'. Even those Domesday vills whose centres were located only a small distance from the main valleys often bear such names: Shenley, the 'bright clearing'; Wormley, the 'snake-infested clearing' (Gover *et al.* 1938, 64, 67, 233).

Villages based in the valleys of the Lea and the Colne tend to have rather elongated parishes which extend up onto the clay uplands (Figure 36) (Barton 1981, 8–9; Wooldridge and Hutchings 1957). Such a pattern presumably developed as valley settlements competed for a share of the pannage and other resources provided by the upland woods. Of particular interest is the way in which, in the area immediately to the south and west of the River Lea, a string of parishes – Essendon, Little Berkhamsted, Bayford, Hertford All Saints, Broxbourne, Cheshunt and Wormley – run up towards an upland tract which was apparently once shared between them, occupying the level interfluve between the Lea and the Cuffley Brook; but no longer. The parish of Hatfield now extends, greatly elongated, far to the east, and has clearly annexed what was once shared territory (Figure 36). It is impossible to say precisely when this might have occurred, but it is tempting to associate it with King Edgar's gift of Hatfield to the Abbey of Ely in *c.*970 (above, p. 136). The area immediately around the present focus of Hatfield comprises fairly well-drained gravel soil within the Vale of St Albans, land which had almost certainly been long cleared, and long settled, when the gift was made. Yet the *Liber Eliensis* nevertheless describes how the estate was given to the abbey 'because, since the country is wooded, the brethren can find timber for the fabric of their church, and wood for other purposes' (Page 1912, 91). It is possible that Edgar had in mind the resources of this remote area of clay upland, which was now severed from the other communities which had formerly shared its exploitation.

This easterly extension to Hatfield parish remained heavily wooded well into the Middle Ages. It was known as the 'Great Park', and the Ely custumals of 1222 and 1251 (made after the abbey's holdings had been transferred to the bishopric of Ely) describe it as a tract of wooded ground covering some 1,000 acres, although in reality it probably covered nearly twice this area (Rowe 2009, 112). Later it was referred to as the Great Wood, although it was mainly an area of wood-pasture (although there was some intensively managed coppice ground) with a scatter of trees (especially oak, hornbeam and beech) thin enough to permit a reasonable growth of herbage. It was exploited not only by the bishop but also by his tenants, who held common rights there. A survey of 1538, made soon after Hatfield was taken over by Henry VIII, reported that the park contained 10,000 oaks and beeches, probably fewer than six per acre (Rowe 2009, 108–13). Another survey, drawn up in 1551, described

> One great park called Hatfield wood containing by estimation 7 miles compas replenished with wood of gret age wherein are 120 dere by estimation not well fensid in all places ... The herbage therof is Comon, the pannage belongeth to her grace ... Excepted ... all Customary holders dwellinge in Bukhamwikhide [modern Woodside] if ther be anye other they cannot tell. (Austin 1995, 2)

By this time some of the eastern parts of the wood had been assarted – cleared for agriculture – but the rest survived until 1611, when it was enclosed by an agreement made between Robert Cecil and the commoners, and much turned to farmland. The 560 acres allotted to Cecil were made into another park, the New Park, but this too was soon made into farmland, and today 'the land which was once Hatfield Great Wood is now a regular pattern of mostly arable fields with few surviving clues to its ancient wooded past' (Austin 1995, 7).

The Great Wood at Hatfield was one of the last surviving remnants of the great pannage woods and wood-pastures which once occupied much of the Southern Uplands. Most of the rest, as we shall see, was converted to farmland or to more intensively managed woodland, or degenerated to open heath, during the course of the Middle Ages. We should not, however, think of these wooded tracts as 'waste'. They were greatly valued in Anglo-Saxon times for the wood, timber, grazing and pannage which they provided – as the strongly parallel and attenuated pattern of parish boundaries on the periphery of the clays suggests.

By the end of the Saxon period Hatfield had not only acquired the area of the Great Wood but also Totteridge, some fifteen kilometres away in the far south of the county. It remained a detached chapelry of Hatfield parish until 1892, the chapel originally dedicated, significantly, to St Etheldreda (Page 1908, 148). The holdings of St Albans Abbey similarly included distant tracts, far to the south on these same clay uplands, including the village of Ridge, first mentioned in 1248 (Page 1908, 386; Barton 1981). Later in the Middle Ages the manor of 'Ridge or Tytenhanger' also embraced the hamlet of the latter name, to the north-west of the Colne, in St Peter's parish – perhaps supporting the conjectures advanced earlier (above, pp. 148–50) regarding the location and extent of the estate attached to Kingsbury. Ridge remained a chapelry, annexed to the parish of St Peter, until the early fourteenth century (Page 1908, 387, 391). It had to the west a small detached section which was separated from it by Shenley parish; beyond *this* was a detached section of Shenley (Figure 36). The two parts of Shenley probably equate to the two Domesday holdings which did not form part of the abbey's properties (they were held by the Count of Mortain and Geoffrey de Mandeville respectively), for they remained in Dacorum Hundred; the detached section of Ridge parish is probably the abbey's Domesday holding in *Titeberst*, usually equated with the hamlet of Theobald Street, now in

Borehamwood. The abbey's Domesday holding in Shenley can probably be equated with what later became Elstree, a property confirmed to the monks by Pope Clement in 1188, together with the 'wood of Boreham' for feeding swine. It remained a chapelry until constituted as a separate parish in 1424 (Page 1908, 351). Northaw, lying at an even greater distance from the abbey, was the *sylvam quae dicitur North Haga*, 'the wood called the north enclosure', which the abbey had to struggle to recover from Robert FitzWalter in the late eleventh century (Riley 1867, 63). It achieved independent parochial status only in the sixteenth century (Page 1908, 358). Lastly, the Barnets – East and High – had, as already noted, been acquired by the abbey by late Saxon times. Friern Barnet in Middlesex was probably taken from the abbey and given to the bishop of London after the Norman Conquest (Javes 1992). The high, remote watershed here divides Hertfordshire from Middlesex: and as we have seen, the boundary has always been strangely defined, dividing North from South Mimms and East Barnet and Chipping Barnet from Friern Barnet, again suggesting that in the earlier Middle Ages much of this area was sparsely settled, debatable ground. Interestingly, early documents, such as the grant of Henry II confirming the abbey's possessions here, refer not to the Barnets themselves but to the woods of *Suthawe* and *Ossridge* or *Huzelhege*.

Conclusion

Many readers will by now have tired of these often speculative reconstructions of Saxon territorial organisation, and may even feel that such enquiries have a rather old-fashioned, antiquarian flavour. Partly for this reason, but also because of a paucity of good evidence, I have said little about some of these estates (Cheshunt) and nothing about others (such as Tring, surely the centre of a major Saxon territory, given its early status as the head of an eponymous hundred). But these matters *are* important, not least to local historians. Those who study the histories of particular places should always be alert to the likelihood that these once formed a part of some larger entity. Moreover, the role of any settlement within such an archaic unit – as a central place, or as an outlying dependency – often laid the basis for its later development, and even for aspects of its present-day character. Indeed, it is Hertfordshire's local historians, more than anyone else, who may be able to test and amplify the picture presented here: for the picture *is* often fragmentary and incomplete, and the evidence currently available open to a range of interpretations. The broad features of middle Saxon geography are, however, tolerably clear. Most of Hertfordshire was divided into a number of large estates – probably around fifteen in all (Figure 30). These contained named subdivisions (Burston, *þwangtune*), some of which were occupied into late Saxon times by what may well have been semi-free kin-groups (the 'Harpsfield people'), others by bond tenants, others – to judge from the detailed bequests in Æthelgifu's will – largely by slaves. These estates seem mainly to have developed from earlier folk-territories – from the lands of the *Hicce*, the *Brahingas*, the *Beningas*, the *Wæclingas* and the rest. Their core areas lay on light land, usually in major river valleys; their central places were often near to where major roads crossed these rivers. The interfluves between were, initially, occupied by tracts of grazing and woodland. In several areas – the Stevenage–Welwyn Clays, on the high Chiltern ridge to the north of Berkhamsted, and above all on the Southern Uplands – particularly extensive areas of woodland survived into the post-Conquest period. In part their existence was a consequence of the poorly draining and/or infertile character of the local soils. But it was also a function of topography, of the width of the clay-covered interfluves and the distance between the major valleys in these places. In these districts complex forms of exploitation seem to have existed, with estates lying some distance away sometimes obtaining shares in the woods and pastures.

What is particularly intriguing is the way in which many of the estate centres suggested above seem to have been closely associated with places of Roman and, in some cases, Iron Age importance. St Albans, Braughing, Welwyn, Berkhamstead – all major estate centres, all the sites of early minsters – lay close to Roman towns and major Iron Age settlements. Bishop's Stortford, Wheathampstead, Hadham, Ashwell and Cheshunt also seem to have located at or near places of Roman and, in some cases, earlier importance. Of course, such 'continuity' is not evident everywhere. While the areas occupied by the estate centres at Hitchin and Hertford were certainly settled in the Roman period, there is no real evidence that these had been important places then. We may have glimpses of continuity, spanning in some cases the whole of the first millennium. But patterns of territorial organisation, ownership and administration evidently continued to evolve over this immense period of time.

Chapter 5
The Saxon Landscape

Introduction

We can reconstruct, at least in general terms, patterns of territorial organisation in Hertfordshire during the early and middle Saxon periods – the configuration of folk-territories and estates, and the location of the principal tracts of woodland and wood-pasture. It is much more difficult to discover the pattern of settlement or the appearance of the landscape in this remote period. In the 'core' areas of estates, were there many settlements or only one – that which formed the estate's focus? And were the wooded tracts of the interfluves devoid of habitation, or did they too contain settlements, perhaps seasonally occupied, to facilitate the exploitation of woodland and grazing? Indeed, how wild *were* these areas? Were they indeed trackless wastes, or were they managed environments, systematically exploited?

It is difficult to answer these questions because, for the reasons already outlined, few settlement sites from the Saxon period are known in Hertfordshire. At the present time, any study of Anglo-Saxon settlement and landscape in the county has to rely mainly on the evidence provided by the boundary clauses of pre-Conquest charters, on the interpretation of place-names and on Domesday Book, which was compiled in 1086 but which looks back into pre-Conquest times. Because Domesday provides our first comprehensive impression of the landscape, it is with this problematic document that we must begin.

Regional contrasts

Domesday describes, in some detail, the tenants and resources on the estates or manors held by various major landholders and their subtenants. These

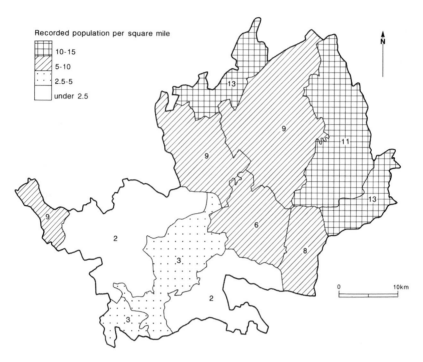

Figure 37. Hertfordshire: Domesday population (after Campbell 1962).

are located in terms of the townships or vills – units of local administration and taxation – in which they lie. Domesday also tells us about each estate's tax liability – the number of hides at which it was assessed – which was broadly related to the area that it covered. Domesday's account makes it clear that by 1066 the extension of settlement and the expansion of agriculture had proceeded some way in Hertfordshire, although to varying extents in different parts of the county. In the north and east – on the fertile soils of the chalky boulder clays, and in the Vale of Baldock at the foot of the chalk escarpment – people were relatively thick on the ground, with population densities ranging from around nine to eleven recorded individuals per square mile, rising to thirteen in the Vale (Campbell 1962, 68–9) (Figure 37). These figures are perhaps equivalent to between fifty and seventy actual people per square mile – Domesday records only landholders. Parts of eastern Hertfordshire thus possessed population densities considerably above the average for England as a whole, approaching those of the populous lands of Norfolk, Suffolk and north Essex (Darby 1977,

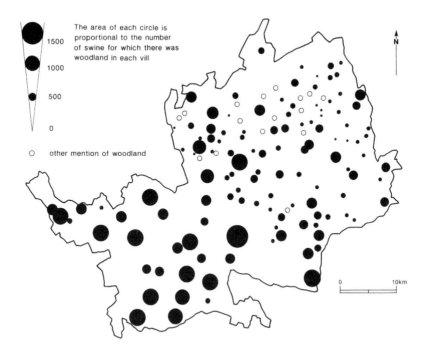

Figure 38. Hertfordshire: Domesday woodland (after Campbell 1962).

90). In the Vale of Baldock there was little or no woodland, but on the boulder clays woods were frequent, although not apparently extensive: most vills here had some woodland, but in moderate quantities. Most places had sufficient, Domesday tells us, for 100 swine or fewer; many had enough only to supply materials for the repair of fences; and only three (Meesden, Much Hadham and Pelham) had sufficient for 300 swine or more (Figure 38). In Hertfordshire, as in other counties in the south and east of England, the Survey thus records woodland mainly in terms of the number of pigs it could support. It is usually stated that this reflects the use of the woods for pannage, in the sense of fattening swine in the autumn on nuts, acorns and mast (Rackham 1986, 75–8). In fact, it may imply a more general use of wooded environments for pig-keeping: pigs are woodland animals, capable of rooting out all kinds of tasty morsels from the woodland floor. But whether all the woods recorded in this manner by Domesday were indeed still being managed in this way, and how such figures should be converted into acres or hectares, remains uncertain.

Given the density of population recorded in the north and east it is not surprising that Domesday suggests that arable land was extensive here: the number of recorded plough teams (a rough indication of the extent of ploughland) was generally around three per square mile. Later medieval sources suggest that one medieval plough could work around seventy sown acres on average soils (Campbell 2000, 121). If, as seems likely, most Hertfordshire townships at this time employed a two-course rotation, allowing half the land to lie fallow each year, then each plough could cultivate around 140 acres of arable land, allowing for fallow: and three ploughs would work 420 acres out of the 640 acres in a square mile. This admittedly rough and ready calculation suggests that something approaching two-thirds of the land in this part of the county may have been under the plough in 1086. Certainly, even the smallest 'upland' vills on the boulder-clay interfluves were at least partly under arable cultivation (Campbell 1962, 64–5).

The south and west of the county present a rather different picture. Domesday shows that here arable was much less extensive and population levels were low. Indeed, the average population density of vills on the Chiltern Dipslope, in the Vale of St Albans and on the Southern Uplands generally varied from a mere two or three recorded individuals per square mile (Campbell 1962, 68–9), perhaps implying a real population density of between ten and fifteen people per square mile (Figure 37). The density of plough teams was generally below two per square mile, and in places below one. These figures are low indeed by comparison with the north and east of the county, but not unique. This area of Hertfordshire formed part of a wider district of sparse settlement extending westwards into the Chilterns of south Buckinghamshire and southwards onto the London Clay of north Middlesex (Darby 1977, 127–33). There were also far fewer manors and vills recorded by Domesday in the south and west of the county than in the north and east, as we have seen. This was a district of large estates, many of which were in ecclesiastical hands. In addition, woodland was apparently much more extensive here, with places like Berkhamsted having enough (to use Domesday's terminology) for 1,000 pigs, and Hemel Hempstead sufficient for 1,200.

Some caution needs to be maintained when examining such figures: it is easy to exaggerate the undeveloped, sparsely cleared character of the south-west of the county compared with the north-east. In particular, mapping Domesday woodland in the form of discrete, variably sized symbols tends to over-emphasise the distinction between the two halves of the county in this respect. In part, vills in the south-west had more woodland simply because they were themselves considerably larger, in general, than those in the north and east. A place like Hemel Hempstead may have had woodland sufficient for 1,200 swine, but it was also a vast tract of land, assessed at no fewer than thirty hides. This said, when the appropriate adjustments are made it is still clear that the south-west of the county (roughly, the area to the south and west of the River Lea) was nearly twice as densely wooded as the north-east, with around twenty-nine swines' worth of woodland per square kilometre, as against fifteen in the north and east. Similar calculations suggest that around half as much land (just over a third) was under the plough in the south and west as was the case in the north and east of the county.

The fact that ecclesiastical houses such as St Albans were keen to acquire shares of distant woodlands certainly indicates that the west of the county was not completely blanketed by forest, at least by late Saxon times. But it also serves to emphasise the fact that woodland was not empty, unexploited and valueless 'wilderness'. Woods provided timber, fuel and grazing, as well as opportunities for hunting and perhaps – as early as this – for farming deer. We should, perhaps, view wooded districts as ones with their own distinct economies in middle and later Saxon times, their produce often of greater importance and value than that from areas of arable farming. We think of cattle and sheep as essentially grass-consuming animals, but the latter in particular will happily eat a wide range of woodland shrubs, even dry twigs in the winter. But the woods were especially valued, as already noted, as swine pastures. Not only does Domesday record (as in neighbouring counties) the extent of woodland almost entirely in terms of the numbers of pigs that could be grazed in it. Pigs and their management also loom large in other documents, such as Æthelgifu's will, which included bequests of a herd of swine 'and the swineherd with it' at *Achurst* in Aldenham; another herd at *Langford*; a herd and swineherd at Standon; what appear to be two separate herds at Gaddesden; and land at Tewin 'as swine-pasture'. A number of individual swineherds are mentioned by name, and pigs were included in the donations of food-rents made to the various minsters (Crick 2007, no. 7). Pigs, presumably grazed at least in part in the abbey's extensive woods, formed a major element of the diet of the Saxon monks at St Albans: no less than 66 per cent of the bones recovered during the excavations of the Chapter House (in a context dating from some time between the fifth and ninth centuries) were from pigs (Crick 2007, 75).

A further 5 per cent were from deer, and it is possible that these were a more important part of the middle and later Saxon economy than we often assume. Æthelgifu left significant bequests to her huntsman Wulfric, and it is probable that deer parks, rather than being simply a Norman introduction, existed in some form in Hertfordshire in the eleventh century and perhaps earlier. Domesday records 'parks for woodland beasts' at St Albans, Ware and Benington, and it is perfectly possible that these were pre-Conquest creations, as all were associated with major Saxon estates (Rowe 2009, 56, 192, 222). Moreover, the term *haga* occurs in the boundary clauses of the charters for Pinesfield and Kingsbury (Crick 2007, nos 4 and 11). It has been suggested that this term, often translated simply as 'hedge' or 'enclosure', may sometimes have had a more specialised meaning, referring to a barrier used to corral or control deer, perhaps in some cases surrounding enclosures similar if not identical to later parks (Hooke 1981, 236, 245; 1998, 154–7). It is probable that only small areas of woodland were being managed as coppices at this time, at least in the south and west where the woods were extensive, but the boundary clauses of Saxon charters make numerous references to 'stocc', in the sense of pollarded trees, perhaps implying the presence of intensively managed wood-pastures (e.g. Crick 2007, nos 4, 10, 11 and 12).

Such intensive but varied uses of woodland, and the active assertion of property rights over distant areas of woodland, explains the numerous charter references to gates and banks in a woodland context, as described below: woods needed to be divided, and portions enclosed. But regular grazing would also have led to the gradual degeneration of woodland, the formation of clearings or *leahs* where the regeneration of felled or fallen timber was prevented by the browsing of stock. Indeed, the available evidence suggests that, by the tenth century at least, even the most densely wooded areas of the county included numerous clearings, and often more extensive areas of open land.

Landscape and settlement: the south and west

The extent of uncleared 'waste' on the Chiltern Dipslope in Saxon times has been emphasised by historians (e.g. Munby 1977, 84–5; Levett 1938, 180–1). This is in part because Domesday records such large areas of woodland here; and in part because Matthew Paris, the author of the *Gesta Abbatum*, recorded that the Chilterns remained an impenetrable forest, harbouring only wild beasts, until Abbot Leofstan cleared the area to the south and west of Watling Street during the early eleventh century (Riley 1867, 39). But as noted, the apparent Domesday evidence for vast tracts of woodland in this district needs to placed in the context of the large size of townships and estates here; while the reliability of Matthew Paris as a source for landscape history is probably limited. Local place-names, mainly coined in the middle Saxon period, do not suggest the presence of dense and continuous forest. Only one major place-name in the district incorporates a term for woodland or its clearance: King's and Abbot's Langley take their names from the *lang leah*, the 'long clearing' (Gover *et al.* 1938, 44). Nor do the majority of the hamlets and isolated farms in the district bear 'woodland' names, although there are some examples, including Apsley ('the aspen wood') in King's Langley and Micklefield Hall ('the large open area') in Rickmansworth (Gover *et al.* 1938, 45, 81). Most places away from the long-cleared valleys in fact have names which refer to the topography, and in particular to the broken nature of the local terrain: Windridge is the 'windy ridge'; Sandridge the 'sandy ridge'; Bovingdon is the place 'above the *dun*', or hill; while Gaddesden, Harpenden, Nettleden and Flaunden all incorporate the element *denu* (Gover *et al.* 1938, 35, 37, 48, 34, 102, 92, 100, 29). Although usually translated simply as 'valley', the distribution of this term in England as a whole suggests that it had a more specific meaning (Gelling 1984), being applied particularly to narrow valleys with steep sides, including dry ones, like the numerous 'gaps' running north-west–south-east down the dipslope of the Chilterns. Nettleden, the 'nettle-infested clearing in the valley' (Gover *et al.* 1938, 48) lies in a particularly pronounced dry cut running into the valley of the River Gade, the name of which is a back-formation from Gaddesden, 'Gaeta's valley' (Gover *et al.* 1938, 34–5). Flaunden takes its name from the dry steep-sided valley running north from the Buckinghamshire village of Latimer; Harpenden from the prominent dry valley located between, and running roughly parallel to, those occupied by the Rivers Lea and Ver. The term is also found in minor names: Whippendell Woods in Watford derives its name from *Wippa denu*, 'Wippa's valley'. Four kilometres to the north, in King's Langley, lies Whippendell Bottom (Gover *et al.* 1938, 46). The two places are connected by the deep dry valley from which both clearly derive their name. The keen awareness of topography indicated by all these names may suggest that the Chiltern dipslope was sufficiently open country for the broad pattern of landforms to be more noticeable to contemporaries than the character of clearings in woodland.

This impression of a fairly open landscape – or at least, of a landscape not completely carpeted with woodland – is also given by the boundary clauses of Anglo-Saxon charters, such as that for Wheathampstead, drawn up around 1060 when Edward the Confessor confirmed Westminster Abbey's possession of the estate. The bounds have been studied in detail by Lionel Munby (Munby 1973) and A.R. Rumble (1977). Beginning at *Maerford*, the modern Marford, the boundary ran up the *Headic* – the Devil's Dyke, the linear earthwork associated with the Wheathampstead *oppidum* – and then along a *denu*, the dry valley which extends southwards to Nomansland Common, as far as the *deorleage*, the 'deer wood'. This is the only reference to woodland included in the clause. The next markers suggest a settled and managed landscape: the boundary ran 'along the hedge' and then to the *lippelane*, the 'lane at the steep place' (Rumble 1977, 9). It then passed the *secgham*, the 'reedy meadow', and unidentified features called the *Pobbenaettoce*, before reaching *herpedenu*, the dry valley now occupied by Harpenden (Rumble 1977, 10). Proceeding thence to the 'ash tree at the ford where thatch is gathered', the 'stile by the plum tree' and the 'hollow tree', the boundary ran past two pools and along the 'boundary valley' before returning once more to Marford (Munby 1973, 8–9). There is little here to suggest a wild and untenanted countryside. Hedges, lanes, stiles and hollow trees indicate, at the very least, a moderately tamed and fairly open landscape, even on the interfluve between the Rivers Lea and Ver. The boundaries of Gaddesden, set out in an undated document appended to Æthelgifu's will of *c*.980, and of Flamstead, described in a charter of 1005, certainly seem to have run through more wooded landscapes, presumably because to the north these estates reached further towards the high, remote watershed of the Chilterns (Crick 2007, nos 7 and 11). The boundary clauses refer to the 'woodman's valley', the 'woodman's clearing', the 'fern wood' and the 'boundary clearing'. Yet even here, again in places which appear to be located away from the principal river valleys, we also learn of ploughed land and outlying dwellings.

Even the Southern Uplands – the poor London Clay soils south of the Vale of St Albans – were, at least by later Saxon times, probably a more tamed and settled landscape than has sometimes been assumed. Vast tracts of pannage woods there certainly were, but these were managed, often enclosed, accessed by defined tracks and interspersed with areas of more open land, again to judge from the boundary clauses attached to charters. One informative example, purportedly describing a grant by Offa of Mercia of thirty *cassati* of land in Aldenham to Westminster Abbey, is unquestionably a later forgery, but the attached boundary clause is nevertheless certainly 'from a pre-Conquest source' (Gelling 1979, 80; Birch 1885, 339–40). The original focus of settlement in Aldenham, as presumably marked by the site of its church, lay in the north-west of the parish, where the soils towards the River Colne are comparatively light and free-draining. But the bounds of the parish, and of the property described in the charter, extend a long way south onto the clay uplands, as far as the county boundary with Middlesex. The boundary first runs along the River Colne upstream as far as the *lange hegge ende*, the 'end of the long hedge', there turning east into the *heidene*, the 'high valley' (Birch 1885, 339). The term *denu*, as already noted, was generally used in Old English place-nomenclature for a steep-sided valley, and the only topographic feature which would really fit this description is the valley now occupied by the sewerage treatment plant below Blackbirds Farm. The boundary is on fairly light soils here, but beyond the valley it runs across heavier land as it makes for the next identifiable feature, the Roman road Watling Street, passing en route a place called *Boiwic* – presumably a farm of some kind (*wic* in such a context usually denotes an outlying dairy farm or ranch) and an unidentifiable feature called the *cupe*. Having reached Watling Street the boundary follows it southwards, through the *hilce sloð*, a swamp which can perhaps be identified with the particularly poorly draining piece of ground where the road descends into the valley of the stream called Tyke's Water. From here the boundary heads towards *Tiðwulfes treow* – Tithwulf's tree, which has given its name to the village of Elstree. The fact that a tree, however prominent, could be used as a landmark suggests that the area cannot all have been covered with dense, continuous woodland. Following, in all probability, the line of the present county boundary with Middlesex, the next two markers again suggest a landscape to some extent tamed and settled, even at this far extremity of the county: the *hæsel hyrst gate*, probably the 'gate to the hazel wood'; and the *fulen gate*, a 'dirty gate'. Passing through the 'west nook', along another hedge, over the 'small bridge' and through the 'cold clearing', the boundary returns to the Colne. Here is a landscape of woods and clearings, but also one of gates and hedges: an area of woodland and grazing, certainly, but a managed landscape, not a wilderness.

A little further down the River Colne lay the estate of Oxhey. Its bounds are described in a St Albans' charter, this time reliably dated to 1007 (Crick 2007, no. 12). The boundary probably ran on or close to the line of the modern parish boundary. It began at *watforda*, the ford where Watford Bridge now spans the Colne; and then proceeded via *wudwyrðe* and *mapuldorgeat* to the *east heale*. The first of these means 'the wooded enclosure' or, more probably, 'the enclosure in the wood'; the second means something like 'the deer gate made of maple wood', suggesting perhaps some feature like a deer leap (the word *geat* often means something like 'gap in a fence or bank through which only particular animals could pass'); the third the 'east nook'. The perambulation then continued to the 'three boundaries', the cross, the 'slender oak', the old thorn, the hollow and the birch-wood (*beorc leah*), before running 'from the wood on to Cuthhelm's tree, from the tree to the stile. From the stile to the spring of Read's people, from the spring to the island in the River Colne.' Once again we get an impression of a divided and exploited landscape, with enclosures, gates, defined areas of woodland and stiles: some of the features were apparently for the management of deer. The very fact that individual trees could be singled out as markers suggests, once again, that the area was not covered in impenetrable forest.

Not only were the clay-covered uplands of the south and west of the county thus carefully divided and quite intensively exploited: by late Saxon times settlements were probably more widely established here than historians often assume, or than Domesday seems to imply. Indeed, the commissioners were not interested in settlements *per se*, but only in units of tenure (estates or manors) and units of taxation and administration (vills). There is little doubt that settlements were much more numerous than vills, and that many of the latter contained several of the former. On the Chiltern dipslope it is clear that huge vills like Hemel Hempstead did not simply consist of the individual settlements which today bear their names. Many of the neighbouring villages, which only appear in documents much later in the Middle Ages, also existed (if only as farms or small hamlets) at the time of the Survey but are passed over in silence. Thus Flaunden and Bovingdon were, until the nineteenth century, part of the large parish of Hemel Hempstead, and were clearly subsumed by Domesday within this manor and vill. We first hear of them in the thirteenth century, but their names are of typical Old English form and strongly suggest a pre-Conquest origin. Indeed, Bovingdon's dependence upon Hemel Hempstead probably explains its name. The place lies in a shallow dry valley in the uplands to the west of the Gade valley, and the editors of the EPNS volume for Hertfordshire expressed some reservations about whether its name was indeed derived from the Old English *bufan dune*, 'above the down' (Gover *et al.* 1938, 29). But such a derivation *does* make sense when the place is viewed from the direction of Hemel Hempstead, for Bovingdon lies high above the steep slopes of the valleys of Gade and Bulbourne in which the former place lies. Nearby Sarratt was almost certainly in existence by the time of Domesday: its name is of obscure Old English form (it probably means 'the dry place') and, if we can trust the account in the thirteenth-century *Gesta Abbatum*, it was alienated from the monastery for a short period during the abbacy of Paul of Caen (1077–93) (Riley 1867, 63).

While Sarratt and Flaunden are located beside and within the valley of the Chess, Bovingdon occupies a position out on the dry interfluves between the Chess and the Gade, and it is probable that there were other late and perhaps middle Saxon settlements on the 'uplands', in some cases only seasonally occupied, for the management of grazing and the exploitation of woodland. Unfortunately, place-names are of limited assistance here. There are a large number of farms and hamlets away from the main valleys which bear what appear to be pre-Conquest names, but in most cases these are of topographic form – that is, they refer to features of the landscape – and the settlements in question may have developed after the Conquest, and merely borrowed some pre-existing name for the immediate locality. On the Chiltern Dipslope places like Pepsall End in Flamstead, Widmore in Great Gaddesden, and Hudnall and Ringshall in Little Gaddesden may thus all have originated as names for areas, rather than places. On the London Clay, similarly, the fact that Letchmore Heath (the *lache mere*, or 'muddy pool') in Aldenham or Pursley Farm ('The clearing with the bitterns') in the far south of Shenley parish (Gover *et al.* 1938, 61, 68) have Old English names does not mean that the settlements established beside the pool, or in the clearing, had the same kind of antiquity. But we should not be over-cautious. Some places with Old English 'habitative' names occur in remote upland locations and are referred to in pre-Conquest documents. Westwick in St Michael's, the 'west farm', does not appear in Domesday but is mentioned in the will of Æthelgifu of *c*.980 and in a charter of 996 (Crick 2007, nos 7 and 9). Further north, on the far side of the Ver valley, is Childwick, *Childewicam*, the 'dairy farm of the young monks' (Gover *et al.* 1938, 92). This, again, is

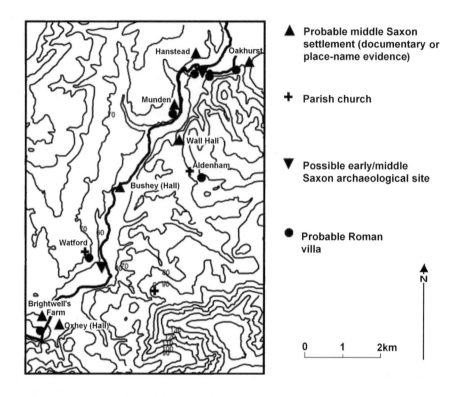

Figure 39. Probable middle Saxon settlements and Roman 'villa' sites in the Colne valley.

absent from Domesday but the place was, according to the *Gesta Abbatum*, in existence by the late eleventh century (Riley 1867, 56). We should also note that a number of isolated upland settlements appear to be mentioned in the boundary clauses of local charters: the obscurely named 'mercing dwellings' in the clause for Gaddesden, for example; the *heale wic*, 'corner farm' in that for Cashio; or *Boiwic* in Aldenham (Crick 2007, nos 1b and 7). It is noteworthy, and probably significant, that many of these places have names incorporating the element 'wic', generally used for an outlying grazing farm. The most striking case is the obscure hamlet of Cockernhoe, on the eastern edge of the Chiltern plateau in the parish of Offley, and now on the outskirts of Luton. This is first mentioned in a document of 1221, but a single chance reference shows that it had then been in existence for more than 200 years, for Æthelgifu's will of *c.*980 ordered that, after her death, a slave called 'Wulfstan of Cockernhoe' was to be freed (Crick 2007, no. 7).

If some middle and later Saxon settlements existed on the uplands, we should not be surprised to find them in greater numbers in the principal river valleys of the south and west. In that of the Colne, for example, in the area near Watford, probable examples are particularly closely clustered. The name of Brightwells Farm (TQ100946) – 'the bright spring' – strongly suggests an early origin (Gover *et al.* 1938, 104). It stands on the north bank of the Colne, opposite Oxhey Hall (TQ103944) (Figure 39). Oxhey does not appear in Domesday but, as already noted, is named in a charter of 1007 (Crick 2007, no. 12). Moving upstream some three kilometres we reach Bushey Hall (TQ122979), the probable original focus of Bushey parish and the location of the main settlement in the vill at the time of Domesday. A little further on, this time on the north side of the river, we come to Munden or Meriden House (TL136003). Again, there is no mention of this place in Domesday, but its name ('at the pleasant valley') suggests an early origin, and the *Gesta Abbatum* certainly indicates that it was in existence by the early twelfth century (Riley 1867, 64). Opposite, on the south bank of the river, stands Wall Hall (TQ137995). First mentioned as *Walenhale* in 1218, its name probably means 'the secluded place of the serfs, or Britons', suggesting a settlement of some considerable antiquity (Gover *et al.* 1938, 99) (Figure 39). Another 1.5 kilometres upstream and we reach Hanstead House (TL143017), on the north side of the river, presumably the focus for the estate of that name, which was one of the first estates granted to St Albans Abbey; and somewhere near here, on the south side of the Colne, was the lost *Acersce*, 'the stubble land by the oak trees', a place first mentioned in the will of Æthelgifu of *c.*980, but not again until the mid thirteenth century (Gover *et al.* 1938, 68). In other words, on this stretch of the river settlements with pre-Conquest origins were spaced at intervals of around two kilometres along each bank, often ranged in pairs, facing each other across the river. Indeed, in the area around St Albans and Hatfield such sites were not restricted to the immediate vicinity of the Ver and Colne, but were scattered more widely across the lighter soils of the gravels and brickearths in the Vale of St Albans: places like Burston, presumably the centre of the estate granted to St Albans in 996, or the lost Faunton, which the community received in the 1040s but which was already in existence by 996 (Crick 2007, nos 9 and 14). Of particular interest in this context are a number of isolated farms in the area of St Albans, Welwyn and Hatfield with names bearing the suffix 'hyde'. Examples include Nast Hyde, Sleapshyde, Roehyde, Hatfield Hyde, Cromer Hyde and

Handside: others, now lost, are referred to in medieval documents. By late Saxon times 'hide' was a term for a unit of taxation; in earlier times it also meant the land held by one peasant family, an area of around 120 acres, and it may well be used in this latter sense here. It has been suggested that these holdings are to be associated with the twelfth-century policy of Ely and St Albans Abbeys of granting out large assarts of 120 acres or more in order to clear formerly forested land. Many subsequently became sub-manors (Munby 1977, 111). But their archaic names may hint at an earlier origin: not only the use of the element 'hide', but also their prefixes, which generally incorporate some Old English topographic terms rather than a personal name. Sleapshyde is the hide at the *slæp*, the watery or slippery place; Cromer Hyde is the hide at the crow's pool; Roehyde is the hide at the clearing (Gover *et al.* 1938, 95). An early origin for these settlements may be indicated by the fact that some played a prominent role in medieval local government. Typically, in 1487 the court rolls for Welwyn record 'John Archer and William Couper are chosen and sworn as constables for Lodeewikhide. Thomas Colyn and William Hilton for Bokenwickhide' (Munby 1977, 111). These places may in fact represent settlements originally held by individuals dwelling on the outlying *warland* of estates based in the Vale of St Albans, men who in other areas of the county would have been categorised as sokemen by Domesday, but who have here – due to the continuing integrity of the abbeys' estates, and the extent of their control over the local inhabitants – been subsumed within the main body of tenant cultivators.

A similar scatter of middle and late Saxon sites probably existed along the other main river valleys in the south and west of the county, the Gade and the lower Lea, although they have left fewer obvious traces in the names attached to existing farms and hamlets. Such places may have become fixed at these points (to judge from evidence elsewhere in England) in the seventh or eighth centuries. Before this, in the early Saxon period, settlements may have drifted around the landscape to some extent, moving every generation or so (Hamerow 1991). One probable example of such a transient, short-lived settlement (although the dating remains debated) was excavated in the valley of the Gade to the north of Watford, in the grounds of The Grove, in 2000. It comprised twelve buildings (some with the characteristic sunken floors of early Saxon domestic buildings) lying within, and orientated the same way as, the earlier Iron Age field system (HER 11495: Le Quesne *et al.* 2001). This said, it is noteworthy how many small valley settlements with 'early' place-names have known Romano-British sites in close proximity (below, p. 181). Settlements may have drifted, but only within a limited area.

Landscape and settlement: the north and east

Although the west of the county was far from being an impenetrable wilderness in middle and late Saxon times, there is no doubt that eastern Hertfordshire was much less densely wooded and more densely settled. Over much of the Boulder Clay Plateau, as already noted, Domesday gives the impression of woodland as a carefully managed resource rather than an abundance. Indeed, it occasionally implies management by coppicing – this, presumably, is the meaning of the phrase 'wood for fences' or its variants used at places such as Hormead and Offley. In addition, certain references suggest that woods were already discrete entities, as they are in the modern landscape, rather than forming extensive blocks. One entry for Munden, for example, mentions woodland for 150 swine and 'another woodland where 200 swine might be fed'.

Large numbers of settlements seem to have existed on the clay plateau by later Saxon times, even in places far from the better soils of the principal valleys. Our knowledge of their existence is often dependent on chance references in, and chance survival of, pre-Conquest charters. Roe Green and Roe Wood in Sandon, on the high watershed between the Cat Ditch, the Beane and the Rib, are first referred to by name in 1222, but a settlement must have existed somewhere in this remote place by 940, when King Æthelstan granted the monastery of St Paul's ten *mansas 'ad Sandon cum Rode'* (Birch 1885, 451; Gelling 1979, 83). Domesday records several very small vills in this region, places clearly no larger than hamlets, located in the higher reaches of minor tributaries of the main rivers. These are often represented today by some minor settlement which appears no different to an adjacent one bearing a respectable Old English name. It is tempting to believe that while the one is mentioned by Domesday because it was a distinct tenurial entity, the other was not because it still formed part of some larger estate. If we take, for example, the tract of country between the Rivers Beane and Rib, we can see from the location of Domesday vills such as Wakeley and Berkesdon that settlement had already spread right to the upper reaches of minor tributaries of the two rivers. Along the south-facing slopes of the valley of the Dane End Tributary, to take one example, settlements of certain or probable pre-Conquest origins are spaced at intervals of a

Figure 40. Settlements in the Dane End Tributary, north-east Hertfordshire. The relatively light clay soils in this dissected landscape ensured that by middle and late Saxon times the area was densely set-tled, as indicated by the number of places with Old English names. In the foreground, left, Little Munden church; beyond, in the middle distance, the hamlet of Haultwick (the 'old dairy farm'); and beyond this, Libury Hall (an estate called *Suterehela* in Domesday book). In the distance, on the valley floor, is Herringworth (*Hæringa worþ*) (the 'enclosure of Hæra's people'); and in the far distance, Great Munden (mentioned in the will of Æthelgifu of c.980) (by courtesy of English Heritage).

kilometre or less (Figure 40): Great Munden (mentioned in the will of Æthelgifu of *c*.980); Herringworth (*Hæringa worþ*) (the 'enclosure of Hæra's people); Libury (*Suterehela* in Domesday book); Haultwick (the 'old dairy farm'); and Little Munden (a separate estate in Domesday). Such a density of settlement should not surprise us, given what has already been said about the population of this region by the time of Domesday.

Even in the more wooded, less fertile soils of the Stevenage–Welwyn Clays, a number of places which never became more than hamlets are listed as vills in Domesday – places like *Leglega*, probably Ley Green, in King's Walden, where three sokemen and four bordars kept one and a half ploughs. Many other places of similar size and status, often assumed to be of post-Conquest origin, probably existed by late Saxon times, although they do not appear in any source before the mid thirteenth century (Cockernhoe, discussed above (p. 176), could just as easily have been mentioned here, lying as it does on the junction of the Chilterns proper and the Stevenage–Welwyn Clays).

To demonstrate that Hertfordshire was peppered with farms and hamlets by late Saxon times – to show, that is, that settlements were more numerous than Domesday appears to suggest – is one thing. To trace the origins of such places is quite another. All the documentary references discussed above date from the later tenth and eleventh centuries. This does not mean that the places in question were first established around this time: merely that we have no earlier sources which could demonstrate their existence. Nevertheless, it seems probable that Saxon farms and hamlets in the 'core' areas of settlement – vale, scarp and valley – were of greater antiquity than those in the more remote parts of the interfluves. Indeed, there are hints that some of the former may have developed from Romano-British settlements – not necessary on the same site, but moving short distances over the centuries. In the Colne valley, for example, the proximity of probable Saxon settlements to major Roman sites is suggestive: Brightwells Farm, Munden, Hanstead and possibly *Acersce* all lie within 200 metres of probable villas (Figure 39).

Settlements on the clay interfluves probably developed later, perhaps from seasonally occupied outstations established for the management of woodland, grazing and pannage. These became permanent as, with the growth of population, more intensive management of these resources became necessary; and later still they developed into farms and hamlets cultivating their own arable land. This development had, by the time of Domesday, advanced further in the north and east of the county than in the

Figure 41. Early co-axial field patterns and watershed tracks on the Chiltern dipslope (source: selected boundaries from first edition 6-inch Ordnance Survey maps of the 1880s and 90s).

south and west. It is possible that this late Saxon shift towards arable cultivation explains the frequency in Hertfordshire of the minor place-name Aldwick and its variants – 'the old dairy farm' (Gover *et al.* 1938, 260), presumably in the sense of 'former dairy farm'. Not surprisingly, this is more common in the north-east of the county than in the south-west: the EPNS lists five examples to the south and west of the River Lea, but fourteen to the north and east (Gover *et al.* 1938).

Ancient landscapes

Although the population of the Hertfordshire area probably fell significantly in the immediate post-Roman period, with much land passing out of cultivation, the lighter land at least evidently continued to be occupied and cultivated: and this in turn raises the possibility that some parts of the basic pattern of roads and field boundaries in the county, rather than dating from the medieval period, could have originated in prehistoric or Roman times. In this context attention should be drawn to a distinctive type of landscape found over large areas of Hertfordshire, consisting of bundles of long, roughly parallel but slightly sinuous axes which run for many kilometres in one direction. Fewer boundaries run for any distance at right angles to this dominant 'grain', so that the field pattern resembles, in plan, slightly wavy brickwork (Williamson 2008). Even on the modern Ordnance Survey maps, in spite of modern hedge removal and urban or suburban sprawl, these 'co-axial' landscapes, to use the jargon of archaeologists, are still striking. Most are found in the centre, south and west of the county: on the Southern Uplands, on the Stevenage–Welwyn Clays and on the Chiltern Dipslope. Here they are invariably orientated at right angles to major rivers, their long axes running up the sides of the valley slopes and far out onto the interfluves (Figure 41). Such landscapes are largely absent from the more fertile soils and more dissected topography found in the north and east of the county. Early maps and surveys, especially from the Chilterns, suggest that some of their constituent fields have always been enclosed and farmed in severalty; others, however, seem to have originated through the early piecemeal enclosure of the open fields which were, in medieval times, a prominent feature of the lighter soils throughout the county.

Similar co-axial landscapes have been noted elsewhere in England, notably in East Anglia and Essex, and here it has been suggested that they represent the much-altered remnants of planned field systems of prehistoric or early Roman date. In part this is because they look remarkably like a type of prehistoric field system surviving in the form of earthworks or tumbled walls in some areas of chalk downland or upland moor, or which have been revealed by excavation or aerial photography: most notably the so-called 'reaves', the remains of which can still be traced over extensive tracts of

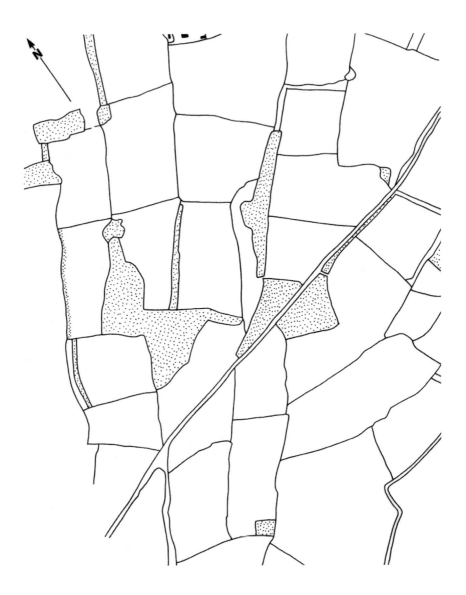

Figure 42. Possible remains of an early co-axial field pattern crossed by a Roman road south-west of Watton. Detail from the Watton tithe award map of 1840.

Dartmoor (Fleming 1978; 1983; 1984; 1988). In part, however, a prehistoric date has been suggested because some of these landscapes appear to pre-date Roman military roads, which cross them at an oblique angle (Rodwell 1978; Drury and Rodwell 1980; Williamson 1987; 1998).

In Hertfordshire, similarly, landscapes of this type have sometimes been explained, tentatively, as remnants of planned prehistoric or Roman field systems. In the area around Arkley, in the far south of the county, this interpretation was reached because of an apparent similarity to prehistoric field systems (Hunn 2004, 115–18), while in the Aldenham area it was simply due to the rectilinear, regular nature of the boundary pattern (Brown 1992). It is not possible to date many Hertfordshire examples on the basis of their relationship with Roman roads, for in the areas in which most examples occur these mainly follow the low ground of the principal river valleys, and thus intersect with the lower parts of the 'systems' more or less at right angles. In the area around Radlett, however, where Watling Street leaves the lower ground of the Ver and Colne valleys and climbs up onto the clay uplands it seems to run hard against the 'grain' of the principal roads and boundaries. More striking is the situation to the south-west of Watton, where the earliest available map (the tithe award of 1839) seems to show the Roman road from Verulamium to Braughing cutting obliquely through a landscape of this type (HALS DSA/112/2 (4/260) (Figure 42). As we shall see, some elements of these landscapes have also been dated to the prehistoric period by archaeological excavation. Nevertheless, there is little doubt that in Hertfordshire, as elsewhere in England, these 'relict field systems' probably have complex origins. Rather than dating from a single 'period', they are the result of many centuries of development, and their distinctive form is largely a consequence of the natural topography.

As noted, the principal axes of such 'systems' invariably run at right angles to major river valleys; and many are formed by roads and tracks, rather than by boundaries *per se*. Thus on the Chiltern Dipslope prominent examples, like that to the west of Great Gaddesden, or those around King's Langley, are all orientated at right angles to the River Gade (Figure 41); while on the Southern Uplands the striking pattern in the Broxbourne–Wormley area lies at right angles to the River Lea, and the extensive landscape in the area of Shenley, Ridge, North Mimms and Aldenham bears a similar relation to the River Colne. Both this chapter, and the last, have emphasised repeatedly the contrast between the 'core' areas of early territories and estates, lying within the major valleys, and the outlying areas of woodland and pasture, on the higher ground and heavier soils. On the Southern Uplands, on the Stevenage–Welwyn Clays and in parts of the Chilterns particularly extensive tracts of woodland and pasture seem to have

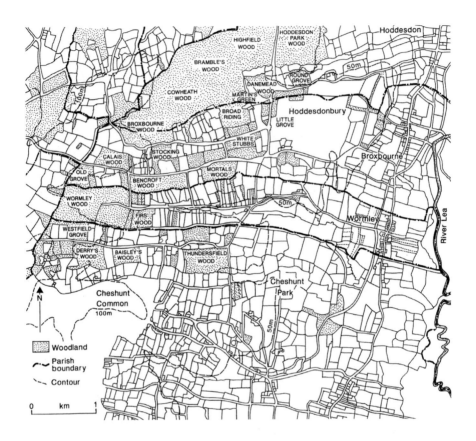

Figure 43. An early co-axial landscape in the Broxbourne–Wormley area of south-east Hertfordshire.

existed in Anglo-Saxon times, exploited by communities living around (or beyond) their margins. Co-axial landscapes are mainly found in these same areas, and they appear to have developed as a consequence of the enduring contrast between 'river and wold'.

The striking arrangement of fields and roads in the area around Wormley and Broxbourne in the south-east of the county is particularly interesting in this respect (Bryant *et al.* 2005) (Figures 43 and 44: the former shows the earliest known boundaries recorded on the available maps for the area).[4]

---

4. Figure 43 is based on the following maps. Hertfordshire Record Office: tithe award maps for Wormley (HALS DSA 4 120/2) and Broxbourne (HALS DSA 4 25/2); survey of Hoddesdon 1792 (HALS B1444), Wormley 1755 (HALS D/Ewb P1), Broxbourne e.19th century (HALS 71013), Broxbourne 1829 (HALS 71014). Hatfield House archives, 1692 estates of the Earl of Salisbury (CP 354); estates of Robert Cecil 1600–01 (CP 349).

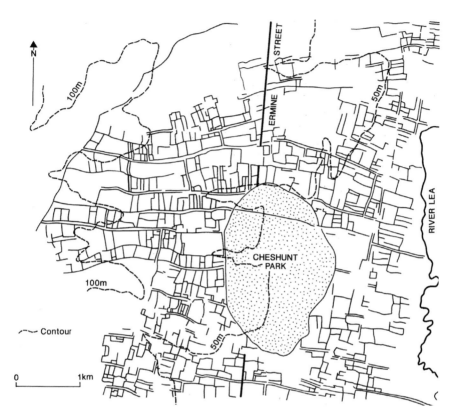

Figure 44. An early co-axial landscape in the Broxbourne–Wormley area: the pattern enhanced through the selective removal of landscape features.

While partly defined by field boundaries and roads, some of the main elements of the 'system' comprise earthworks surrounding, and subdividing, ancient hornbeam woods (Figure 45). The areas thus enclosed are much larger than the hedged fields outside them, suggesting that originally the landscape consisted of a network of tracks and rather large enclosures suitable for grazing and the management of woodland, which were only later broken up into smaller fields (Bryant *et al.* 2005, 14). It is, unfortunately, hard to establish the date of the earliest elements in this landscape. The relationship of the pattern with Ermine Street is typically unclear. The road follows the side of the Lea valley and thus runs more or less at right angles to the network of co-axial lanes and boundaries, and much of the field pattern where the two would have intersected has been disrupted by the creation of Cheshunt Park, probably established in the thirteenth century (Rowe 2009, 78) (Figures 43 and 44). However, an excavation carried out in the centre of this area revealed lost field ditches which shared the orientation to the surrounding landscape. These contained first- and second-century AD pottery in their basal infill, and had apparently been filled in during the construction or expansion of a small Roman settlement (Ely and Edwards 2003, 15; Bryant *et al.* 2005, 12–14). The prevailing orientation of boundaries in the area had thus been established by the start of the Roman period.

On the other side of the county, just to the north of Watford, similar evidence was recovered during the excavations carried out at The Grove in 2000. The site – over four hectares of which was systematically stripped prior to the construction of a golf course – lies within an eighteenth-century landscape park in the valley of the Gade. The landscape in the immediate area is dominated by an extensive co-axial field pattern, but all field boundaries had been erased within the excavated area by the creation, in the 1760s, of the park. The excavation, however, revealed (along with a wide range of other features) a number of ditches which were clearly part of this surrounding pattern. Several contained, in their basal fills, sherds of unabraded Iron Age pottery (Le Quesne *et al.* 2001), while the line of one is directly continued, beyond the boundary of the park, as an upstanding boundary, the northern edge of Whippendell Wood. Again, some of the elements in a co-axial landscape seem to have come into existence by late prehistoric times.

One noticeable feature of Hertfordshire's co-axial landscapes is that they often have a hard 'edge' formed by some continuous linear feature – usually a road or track – which runs at right angles to their general 'grain'. On the far side of this we find either field patterns arranged on more irregular lines or another co-axial landscape running up out of the next valley. The western edge of the Broxbourne–Wormley 'system' is thus formed by a long boundary line which formed the division between the Dioceses of London and Lincoln; the probable frontier, therefore, between the East Saxons and Mercians, and which perhaps originated as the edge of an ancient territory centred on Cheshunt (above, p. 100). On the Chiltern Dipslope these terminal lines are particularly noticeable, generally taking the form of long, gently sinuous tracks which not only run continuously for many miles, but which seem to follow, uncannily, the line of the watershed between two drainage systems. One example thus follows closely the watershed between the Gade and the Chess. It begins as a minor road near the county boundary

Figure 45. Details of the co-axial landscape in the Broxbourne–Wormley area: note how the earthworks within and around the blocks of ancient woodland generally define areas larger than the surrounding fields.

with Buckinghamshire at Bovingdon (TL012040). Running through the village (close to the parish church) it continues through the hamlet of Bulstrode and then forms the north-eastern edge of Chipperfield Common (passing, significantly, close to the two Bronze Age round barrows discussed in Chapter 2 (p. 29)). Continuing through Bucks Hill and Bucks Hill Bottom, it finally reaches Chandlers Cross (Figure 41). Beyond this point its course is not apparent, for the watershed itself peters out as it approaches lower ground and the confluence of the Gade and the Chess. Another example marks the watershed between the Gade and the Ver. This runs from the southern end of Abbot's Langley, at Leavesden Green, northwards through Abbot's Langley village and on through Bedmond, Pimlico, Leverstock Green and Adeyfield to Cupid Green. Here it ends, but it is possible that it originally linked up with the long straight section of road along which the hamlet of Gaddesden Row is strung. Co-axial patterns exhibiting varying degrees of regularity butt up against it from both east and west (Figure 41).

These watershed lines may represent ancient divisions of the upland woods and grazing grounds between groups living in the principal valleys: divisions fixed, in some cases, close to the line of the watershed. The co-axial lines running up to them presumably emerged gradually, partly as access tracks to the woods, and partly as further subdivisions of the uplands among those living *within* each valley, created as population rose and a closer definition of rights became essential (Williamson 2008). As further subdivisions were made over the centuries the 'bones' of the distinctive co-axial patterns emerged. But there are signs that, while the overall 'systems' thus developed gradually and organically, some areas within them may have been laid out with care, to some predetermined scheme. These landscapes, that is, may contain some planned sections. Notable examples include the highly regular field pattern to the south-west of Gaddesden Row and parts of the Broxbourne–Wormley landscape, especially the area between Beaumont Manor and Westfield Grove, where two principal axes maintain an almost precise separation of 275 metres for nearly two kilometres (Figure 45).

Hertfordshire's co-axial landscapes are thus not simply the much-altered remains of vast planned field systems of prehistoric date. They developed organically and represent the end result of many centuries of expansion and abandonment, replanning and remodelling, infilling and alteration. Nevertheless, there are good grounds for believing that some of their principal elements originated in the late prehistoric period. Some of Hertfordshire's hedges and lanes, in other words, are prehistoric monuments, as old and, in their way, as impressive as any hillfort, barrow or linear earthwork.

Chapter 6
Manor, Vill and Parish

Manor and vill

At the time of Domesday some large unitary estates still existed in Hertfordshire, especially in the west of the county, but the majority of manors were small or medium-sized units, extending over ten square kilometres or less. Precisely when the process of estate fission occurred remains uncertain, but Æthelgifu's will of *c*.980 (Crick 2007, no. 7) suggests that a century before Domesday great landowners already possessed widely scattered, rather than compact, properties. Precisely *how* the great estates disintegrated also remains unclear. In general terms, this process was associated with the transition from the redistributive, 'chiefdom' forms of social organisation characteristic of middle Saxon times to more sophisticated, state-based systems. It was closely connected with demographic growth, with the development of market exchange (which allowed elites to purchase particular commodities rather than produce them themselves), and with changes in the nature of political power and concepts of land ownership.

Over time, many large estates became alienated from the royal patrimony. Those that passed into lay hands were subject to the divisive effects of partial sale and divided inheritance. At the same time, smaller estates were increasingly carved out of ancient territories to provide endowments for minor warriors, and in particular for individuals involved in the administration of large estates. Outlying *warland* was converted into such properties by royal grant, usually accompanied by a charter, or 'book', to use the Old English term: Buckland in north Hertfordshire presumably represents an outlying portion of the Braughing estate, 'booked' to some local landowner at some unknown point in the later Saxon period (Gover *et al.* 1938, 175). Lastly, new estates could be created by usurpation, as – with the growth of population, and the expansion of farmland – some of the dependent tenants of the outlying *warland* prospered, attracting dependent cultivators to their holdings and carving out what became, by default, small manors (Maitland 1897, 325–6). Whatever the precise way in which estate fission occurred, it had important social consequences. According to most historians the obligations of the mass of the rural population – the dues owed by those dwelling on the outlying *warland* to the estate owners – increased, and their degree of personal freedom declined (Faith 1997; Sawyer 1979). A local lord was a more insistent and demanding presence than a distant one.

The process of estate fission was highly complex, the resultant pattern of smaller estates regionally varied. Such diversity was the result of the interaction of two factors. The first was the nature of the local environment, and especially the extent to which this allowed the extension of cultivation and thus the creation (by default or otherwise) of new, small estates within old, larger ones. In areas of poor soil it was less easy to hive off portions as self-sufficient economic units: in general, fertile soils encouraged and poor soils discouraged the fission of estates. The second was the character of estates *before* their disintegration. Those ancient territories which had, in middle Saxon times, always been retained for the use of the king, and not regularly granted out as an endowment for a warrior or administrator, had usually functioned primarily as places where food-rents, *feorm*, could be collected, in order to feed the itinerant royal entourage. In Faith's words, 'many royal vills remained collecting centres rather than agrarian enterprises' (Faith 1997, 42). Hitchin, with its central but comparatively small agricultural 'core' and its great penumbra of outlying sokes, was perhaps an estate like this. Where such territories remained in the hands of the Crown, the wealth and independence of the outlying sokemen doubtless increased as population rose and as the frontiers of cultivation expanded. Distant farms in woodland and pasture developed into arable villages and sokemen came to have their own under-tenants. They often became, in effect, local lords, although they continued, as we have seen, to owe some residual dues and obligations to the old *caput*.

Where estates had normally been granted out to resident noble families, in contrast, the size of the central agricultural enterprise had generally been larger, and so too the obligations demanded of the outlying dependencies. Such burdens will have increased further as these estates passed permanently into lay hands and began to divide – as they generally did – into smaller units, so that more and more of the peasant population were subjected to the demands of a local lord. Where large estates had passed into ecclesiastical hands, however, not only were particularly strenuous attempts made to maximise production, and thus to increase the demands placed on those dwelling on the peripheral *warland*, but the estates themselves were much more likely to survive as large units. The holdings of permanent institutions could not be divided by inheritance, although portions might become detached by usurpation – as, in particular, when leases (common by late Saxon times) were falsely claimed as sales.

The end result of these various and complex processes was the bewildering variety of landholding patterns which we discover in the pages of Domesday Book. This was compiled in 1086, when the new regime was firmly in place, but it was largely organised within the administrative frameworks of late Saxon England. Thus, in particular, the manors of the main tenants-in-chief of the Crown are arranged in the order of the hundreds in which they are located, and described in terms of the vills in which they lie. Vills, as we have seen, were units of administration and taxation, rather than of ownership: many bear the names of, and in time developed into, ecclesiastical and civil parishes. Their origins are obscure and debated – they were probably long-established by the time of the Conquest, and, like the hundreds (and shires) into which they were grouped, they were presumably defined by late Saxon administrators as part of the process by which the burdens demanded by the emerging state, including responsibility for the maintenance of defences and public works, were increasingly tied to specific areas of land, measured in the fiscal units called *hides* (Faith 1997, 58–85). Again like hundreds, the configuration of vills was determined in part by earlier structures of territorial organisation; and it is clear that when the framework of vills was first imposed upon the countryside large estates had fragmented to varying extents, so that in some places extensive territories under the control of single institutions or individuals still existed, while in others much smaller properties predominated. Some vills were thus formed out of single properties, others through the grouping together of several. These properties, large or small, might themselves subsequently become subdivided through sale or inheritance. Given all this, it is hardly surprising that by 1066 the relationship between the two entities – the manor as a unit of property, the vill as a unit of administration and taxation – varied considerably from place to place. In some parts of Hertfordshire there were very large vills, embracing thirty square kilometres or more; in others, there were vills little larger than small hamlets. Some vills contained a single estate or manor; others contained two, three, four or more.

The complex history of estate fission, coupled no doubt with a range of economic and environmental factors, ensured that the composition of the rural population also varied considerably from place to place. Domesday divides the bulk of the county's population into five main classes. *Villeins* were substantial peasant cultivators, normally with holdings of thirty acres or more; *bordars* and *cottars* (the difference between the two groups is unclear) held smaller farms, and many probably also worked as craftsmen or artisans. Slaves were unfree landless farmworkers. Sokemen, as already intimated, were a small group of men with a privileged position in rural society, survivors of the more independent and prosperous peasantry dwelling on the outlying *warland* in a former age. In Domesday they are often listed as the holders of minor estates, sometimes as joint holders. Not all of these groups were present on every estate, or in every vill. In some places villeins formed a prominent element of the population; elsewhere they were absent. Sokemen were recorded in some districts, but not in others. In some places bordars were numerous, in others they were not.

Patterns of tenurial and social organisation thus varied greatly from place to place: but it is possible to see some structure and patterning in Domesday's record. Beneath the superficial chaos, Hertfordshire's vills can in fact be divided into a number of distinct categories on the basis of their size, their tenurial composition (whether they comprised one manor or several) and the character of their constituent population (i.e. the relative proportions of villeins, bordars and the rest).

The first identifiable category comprises very large vills, assessed for taxation at ten hides or more, which had fairly simple tenurial structures. The majority (twenty-five, or over three-quarters) were unitary vills – that is, they contained only one manor or estate. The rest contained only two holdings, often of very unequal size – as, for example, in Cashio, where St Albans Abbey held nineteen hides and Geoffrey de Mandeville only one. Most of these estates possessed extensive tracts of woodland – of the thirty-three vills which fall into this category, twenty-three had woodland sufficient

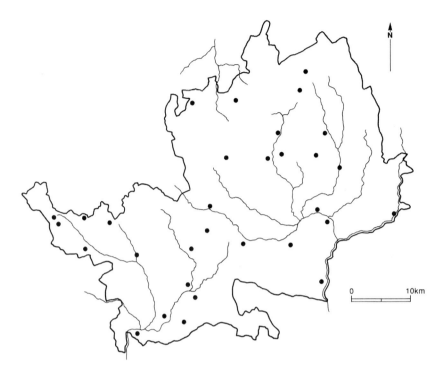

Figure 46. Domesday vills: 'category 1' vills.

for 300 swine or more. Their populations generally comprised a full complement of villeins, bordars and/or cottars and slaves. In just under half (sixteen) Domesday records priests, and all except two (6 per cent) developed into medieval parishes. Sokemen, however, were not common in vills of this type, being listed in only ten (30 per cent) in 1066. They generally held fairly substantial sub-tenancies, in some cases amounting to a hide or more, but in only one place did they constitute more than a tenth of the recorded population. Vills of this kind were fairly evenly distributed across the county (Figure 46) but in the south and west they predominated, and other kinds of vill were few in number.

The second category comprises a group of forty medium-sized vills, assessed at between four and ten hides, each containing a single manor or (more rarely: around a fifth of examples) two manors. A very high proportion of these places (85 per cent) became medieval parishes, although in only thirteen (33 per cent) were priests recorded. The majority had moderate amounts of woodland, sufficient for between 50 and 200 swine,

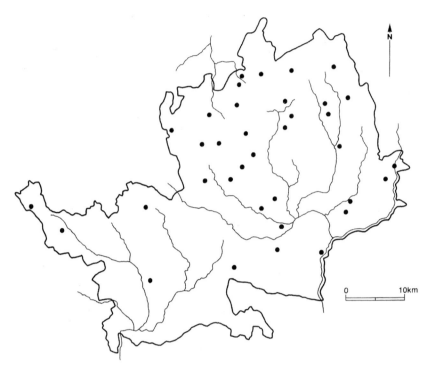

Figure 47. Domesday vills: 'category 2' vills.

although a significant proportion had negligible quantities or none at all (around a third had sufficient for only ten swine or fewer, or 'wood for fences' only). Most of the manors in vills of this type had a full complement of villeins, bordars/cottars and slaves; and just under a quarter of such vills contained estates held by a sokeman, or by a group of sokemen, at the time of the Conquest. Vills of this type were widely scattered across the county, but were a particular feature of the centre and north-east. Most were to be found in what appear to be favourable locations, in terms of soils and water supply: the bulk of their territory, that is, lay within the valley of a major river (vills such as Tewin, Hertingfordbury, Braughing and Widford); on the more dissected areas of the boulder clays of the north-east (Hunsdon, Cottered); or beside exposures of light soils on, or below, the Chiltern escarpment (Bygrave, Hitchin). Only a small proportion of such places were in more marginal, peripheral locations, usually on the clay-covered interfluves in the centre or north of the county (Langley, Rushden) (Figure 47).

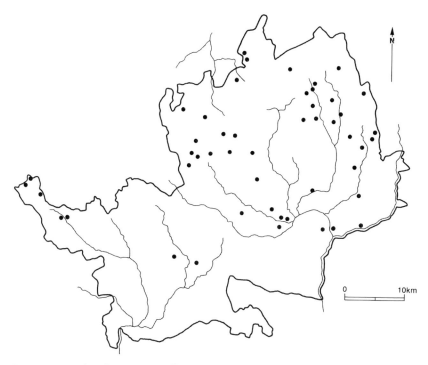

Figure 48. Domesday vills: 'category 3' vills.

The third category comprises a group of rather smaller vills, assessed at less than four hides, which again contained a single manor or (more rarely) two manors. These were the most numerous class of vill in late Saxon Hertfordshire, with a total of fifty-two examples recorded in Domesday. In contrast to those in the previous two categories, most seem to have been little more than hamlets, with just under half having total tenant populations of five or fewer. In nearly half of these places Domesday records only cottars, bordars or slaves, and in only five are priests mentioned. Indeed, only a small minority – nine out of fifty-two (17 per cent) – were destined to become medieval parishes, and most today survive as small hamlets or single farms, like Boarscroft, Gubblecot or Epcombs. Some, such as Berkesdon, disappeared altogether later in the Middle Ages: indeed, in some cases the precise location of vills in this category is doubtful (*Bricewold* in Hertford Hundred, *Lampeth* in Cashio). Although a fair number of these places have names with woodland associations, in only a handful were significant quantities of woodland recorded. In only nine (17 per cent) was there

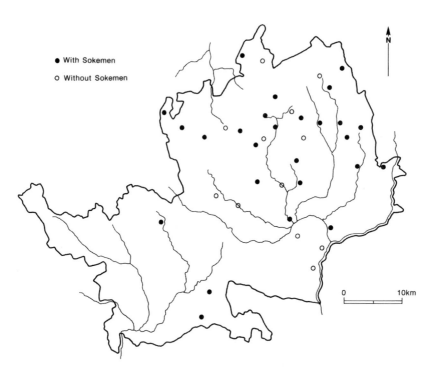

Figure 49. Domesday vills: 'category 4' vills.

woodland for more than fifty swine, and 40 per cent had no recorded woodland at all, or quantities sufficient 'for fences' only. A fairly high proportion of these places (around a fifth) had been held exclusively by sokemen before the Norman Conquest. The overwhelming majority of vills of this type were located in the north-east of the county, on the fertile boulder-clay soils, but generally in fairly peripheral locations away from the major valleys, either on the high interfluves or in the minor tributary valleys which run up into them (Figure 48).

The fourth category comprises what we might term *subdivided vills* – that is, places which contained three or more separate manors or estates at the time of the Conquest. In some cases, the degree of subdivision could be considerable: Bengeo, for example, appears under nine Domesday entries, Pelham under seven. Although there were some fairly small vills in this category – such as Throcking or Bozen, rated as low as three hides – these were for the most part moderately large territories, with nearly half having fiscal assessments comparable to those in the first category discussed, and with an average assessment of around nine hides. Perhaps the most distinctive feature of vills of this type was the prominence of sokemen. Three-quarters contained at least one estate which had sokemen holders, or sokemen as under-tenants, at the time of the Conquest. In some cases, such as Bozen or Wickham, all of the listed estates had been held by sokemen. More usually, there was at least one manorialised 'core', with the usual combination of villeins, bordars/cottars and slaves, alongside a number of smaller estates held by sokemen, which generally contained a dependent population consisting of bordars and/or cottars only. Most of the vills of the first type, containing only sokemen, and many of the second, lay in peripheral locations, and often bore woodland names – Barley, Box, Broadfield, Graveley, Offley, Shenley, Wakeley and Wormley. But some, including many of the largest and most subdivided examples, were in prime river-valley locations – Stanstead, Pelham, Hadham, Redbourn and Bengeo (Figure 49).

The quantities of woodland recorded in these 'subdivided vills' varied considerably, with sixteen having woodland for fewer than 50 swine, eleven for between 50 and 200, and ten with sufficient for more than 200. Domesday records priests in just over a third of the vills in this category. It is noteworthy that these were generally those in which no sokemen were listed, and where priests are recorded in vills which did contain sokemen they were normally found on one of the 'manorialised' holdings. Sokemen and priests were not entirely mutually exclusive, but the pattern is clear enough. Lastly, we should note that only nine of these places failed to achieve parochial status in the Middle Ages.

What are we to make of this fairly structured pattern of variation? A broad range of geographical, demographic and economic factors, as well as particular idiosyncrasies of historical development, have clearly contributed to its crystallisation, and it is evident that superficially similar vills sometimes had very different histories. Nevertheless, certain general observations can be made. Vills in the first category – extensive, and usually containing a single main manor – seem to fall into two main types. Some were simply sparsely settled, well-wooded tracts in the south and west of the county, on the Southern Uplands or the Chiltern Dipslope: places like Aldbury, Aldenham and Bushey. Others, both here and in the north and east of the county, seem to represent ancient estates which have simply undergone a limited degree of fission. A high proportion of the vills of this type (fourteen, or 42 per cent) had been held before the Conquest by major religious houses – St Albans, Ely, Westminster and the Canons of St Paul's in London. Many of the remainder formed the principal estate of some of the most important members of the late Saxon nobility in the county – men like Askell of Ware, Ælmer of Benington, Edmer Ator at Berkhamsted and Engilric at Tring.

Two factors thus seem to have encouraged the survival of these large territorial units. The first was the character of ownership. For reasons already outlined, properties owned by large religious houses were unlikely to experience the same forces of fission as lay estates. In addition, estates in the hands of the families of men like Ælmer of Benington were also more likely to remain intact because, in the event of a divided inheritance, sufficient property existed (in the form of lands often widely scattered across the country) to endow individual heirs without breaking up individual estates. But environmental factors were also clearly important. For the most part large estates remained dominant in areas with low population densities, in the south and west of the county: the low agricultural productivity of these areas was insufficient to maintain a plethora of local lords. Indeed, these two factors – the character of ownership and the agricultural potential of the areas concerned – were to some extent connected in late Saxon Hertfordshire, as elsewhere in England, for it was under-populated, sparsely settled districts which kings like Offa and Æthelred, and large late Saxon landowners, often used to endow monasteries. Their possessions in such districts were of less economic importance than those in more fertile areas, and could be granted away without greatly damaging the fortunes of owner and kin.

Vills in the second category – medium-sized vills again containing only one or, more rarely, two manors – were widely scattered across Hertfordshire in 1066 and clearly had a variety of origins. Some, like Braughing, represent the residual cores of old estates which had lost their outlying portions by the time the network of vills was created at some point in the later Saxon period. Others represent portions of such estates – usually located in prime river-valley areas – that had been alienated from the parent territory. Either way, such vills were strongly manorialised, approximating to the medieval 'norm' of unitary manor/vill. These places were overwhelmingly the property of lay landowners at the time of the Conquest.

The small vills in the third category – those with less than four hides, and again containing one or (more rarely) two manors – seem to represent the outlying sokelands of large estates, places which had begun life as distant grazing establishments but which had attained a measure of independence as the frontiers of cultivation expanded. Their origins are indicated by the frequency with which their names incorporate elements with woodland associations (*ley*, *hanger*, *wold*) or which mean something like 'small farm' or 'outlying ranch' (*-wic*, *-cot*). Some of these places were the outliers of the great royal manor of Hitchin, discussed in the previous chapter: here the residual obligations of their sokemen owners were still remembered at the time of Domesday, although many sokemen were now, in effect, lords of their own manors. In other cases the duties owed to distant estate centres had either lapsed or were not noted by Domesday. Indeed, many of the holders of these former sokelands were no longer classified as sokemen, but as thanes or free men. The majority of these vills were found on high, remote interfluves of the Boulder Clay Plateau in the north and east of the county, or on the Stevenage–Welwyn Clays. Many doubtless originated as outlying parts of the Braughing and Benington estates. Their populations had increased as arable expanded around them but they had seldom grown into large villages. Most remained as hamlets, and several had ceased to exist as separate vills by the later Middle Ages.

The last category of vill – those divided between several estates, some at least of which were usually held by sokemen at the time of the Conquest – are the most problematic, for they clearly originated in at least two different ways. Some probably represent the river-valley 'cores' of ancient territories, in which the manorialised centre had not yet come to absorb the outlying *warland*. This suggests that some at least may until relatively recently have been royal estates like Hitchin, with a small core and extensive sokelands, parts of which had been hived off to endow soldiers or administrators. At the same time, some of the dependent sokelands had been acquired by neighbouring landowners and attached to their estates. Ashwell, Bengeo, Buntingford, Hadham, Pelham, Redbourn, Stanstead and Welwyn may all have developed like this. At Bengeo, for example, at the time of the Conquest nine sokemen held three hides and two and a half virgates[5] paying customary dues to the king, in whose *soc* they lay. There were three substantial manorialised cores, one of five hides and one virgate held by Anand, a housecarle of King Edward; one of six hides held by Brand, another housecarle; and one of six and a half hides, held by Elaf, one of King

---

5. A virgate is a fourth part of a hide.

Edward's thanes. Anand could alienate his land, but it is possible that Brand and Elaf could not – proprietary rights, that is, remained in the hands of the king. In addition to these holdings, half a virgate was held by Ælmer of Benington, one virgate by Snerri, 'Edeva the Fair's man', and three hides and one virgate by one Thorkell, the 'man' of Asgar the Staller.

The majority of places in this fourth category, however, probably originated in a rather different way: as groups of outlying woodland and pastoral establishments (of the kind we have already encountered in the previous category) originally attached to a variety of different estates, which had been grouped into vills in a somewhat arbitrary fashion by administrators simply to make convenient units of taxation and local government. Ayot, Barkway, Barley, Box, Bozen, Brickendon, Broadfield, Chells, Clothall, Datchworth, Graveley, Hoddesdon, Hormead, Libury, Luffenhall, Offley, Reed, Sacombe, Shenley, Throcking, *Titeberst*, Wakeley, *Welie* and Wormley and all probably originated in this way. In several cases these farms were still attached to a neighbouring estate at the time of Domesday. A hide and a half of Chells thus 'lay in Welwyn'; one of the Clothall holdings 'lay in Weston' while another lay in Munden; while part of Libury was assessed in Watton and part was an outlier of Munden. Some of these connections were perhaps of comparatively recent date, some were probably more ancient. It is noteworthy that many of these vills, like those in the previous category, lay on the high watershed of the East Anglian heights, or in the district of the Stevenage–Welwyn Clays.

Variations in demographic growth and in the expansion of arable, together with differences in the character of ownership (especially between lay, ecclesiastical and royal estates), had by 1066 thus produced a bewildering variety of vills and manors. On closer inspection, however, broad patterns do emerge. In the south and west, in particular, many large estates, often conterminous with vills, could be found. Most were territories which had passed out of royal hands at an early date and which had remained largely intact as a result of a combination of factors – principally the character of ownership and the nature of the local environment. In the more fertile lands of the north and east, such estates were rarer. Most had probably fallen into lay hands and their core lands been divided at a relatively early date, leading to the existence of a number of medium-sized, separately named and highly manorialised vills. Hitchin, however, had remained in royal hands probably until the middle of the eleventh century and still displayed elements of its archaic structure, of estate core and outlying sokelands, when Domesday was compiled: and a number of other complex vills in the principal valleys of the north-east may have remained royal until a comparatively late date, and in 1066 were complex mosaics of sokelands and small manors. In upland, interfluve locations, especially in the north and east, places which had originated as isolated farmsteads, as distant sokelands in woodland and pasture, had often developed into hamlets or small villages. Their owners had prospered as cultivation expanded: some remained as sokemen, others were accounted thanes or freemen, their ancient obligations to distant estate centres perhaps forgotten or commuted. Some of these outlying places had been acquired by large landowners, like Ælmer of Benington, by the time of Domesday. Where arable expansion had been greatest, such units had often achieved sufficient size to be recognised as vills in their own right. Often, however, a number of neighbouring farms or hamlets had been grouped together by administrators to make a vill, its name usually derived from some topographic feature, often that of a local wood.

I should stress that this account of territorial development is, like the account of Saxon settlement presented in the previous chapter, only a *model* – an explanation which seems to fit many of the observed facts, and which is in accord with what is known about the development of late Saxon society from other, better-documented areas of England. Alternative interpretations are possible: but in the last analysis we shall probably never know for certain the processes which produced the rich and varied territorial kaleidoscope that was Domesday Hertfordshire.

Minster and parish

By the time that Domesday was compiled the fission of ecclesiastical territories – the break-up of minster *parochiae* and the development of local parishes – was far advanced, especially in the north and east of the county. We have no real idea how early this process began but the will of Æthelgifu, drawn up in the 980s, as well as containing bequests to the minsters at St Albans, Hitchin, Ashwell, Welwyn and Braughing, also includes bequests to individual priests (Crick 2007, no. 7). Æthelweard and Boga may have been household priests, but Edwin was 'to have the church for his lifetime on condition that he keep it in repair', clearly suggesting the existence of a church quite separate from and independent of the minsters. The fact that the two processes of fission – secular and ecclesiastical – occurred at roughly

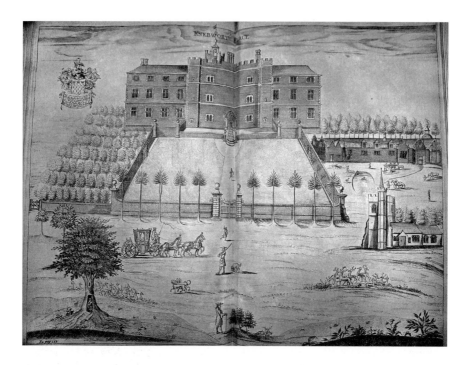

Figure 50. Drapentier's engraving of Knebworth Hall, c.1700, showing the close association of manor house and church so common in north and east Hertfordshire.

the same time, and at similar rates in the same areas, has meant that historians have sometimes assumed a direct causal link between them. In general this is probably true: as individuals acquired portions of estates they built churches on their property, both to serve the needs of their households and estate workers and also as a source of profit and status. Church-building was a sign of status – was, indeed, one of the necessary legal requirements for thegnly rank (Morris 1989, 253). Sometimes two local lords might work together to establish a church, but either way, because lay owners endowed the church with tithes from their tenants and glebe from their own estates, parish boundaries tend to follow the boundaries of pre-existing secular territories. The role of landowners – whether before or after the Norman Conquest – in church foundation is still very evident in the Hertfordshire landscape. Even today church and manor house often stand in close proximity, forming what some archaeologists call a 'hall–church complex', as at Barkway, Digswell, Hunsdon, Little Wymondley, Westmill and Widford (Figure 50). Elsewhere the hall has declined to the status of a farm, but still

Figure 51. Reed parish church contains a number of 'Anglo-Saxon' architectural features, such as this 'long and short' work in the angles of the nave, but, as in many such cases, architectural historians disagree over whether these pre- or post-date the Norman Conquest.

bears a name like Hall Farm (Graveley), Bury Farm (Wheathampstead), or Old Hall (Pirton). In a number of cases the presence of lordship is further emphasised by the existence of moats or castle earthworks in close proximity to the church, as at Benington, Pirton, Therfield and Great Wymondley.

But local parish churches did not always emerge in precisely this way, or for these reasons. When Æthelgyth and Oswulf entered the monastery of St Albans and granted the community their estate at Studham (just over the county boundary in Bedfordshire) some time between 1053 and 1066 they asked Abbot Leofstan to give them wood to build a church there, which might serve as a symbol of the abbey's ownership (Crick 2007, no. 17). St Albans itself erected churches on its land, creating parishes within what was effectively the minster territory of the abbey. The *Gesta Abbatum* records how Abbot Wulsin built the three churches of St Michael's, St Peter's and St Stephen's (each of which served what became separate parishes) in the mid tenth century (Riley 1867, 22; Niblett and Thompson 2005, 188–9). In reality, the churches were probably established early in the following century (Hunn 1994, 70), but the story shows how local churches could be erected within large estates as symbols and statements of ownership, or simply to meet the spiritual needs of an expanding population.

The rate at which local churches became established in the landscape is unclear. It is notoriously difficult to distinguish pre- from post-Conquest architectural details (English masons were not all killed off at the battle of Hastings) and the fragmentary remains at Little Munden, Reed and Westmill may be of post-Conquest date (Smith 1973, 17, 19, 34; Taylor and Taylor 1965, 509–10, 645–6) (Figure 51). Only a handful of the county's churches contain structural remains which are generally accepted as being of Anglo-Saxon date: those at Northchurch (Figure 33), Wheathampstead and Walkern, together with St Michael's and St Stephen's in St Albans (Smith 1973). In addition, a fragment of what appears to be late Saxon interlace sculpture has been found in the walls of the parish church at Braughing (HER 4332). The churches at St Albans have already been touched upon, while Braughing was a minster church, Northchurch and Wheathampstead were, as we have seen, probably minster churches, built at the centres of their respective estates, and Walkern may well have served as the minster for the large estate based on the neighbouring settlement of Benington.

In spite of this paucity of surviving pre-Conquest fabric there is no doubt that parish churches were already a fairly common feature of the landscape by the time of the Conquest (Weale 1987). The principal evidence for this is Domesday Book. Although it specifically mentions only four churches – the minster (*monasterium*) at Hitchin, the church at Welwyn and two in Hertford – their presence elsewhere can be inferred from references to priests. These are recorded in a total of fifty-one vills in the county, excluding places which now lie in Bedfordshire; and, in addition, a *clericus* is mentioned at Sacombe, bringing the total to fifty-two. Most of these individuals presumably served churches located in the vills where they are recorded, although there are grounds for believing that the priest at Epcombs served the church at Hertingfordbury, in which parish that hamlet now lies: there are no subsequent references to a church at Epcombs while, conversely, a minster at Hertingfordbury is mentioned in Æthelgifu's will of *c.*980 (Crick 2007, no. 7) but no priest appears there in Domesday. If we add to this total Hitchin and Hertford, where churches but not priests are recorded, we arrive at a grand total of fifty-five places in which churches had probably appeared by the time of Domesday.

This, however, is clearly not the total number then in existence, for none of the churches allegedly built by Wulsin at St Albans (nor, indeed, the abbey itself) are mentioned. What is particularly striking, moreover, is the kinds of vills where priests (and therefore, presumably, churches) were to be found by 1086. They occur, not surprisingly, where churches are mentioned in earlier documents (Welwyn, Hitchin, Braughing, where minsters or churches are mentioned in the will of Æthelgifu of *c.*980); in those places (St Albans excepted) where churches contain surviving 'Anglo-Saxon' work; and in most of the places which have been suggested, in the previous chapter, as the likely centres of early estates. But priests are also listed in obscure or even lost vills like Minsden, *Bricewold* and Berkesdon. If places like these had churches, then it is arguable that they also existed in large vills like Hemel Hempstead, where no priests appear. This could, indeed, be taken as evidence that large numbers of priests, and therefore churches, were omitted by Domesday, and that most of the county's parish churches had in fact come into existence by this time.

While there is indeed little doubt that the St Albans churches are not the only ones of which we find no hint in Domesday, this argument should not be taken too far. There are in fact good grounds for believing that the overwhelming majority of churches which were in existence at the time of Domesday *were* obliquely recorded and that – conversely – most vills without recorded priests really did lack churches. Some light can be thrown on this problem by comparing those churches whose structure unquestionably contains some surviving Anglo-Saxon or Norman fabric (suggesting that they were built within a century or so of Domesday) with the entries in Domesday book.[6] There are 141 churches in Hertfordshire with medieval origins (parish churches or major chapelries), excluding sites such as Berkesdon, where no trace or record of the church fabric survives. Of these, forty-six (33 per cent) display certain evidence of Anglo-Saxon or Norman fabric, and nineteen (41 per cent) of those are in places in which churches are implied by Domesday. Of the ninety-five parish churches *without* obvious eleventh- or twelfth-century fabric, twenty-nine (31 per cent) are in vills in which priests are recorded by Domesday. These figures become more striking, however, when the character of the twenty-seven Anglo-Saxon and Norman churches found in vills *without* Domesday priests are examined. No less than ten are on manors belonging to the two great monastic houses, St Albans and Westminster; another was on one of the two Hertfordshire manors of the Canons of Waltham Cross (Wormley). This may suggest the systematic omission of priests from monastic holdings, rather than any random tendency to omit; and, indeed, priests seem to be under-represented on St Albans holdings in particular, with only two listed on nineteen principal manors.

It is also interesting to look at the problem the other way round. As already noted, nineteen of the vills in which Domesday implies the presence of a church still have churches with some surviving Anglo-Saxon or Norman fabric – in other words, 35 per cent of the total of fifty-five (the comparable figure for the Hertfordshire vills in which Domesday does not imply the existence of a church is 16 per cent, although this is a rather misleading statistic given that many, as we have seen, never became parishes). Five of the vills in which Domesday implies the presence of a church are now lost or deserted, leaving a total of thirty-one vills in which Domesday implies the presence of a church, but in which the existing structure shows no trace of pre-thirteenth-century fabric. Of these thirty-two churches (Hertford has two), five lie in prosperous medieval towns and were completely rebuilt, from the foundations up, in the late Middle Ages; while a further thirteen were

---

6. This discussion is based on the information contained in the various volumes of the *Victoria County History,* and in Pevsner's *Hertfordshire* (1977).

largely or entirely rebuilt in the post-medieval period (mainly in the nineteenth century), leaving no trace of earlier fabric. This leaves a mere fourteen churches which developed in a gradual, piecemeal fashion through the Middle Ages and have not been completely rebuilt in the late or post-medieval periods; and which are found in vills in which priests are mentioned in Domesday; but which nevertheless retain no *obvious* traces of early fabric.

The evidence upon which this somewhat convoluted argument is based is poor: relatively few Hertfordshire churches have yet received the archaeological investigation they deserve. Nevertheless, the broad coincidence of churches containing eleventh- or twelfth-century fabric and places where Domesday records priests is probably significant, and has two implications. Firstly, it suggests that Domesday is in fact a fairly reliable guide to the numbers of churches established by the late eleventh century in the county, with the notable exception of major ecclesiastical estates. Allowing for these, we might guess that there were around sixty-five or seventy churches in the county by 1086, rather less than half the late medieval total. Most, although not all, had probably been established before the Conquest. Secondly, the fact that only six Hertfordshire churches contain substantial evidence of pre-Conquest fabric, whereas more than forty incorporate Norman material, suggests that the vast majority of pre-Conquest churches were wooden structures, and that the century or so following the Conquest saw a sustained campaign of rebuilding in stone – a pattern evident in many other parts of England (Morris 1989, 165).

Some historians have argued that we can learn something about the development of the parochial system by examining church dedications (Everitt 1986, 225–58). Different saints were fashionable at different times or considered suitable for particular kinds of church. There are problems with this approach, not least the fact that most dedications are only first recorded in the later eighteenth or nineteenth century, and they could, and unquestionably did, change over the previous centuries. That of Aston church, for example, was altered from St James to Our Lady some time between 1490 and 1509, while Sacombe was originally dedicated to St Mary and only later to St Catherine (Doggett 1988, 22). Some changed their dedication more than once: Braughing, originally dedicated to St Andrew, was by the late fourteenth century dedicated to Saints Peter and Paul, and by the fifteenth century to St Mary (HER 4332). Against this, however, we should note that the early-eighteenth-century lists produced by antiquarians

William Wake and Edward Steele, which are discussed by Nicholas Doggett, indicate that there have been few changes over the last 300 years (Doggett 1993); and on careful inspection there does seem to be some structure and pattern to Hertfordshire's church dedications. This becomes apparent when we compare those of churches with unquestioned pre-1100 origins (i.e. churches with pre-Conquest fabric or whose existence is implied by Domesday), with those of churches for which there is neither documentary nor archaeological evidence for an existence before this date (eighty-six in all: a proportion of these certainly were in existence, as we have seen, but these should not be numerous enough to affect the comparison).

The most striking feature of the dedications in the first category, churches with pre-1100 origins, is the preponderance of those to St Mary – twenty-one out of a total of fifty-six known dedications (38 per cent). Overall, Mary was the most popular dedication in England, probably becoming more popular over time, but this figure is well above the 20 per cent average for the country as a whole, although comparable to that in the adjacent counties of Bedfordshire and Buckinghamshire, and with that in Suffolk (Jones 2007, 31–4, 81–2). The next most popular dedication of 'early' churches is Andrew, with five examples (9 per cent), followed by Mary Magdelene and Peter, with three dedications each. John the Baptist, Margaret, Nicholas, Michael, James and All Saints are each represented by two. There are fourteen saints represented by single dedications: these include a number of comparatively obscure British or Anglo-Saxon saints (Alban, Augustine, Botolph, Dunstan, Etheldreda and Helen). The dedications in the second category, churches for which there is no evidence for a pre-Conquest existence, show a number of differences. Mary is again the most popular dedication but accounts for a more modest 29 per cent of the total, while Andrew has only 3 per cent, less than John the Baptist (7 per cent), All Saints (7 per cent) and Nicholas (6 per cent). There are two dedications to Etheldreda but none to any other archaic Anglo-Saxon saints: in their place are a range of new dedications, popular on the Continent, including Giles, Lawrence, Bartholomew, St Faith, John the Evangelist, Martin, Ipploytus, Holy Trinity, Thomas the Martyr, Vincent and Cecilia. The virtual disappearance of dedications to 'native' saints in the period after the Conquest, and the introduction of new dedications, fashionable on the Continent, is notable, if unsurprising.

Students of church dedications have claimed that some may have had a particular iconic significance, and were considered suitable for certain locations (Jones 2007, 179–212). The only example that really makes sense in a Hertfordshire context is St Lawrence, which is said by some to have been considered peculiarly suitable for remote settlements in woodland environments and with pastoral functions (Everitt 1986, 250–8, 270). St Lawrence dedications are thus found in Nettleden, which originated as a detached chapelry of Pitstone in Buckinghamshire located in the high Chilterns; Ardeley, 'Earda's clearing', a remote wooded area on the periphery of the ancient Benington estate; Ayot, in the wooded uplands of the Stevenage–Welwyn Clays; Bovingdon, on the interfluve between the Chess and the Gade; and Wormley, 'the snake-infested clearing', on the heavy clay soils above the Lea valley. None of these churches appears to have existed at the time of Domesday and only Wormley contains any fabric dateable to the period before *c.*1200.

Towns

Hertfordshire was not entirely rural in 1066. Two places, Hertford and Ashwell, are specifically described as 'boroughs' in Domesday; a *burbium* and burgesses are mentioned at Berkhamsted; there are references to 'burgesses' at St Albans and Stanstead; while at Cheshunt there is no mention of a town or market but Domesday notes the presence of ten *mercatores* (merchants). Some of these places must have been truly urban in character. At St Albans, for example, the forty-six burgesses made up over half the total recorded population, as did the fifty-two recorded at Berkhamsted (although here it is possible that this figure is a scribal error for twelve, for it is higher than any subsequent figure for the number of burgesses residing in the town (Doggett and Hunn 1985, 22; Page 1908, 171). At the other extreme, at Ashwell and Stanstead, the burgesses made up only 17 per cent and 22 per cent of the population respectively, which was otherwise apparently no different in character from that in neighbouring vills.

It is possible – indeed, likely – that there were other urban or semi-urban centres in the county by late Saxon times whose presence is not expressly stated in Domesday. The existence of some kind of trading place is, for example, implied by the place-name *Langeport* – 'the long market' – which Domesday records in Edwinstree Hundred: this is a place usually identified with the hamlet of Hare Street in Great Hormead (Gover *et al.* 1938, 179–80). The name of Chipperfield, a hamlet in King's Langley, means 'open land used by traders' (Gover *et al.* 1938, 45). These may have been short-lived or transient trading places: more important, perhaps, is the possibility that larger, more permanent commercial centres may have been missed. Domesday, as should by now be apparent, is a frustrating document, its coverage of many aspects of eleventh-century life uneven and its omissions many and inexplicable.

The terms *burh*, used for a settlement, and *burgenses*, for its inhabitants, were legal and tenurial rather than economic and functional labels. They denoted that the places or individuals concerned owed dues and obligations, or enjoyed rights and privileges, distinct from those of their rural neighbours. Such legally distinct communities continued to be created in the period after the Conquest, as great magnates or more local lords became involved in urban development, keen to cash in on the economic expansion of the twelfth and thirteenth centuries: money could be made from renting out burgage plots as well as from the tolls charged on traders using the market. They often granted special privileges to a town – gave it a charter, which made it a borough – while the Crown granted the right to hold a market as a mark of favour, or in return for services or cash (Lilley 2002, 42–9). In theory, the documentary evidence generated by these formal and legislative procedures should allow us to chart with reasonable confidence the pattern of urban growth within any region, but in practice there are problems. Not all medieval towns received a charter, and many markets were claimed by prescription or 'ancient custom' and never received a formal grant. Above all, a charter or market grant does not necessarily provide a date for the inception of urban development. The town or market in question might have been in existence for many years, the legal documents merely signifying the point at which local lord or central government began to cash in on a spontaneous economic development (Lilley 2002, 47–8). Documentary evidence for town formation, in other words, can be highly misleading. In the twelfth and thirteenth centuries urban communities could, and did, come into being without legal recognition: and the same was presumably true at the time of Domesday, for the Survey was not concerned with listing in detail the economic role of the population. Some members of the rural population clearly functioned as traders or specialised producers without any special tenurial or legal status, but Domesday does not list them by occupation, as blacksmiths, carpenters and so on, presumably recording them instead as 'bordars' or 'cottars', people holding less land than the more substantial farmers, the 'villeins', who formed the core of the agrarian community.

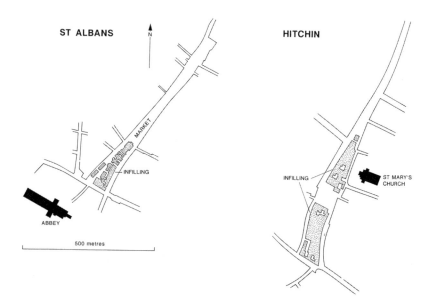

Figure 52. The marketplaces at St Albans and Hitchin. Both have been infilled to varying extents, but are otherwise broadly comparable in size and shape. Domesday records a borough at St Albans, but makes no direct reference to one at Hitchin.

Places where Domesday records large populations, of which a high proportion comprised individuals described as bordars or cottars, might thus already have gained urban or quasi-urban functions.

Another possible indication of early towns and markets may be provided by the location and topography of settlements. Medieval towns, in Hertfordshire as elsewhere, possessed very varying plans, but all had the essential feature of a central marketplace onto which fronted plots for shops that were laid out with varying degrees of regularity. In almost every case the original size of the marketplace has been obscured by infilling, as stalls developed into islands of permanent buildings, sometimes leading to severe contraction and fragmentation of the original area. In many cases it is, indeed, difficult to ascertain the original extent of the marketplace. But, this said, it is clear that many of the towns created in the pre-Conquest period were supplied with particularly large examples, and sometimes with more than one. Those at St Albans and Ashwell both appear to have been particularly extensive, although the latter has undergone so much infilling that its original form is unclear (Short 2008, 165–6) (Figure 52). At Hertford there were two markets, one associated with each of the Edwardian *burhs*, and although their precise form and location remains uncertain the southern one at least appears to have been large (Garfi 1995). Such large marketplaces may, as J.T. Smith has suggested, have originally served the whole of the hundreds in which they lay (Smith 1992, 137). Hertford may have served Hertford Hundred, with Ashwell serving Odsey and St Albans Albanstow. In all these places the market lay close to the church: its proximity may have served as a pressing reminder of the need for probity in transactions. Towns created in the post-Conquest period were generally rather different. Their markets, as we shall see, were normally smaller, often no more than slight widenings in major roads; and, in the case of the later ones especially, they were less closely associated with the sites of parish churches.

With all this in mind – the possible role of bordars as petty traders and craftsmen, and the character of pre-Conquest marketplaces – we can look again at the evidence for late Saxon urbanism in Hertfordshire. We might consider first the case of Hitchin, which by the time of Domesday already had a long history. As we have seen, it was an ancient estate centre, almost certainly a middle Saxon *burh* as well as the location of a minster and the meeting place for the hundred of the same name. Yet it is not described by Domesday as a town; nor is there any mention of *burgenses* or *mercatores* dwelling there. The town is, in fact, first described as a formal borough as late as the thirteenth century but, significantly, its market was then said to be held by 'ancient prescription' (Page 1912, 6), and its marketplace is not dissimilar in size and shape to that at St Albans (Figure 52). Domesday records a very high population here – ninety-one individuals, the same as in St Albans. What is particularly noteworthy is that just over half – forty-six – were described as bordars or cottars. It is more than likely that some of these people were traders who, had the legal status of the place been different, would have been termed 'burgesses'. There seems little doubt that Hitchin already operated, in some sense, as a town. It presumably served as the market place for Hitchin Hundred, as St Albans did for Albanstow and Ashwell for Odsey.

Bishop's Stortford is also interesting in this respect. We first hear of a market here as late as the fourteenth century and it would be easy to assume that it was then a relatively recent creation (Smith 1992, 136). Yet the marketplace appears originally to have been a large one – though now much infilled – and lay close to the parish church. Moreover, Bishop's Stortford was, like Hitchin, apparently a place of early importance – a probable Saxon estate centre with a possible Roman precursor. As Page noted, the parish of Bishop's Stortford has a marked 'salient' extending across onto the eastern, Essex, side of the Lea: given that this line also forms the county boundary, we would expect that this arrangement was of considerably antiquity (Page 1920). The large estate of Edeva, which was apparently centred on the town, was taken by William I after the Conquest and subsequently purchased by Bishop William of London. A castle was raised outside the town by his successor, Bishop Maurice. Not surprisingly, when we look closer at the earliest references to the market we find that there was no actual market grant: instead, the market was said to be held by ancient, prescriptive right (Page 1912, 292). It is more than likely, then, that the market was in existence long before the fourteenth century, and it is possible that it was already functioning by the time of the Norman Conquest, serving the southern and eastern portions of Braughing Hundred. Domesday, although showing only a modest population, indicates a marked preponderance of bordars and cottars (twenty) over villeins (six).

Braughing is another interesting case. This, again, was unquestionably a place of ancient importance – an Iron Age *oppida* and a Roman town, subsequently the centre of a major Saxon estate and the site of a minster, giving its name to both the hundred and the archdeaconry (Short 1988). Located on a major Roman road, and presumably serving as the meeting place for the hundred to which it gave its name, it probably remained as a royal manor into the eleventh century. It is precisely the kind of place where we might expect an early market to have developed. While the former marketplace does not seem to have covered a huge area, it was clearly much more than a widening in the main road, and it abutted directly upon the churchyard of the minster. By the time of Domesday the place had lost its ancient importance and was divided between a number of manors, but it remains possible that a market, once established, continued to function here. The pre-Conquest holdings, united under Eustace of Boulogne, came by inheritance to Queen Maud, wife of Stephen. Between 1146 and 1148 Stephen granted 100s rent in the manor to the Priory of Holy Trinity, London, and at the same time gave six *librates* of land in exchange for the mill and land which the queen had granted the priory near the Tower of London. These six *librates*, as the charter explains, included the site of the mill – and the market (Page 1912, 308). An established market, presumably held in a marketplace beside an ancient minster church, is thus recorded within sixty years of Domesday at a place of ancient importance. It is quite possible that it existed, in some form, at the time of the Conquest, perhaps serving the central and northern sections of the Hundred of Braughing. The majority of Braughing's admittedly small population (of twenty-two) was listed as bordars and cottars.

Lastly, we have the case of Ware. This has two spacious marketplaces, one of them close to the church. It was a place of ancient importance, with Roman and Iron Age roots; it may have formed the core of a major middle Saxon estate; and it was certainly an important estate centre at the time of Domesday. It seems unlikely that it became a town and market only in the late twelfth century, as the documents seem to suggest. Domesday records a large population here, of whom thirty-eight were villeins but thirty-nine bordars and cottars, together with thirty-two individuals who were – perhaps suspiciously – simply recorded as 'men'.

Not too much should perhaps be made of any of these arguments – in particular, there were other places in the county in which villeins were equalled or outnumbered by other kinds of landholder. Nevertheless, it is easy to see how, and why, markets might grow up at places like these, with their high-status residences, courts and minsters; places where people would anyway congregate, forming a ready market for goods and services. Many of Hertfordshire's towns – like so many things which we study in landscape history – may be older than we think.

Chapter 7
The Norman Conquest and Beyond

Castles and conquest

The Norman Conquest of 1066 had an almost immediate impact on Hertfordshire. Following his victory at Hastings, William 'marched inland … and harried that part of the country through which he advanced until he came to Berkhamsted' (Swanton 1996, 200). Here he was met by some of the key political figures of the time, together with the 'chief men of London'; 'and many more came to him, and giving hostages, surrendered and swore fealty to him. So he entered into a treaty with them: yet, nevertheless, he permitted his army to burn the villages and keep on pillaging' (Stevenson 1864, 135).

Domesday shows that the value of many Hertfordshire estates declined in the aftermath of the Conquest. F.F. Baring suggested in 1898 that the distribution of deteriorating values could be used to chart the progress of the Norman army, and indicated that the English surrendered not at Great Berkhamsted in the west of the county, as had always been supposed, but at *Little* Berkhamsted (Baring 1898). A surrender at the latter place made more sense, Baring believed, because it lay a few miles outside Hertford. But the decline in estate values was probably caused by the economic upheaval of the Conquest and the reorganisation of landholding (Fleming 1991, 124–6), rather than by the direct effects of military action; and Great Berkhamsted was, as we have seen, a place of some importance in late Saxon times. At the time of the Conquest it was the property of 'Edmer, a thane of Earl Harold's', who also held Little Gaddesden. Great Berkhamsted's continued significance after the Conquest is signalled by the fact that, by the time of Domesday, a castle had been raised here: a substantial defended mound or *motte* with an

Figure 53. Berkhamsted Castle was established soon after the Conquest and is the most impressive Norman motte-and-bailey castle in the county (© CUCAP).

associated enclosure or *bailey* (Figure 53); in addition, Domesday records the presence of a *fossarius* – an individual trained in the construction and maintenance of defence works.

Castles were new forms of fortification; in so far as private defences had existed in late Saxon England, they had generally been on a smaller scale. Other examples appeared soon after the Conquest at Bishop's Stortford, Hertford and Benington. It is sometimes suggested that these were sited according to some strategic plan, forming a 'defensive ring' on the northern approaches to the capital (Renn 1971, 4), but such an argument can hardly apply to Bishop's Stortford or, in particular, to Benington. With the exception of Hertford – the only royal castle in the county, located (as was normal practice) in the county town – all are best regarded simply as the *caputs* or headquarters of great feudal estates. As such, their location owed much to pre-Conquest arrangements, because of the way in which the principal properties of the old elite passed to the new (Liddiard 2000). In the case of Berkhamsted, Edmer's estates were granted by William to his half-brother, Robert Count of Mortain, and Domesday shows that he or his men held numerous manors nearby, including Hemel, Langley and Wigginton. Berkhamsted itself had long been the main estate centre in the region and – with a slight change of focus from Northchurch to Berkhamsted – it duly became the centre of a great honour, with jurisdiction extending into the above-named vills and also into Aldbury, and Betlow in Buckinghamshire.

Benington is a similar case. Whether or not it represented some kind of 'central place' within the ancient territory of the *Beningas*, it had certainly become a major estate centre by 1066, when it was the residence of Ælmer or Æthelmar of Benington, one of the most important Saxon landholders in Hertfordshire. William granted most of his lands to his nephew Peter de Valognes who, like his *antecessor*, made his main residence at Benington, which thus became the head of the Valognes Barony. The castle was probably built in the 1080s or 90s, before the official recognition of the barony in the reign of Henry I. It was a 'ringwork', a single defended enclosure, rather than a motte and bailey (Renn 1971, 14).

Bishop's Stortford castle was erected by the bishop of London. Stortford itself, although probably a place of importance in middle Saxon times, was not anciently a possession of the bishopric. At the time of the Conquest it was the centre of an extensive estate held by Edeva the Fair, and was purchased from the Crown by Bishop William soon afterwards. The bishops had always had interests in this old, East Saxon portion of the county. The actual site of the castle appears to have been given to Bishop William's successor, Maurice, by King William (Renn 1971, 24).

These early castles were residences and administrative centres as much as strongholds. None occupied particularly strong defensive positions (Berkhamsted and Stortford are in low-lying sites beside rivers, overlooked by higher ground). They were provided with the facilities expected of a noble residence: Berkhamsted had 'two arpents of vines' while Benington had a *parcus silvaticarum bestiarum*, 'a park for woodland beasts'. There were no other large, early castles in Hertfordshire, mainly because all other major lay landholders in the county had more extensive possessions elsewhere. Robert Gernon, whose properties were largely located in the Hundreds of Broadwater and Edwinstree, thus held the majority of his lands in Essex and erected a castle at Stansted Mountfichet, just over the county boundary. Landowners with large local estates but who were not major players on a national scale did not erect castles, although they might have residences of some pretensions. Hugh of Grandmesnil, who eventually acquired the vast estate of Askell at Ware, did not raise any fortification there, but Domesday records a 'park for woodland beasts' and four *arpents* of vines, *nuprimae plantatae*, 'newly planted'.

There are other examples of early medieval castles in Hertfordshire, but all are on a smaller scale than Berkhamsted, Benington, Stortford or Hertford. Indeed, in some cases there is doubt over whether particular sites really fall into the 'castle' class at all, rather than being large domestic moats. Most comprise small mottes, usually with associated 'baileys' or outer enclosures, although that at Walkern is a ringwork. With the possible exception of the example at Anstey, all seem to have been raised some time after the Conquest (Renn 1971, 13, 20, 22, 25). It is customary to assume that they were associated with the period of dynastic warfare during Stephen's reign (1135–54) conventionally known as the 'Anarchy', which had a significant effect upon the county, but there were other periods of unrest in the twelfth and early thirteenth centuries when local fortifications might have been required by landowners to protect their property. While it is thus possible that the small uncompleted motte at Therfield was raised by the Abbot of Ramsey during the 'Anarchy', and the castle at South Mimms was almost certainly built around 1141 by Geoffrey de Mandeville, in most cases the dates of these sites are unknown. They are strongly concentrated in the east of the county, perhaps reflecting the fact that landholding was more complex here than in the west (where most of the land was in the hands of St Albans, Ely and Westminster), and opportunities for conflict between rival magnates thus greatest. Some are associated with villages (Anstey (HER 27), Great Wymondley (HER 34), Buckland (HER 1940), Therfield (HER 67) and Pirton (HER 746)), and in some cases there are signs that the defences embraced a portion of the adjacent settlement. But other examples are in remote and isolated locations, often closely associated with areas of ancient woodland (Hoddesdon (HER 1110), South Mimms (HER 95), Ardeley (HER 391), Widford (HERE 503), Walkern (HER 33)), and it is probable that these were raised to protect manorial herds, grazed in upland wood-pastures, from baronial rustling in times of unrest.

Castles such as Berkhamsted were impressive statements of power and wealth. But more ubiquitous were the churches raised by Norman landowners within a generation or two of the Conquest. The most striking

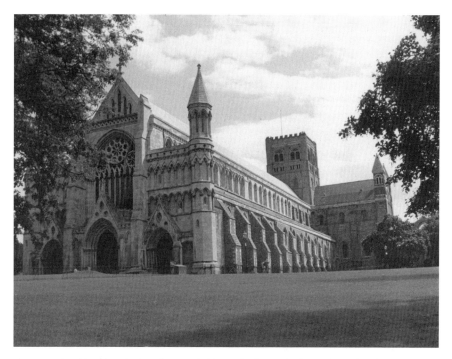

Figure 54. The abbey church of St Albans probably stands close to the burial place of the third-century martyr, Alban, in a cemetery above the Roman town of Verulamium. The present structure is largely of Norman date and the tower is built of Roman brick.

was St Albans Abbey, begun by Paul of Caen in 1077, soon after he had been appointed to reform the allegedly lax Saxon monastery. The building, mainly constructed of brick quarried from the nearby ruins of Verulamium (Figure 54), was largely completed within eleven years and its tower, rising high above the city, was the tallest structure by far in the county (Niblett and Thompson 2005, 221–2; Buckler and Buckler 1847). Paul of Caen's achievement was mirrored by local lay landowners throughout the county. As we have seen, between sixty-five and seventy churches probably existed in Hertfordshire by the time of the Conquest, but most were wooden structures. In the century or so following the Conquest almost all were rebuilt in stone, perhaps in part making a symbolic statement about the permanence of the new elite, and about its superiority over the old order. Most have subsequently been extensively altered but notable exceptions include Hemel Hempstead, Abbot's Langley and Bengeo, with its striking eastern apse (Figure 55). The post-Conquest elite also built churches on new

Figure 55. Bengeo, with its striking eastern apse, is a fine example of a small village church erected soon after the Norman Conquest. Like many others in the county, it probably replaced an earlier wooden structure.

sites, although how quickly remains uncertain: all that is known for certain is that the number of churches in existence at the time of Domesday had more than doubled by 1291, when the *Taxatio Ecclesiastica* was compiled: by this time all the parish churches (and major chapels) in the county had come into existence, together with a number of others (such as that at Berkesdon) which have since disappeared.

The tenurial revolution

The transfer of power and property from English to Norman landholders was gradual. William claimed to be Edward the Confessor's legitimate heir, not an unlawful conqueror, and initially only the estates of those who had fallen at Hastings were distributed to his followers. A series of revolts, however, saw the gradual elimination of the English elite, and few Englishmen of any consequence held manors at the time of Domesday.

As important as any change in the composition of the elite were alterations in the way in which they held their land, although discussion of this matter is complicated by disagreements over the nature of land tenure in the immediate pre-Conquest period. By the time of Domesday landholding in England was organised according to what historians normally describe as the 'feudal system'. All land was held from the Crown by a small elite of great magnates, who granted it out in smaller blocks to local knights in return for military support and other services. Most historians accept that this system was introduced by the Normans: but some believe that, on the eve of the Conquest, something very close to it had already developed, or was developing. The Domesday entries for Hertfordshire in particular have been used as evidence for this assertion, because – like those of other south Midland counties on the same Domesday 'circuit' – they often describe how particular pre-Conquest landowners were the 'man of' some more important figure (Fleming 1986). Æthelmar of Benington, for example, held land at Benington, Ashwell, Hinxworth, Radwell and Bengeo, but his 'men' – either thegns or sokemen – had property in Pelham, Luffenhall, Chells, Woolwicks, Welwyn, Willian, Digswell, Flexmore, Graveley, Libury, Sacombe and Buntingford. Some of the sokemen may have owed ancient obligations to the Benington estate (those at Libury and Sacombe) but most of these individuals were Æthelmar's 'men' because they had sworn fealty and allegiance to him. Some historians (such as Robin Fleming (1991)) believe that this relationship was the same as the feudal bond of post-Conquest times, and that the land occupied by the thegn or sokeman was thus, in effect, the property of the superior landowner.

This argument is at best an oversimplification, however, for Domesday tells us that in the majority of cases the local holder *vende potuit* – 'could sell' – the land in question. Most pre-Conquest landholders listed by Domesday were thus, in effect, possessors of their own property, under the king. Most had commended themselves to some powerful lord and owed him service in return for aid and protection: but this did not affect their proprietary rights. Even sokemen, while they may still have owed certain duties in return for their land, were proprietors in the sense that they could sell their property, passing these obligations with it to the new owner. Only a small number of landholders in the pre-Conquest period were, as far as we can tell, unable to alienate their land. Most seem to have been men holding on long leases from one of the great ecclesiastical houses.

The properties of large Saxon landowners thus passed to individual

Norman lords, while the holdings of the lesser men commended to them were generally treated as the property of these men's successors. But such a smooth and direct transfer occurred only to a certain extent. Thus, as Fleming has pointed out, of the forty hides held by the men of Asgar the Staller in the county in 1066 fewer than half were in the hands of Geoffrey de Mandeville, his successor, in 1086. 'The others were in the possession of Maurice Bishop of London, Odo of Bayeux, Eustace of Boulogne, Robert Gernon, Ralph Bayard, Geoffrey of Bec, Edgar Ætheling and a king's thegn named Alwin Doddason' (Fleming 1986, 89). Quite possibly the twenty years between the Conquest and the Survey had seen more fluidity in landholding, more movement and exchange of land, than Domesday implies.

The Conquest had other important effects on the character of landholding. The number of sokemen in the county declined dramatically. In 1066 there had been around 250; in 1086 there were only 43. These relics of a bygone age were incorporated wholesale into the new feudal order. Those holding small manors fared no differently from other minor landowners: those with the smallest properties were downgraded to the status of the semi-free villeins, their land now regarded as part of the local manor. Typical is the example of Ware, where, according to Domesday, two sokemen 'have, since the coming of King William, been annexed to this manor, to which they did not belong in the time of king Edward'. Where vills consisted largely of the holdings of sokemen the manorial 'core' normally expanded to embrace their land, as at Hormead, where the one and a half hides held in 1066 by thane Alnoth had by 1086 been increased through the incorporation of three and a quarter hides held by seven sokemen, and of two hides belonging to Wulfwin and Alfward, the 'men' of Asgar the Staller and Æthelmar of Benington respectively. This diminution in the status of sokemen was almost certainly accompanied by a more general reduction in the freedom of peasant cultivators, although the majority of the rural population of Hertfordshire on the eve of the Conquest had, as far as we can tell, already owed onerous dues and services to their social superiors.

The impact of the Norman 'tenurial revolution' on systems and concepts of landholding should not be exaggerated. In a relatively short space of time aspects of the old order re-asserted themselves, and, in particular, the various manors held by minor knights were soon passing by inheritance, and ultimately by sale, as if they were private property. Moreover, one important feature of landholding in Hertfordshire remained unchanged. William had neither the desire nor the ability to expropriate the ancient religious houses. These experienced some losses (Great Gaddesden, for example, granted to St Albans as early as 980, had been seized by Edward of Salisbury) but for the most part the holdings of St Albans, Ely and Westminster, which dominated the south and west of the county, remained intact. This area thus continued to be dominated by large monastic estates, while the north and east of the county was characterised by smaller properties in the hands of lay landowners, although the sharpness of this contrast was to some extent softened in the course of the following centuries as ecclesiastical lords, as much as their lay counterparts, entered into the process of subinfeudation, the creation of sub-manors, to meet military obligations or for financial gain. Nevertheless, throughout the Middle Ages this contrast remained an important factor in the county's social and economic development.

The new elite may have revolutionised ideas of land tenure but they perpetuated existing systems of civil administration and justice with little immediate change: as we have seen, the structure of Domesday is framed not only by manors and fees, but also by shires, hundreds and vills. These institutions continued to change and develop, however, in the course of the twelfth and thirteenth centuries. The shire remained of crucial importance, although Hertfordshire did not have its own sheriff, sharing one with Essex to the east; whether this was a new, post-Conquest development or a continuation of later Saxon practice remains unclear. Either way, the sheriff continued to fulfil a wide range of administrative, judicial and military functions. He remained responsible for local defence, for the summoning of the shire levy or *posse comitatus*, although the importance of this militia slowly declined as the king came to rely increasingly on more professional forces, the knight service supplied by honours and fees, which cut across the boundaries of the shire (Jewell 1972, 44–5). The sheriff also continued to preside over the shire courts, although gradually their independence declined as justices began to be sent out into the shires from the king's court in order to prevent maladministration by domineering local magnates. This practice became more regular and formalised with the development of more general sessions and specific circuits, ultimately destroying the independence of the county court, although it remained of central judicial importance, and its *administrative* significance was retained. It was in the shire court that the king's orders were received and promulgated by the sheriff; it was here that the local coroners and, in time, members of parliament, were selected (Jewell 1972).

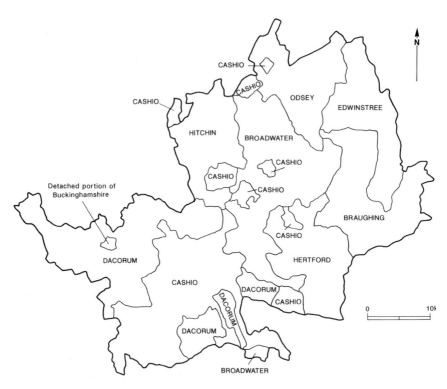

Figure 56. Hertfordshire: medieval hundreds.

The hundred courts also survived the Conquest, although their functions likewise continued to change and develop. Their civil jurisdiction was gradually eroded in the course of the twelfth and early thirteenth centuries, and their criminal business was concentrated in twice yearly 'tourns', presided over by itinerant justices. There were changes, too, in the configuration of Hertfordshire's hundreds (Figure 56). In particular, the Hundred of Tring had disappeared by *c.*1200 (Page 1908, 141), having been absorbed into Dacorum. The latter, however, continued to lose vills to Albanstow, or Cashio, as that hundred had come to be known by the thirteenth century (Gover *et al.* 1938, 69). Abbot's Langley, Napsbury, Windridge and Redbourn were all part of Cashio by the mid thirteenth century (Page 1908, 141). Cashio also gained isolated vills in other hundreds, where the holdings of St Albans were more scattered. Shephall, Codicote and Newnham had thus, by the thirteenth century, become detached islands of Cashio within Broadwater Hundred; Hexton and Bendish lay isolated within Hitchin; Bramfield was an outpost within Hertford Hundred; Norton an island sandwiched between Odsey and Bedfordshire. There were also a number of other minor changes: thus Langley and Minsden, which lay in Broadwater Hundred at the time of Domesday, were by the thirteenth century placed within Hitchin, while Widford passed from Edwinstree Hundred to Braughing. The precise reasons for the latter adjustments is unclear, but the growth of Cashio is easy to explain: it reflects the desire of the Abbot of St Albans to bring all his tenants under a single jurisdiction – his own. For the increasing tendency of the Anglo-Norman state to control traditional local courts was paralleled by the proliferation of private hundreds and other local franchises under the control of powerful magnates. The abbey enjoyed continuing support from the new Norman kings, and especially from Henry I, who celebrated a number of major festivals at St Albans and attended the dedication of the great new church in 1115. In the course of the twelfth century the abbots obtained important privileges from the Pope which guaranteed the house's independence from the diocesan (since 1072, the bishop of Lincoln), thus granting them archidiaconal powers over their Hertfordshire territories (Crick 2007, 30–6). As a result 'St Albans came nearer the exemption of certain major European houses than any other English community' (Sayers 1976, 182). The Hundred of Cashio thus developed into the Liberty of St Albans, over which the abbot had wide powers of civil jurisdiction, an important source of profit for a community which was only poorly endowed with landed wealth (it was the tenth wealthiest monastic house in England in 1066; by the Dissolution it was the fourth, although it had not expanded its landholding significantly (Golding 1986, 111; Crick 2007, 33)). Other great landowners claimed less dramatic privileges; thus the honour of Berkhamsted was outside the direct jurisdiction of the sheriff and, at each circuit, the bailiff went before the justices and demanded the liberties of the honour: one of their number was dispatched to hear all the pleas there (Page 1908, 164).

The making of the medieval landscape

With the dramatic changes in tenurial organisation effected by the Norman Conquest – and with the striking castles and numerous stone churches erected by the new elite – it might be thought that the landscape of the twelfth and thirteenth centuries was largely moulded by the decisions of great feudal lords. To some extent it was: but far more important than the dictates of great men were the patterns of territorial organisation that they had inherited from the Saxon past, and, above all, the structures of the natural environment – geology, soils and topography, especially the ancient contrast between vale, scarp and valley on the one hand, and clay-covered interfluves on the other.

In Hertfordshire, as in other areas of England, the two centuries following the Conquest saw rapid population growth and the steady expansion of settlement and cultivation. Between 1086 and 1307 the population of the county probably more than doubled, from around 30,000 to 69,000 (Bailey *et al.* 1998, xxii). The woods and wood-pastures of the interfluves dwindled: where they survived it was often because they had been preserved by manorial lords as enclosed woodland or private deer parks – the venison farms and hunting grounds that were an essential symbol of status of the medieval elite. Farmland expanded everywhere at the expense of woodland but, by the thirteenth century, when documents become sufficiently abundant to provide a reasonably clear picture of the countryside, the landscape of Hertfordshire displayed a clear pattern of regional variation.

In the far north of the county, in the Vale of Wringtail and parts of Odsey and Hitchin Hundreds, classic 'Midland' landscapes, with nucleated villages and 'regular' open-field systems, could be found. There was little woodland here. Farms were clustered in a single settlement and the holdings of the farmers were scattered in strips throughout the territory of the township, intermingled with those of their neighbours in two, three or more great arable fields (Roden 1973). In post-medieval times these 'champion' landscapes were eventually transformed by large-scale, planned and usually parliamentary enclosure, and were thus replaced by the classic 'planned countrysides' of neat, rectangular fields surrounded by flimsy hawthorn hedges. Nevertheless, so deeply entrenched was open-field agriculture in this district that in some parishes the land still lay partly or even largely unenclosed into the early years of the twentieth century.

Outside these northern parts of the county settlement was more dispersed in medieval times, with a mixture of villages, isolated farms and small hamlets, and farming was generally organised on less rigidly communal lines. It is sometimes suggested that open fields were only ever important in the northern 'champion' parts of the county, and that elsewhere land was always farmed in hedged fields. In reality, open fields *of a kind* could be found almost everywhere in medieval Hertfordshire, but they were normally of 'irregular' form. That is, there were usually many individual fields in a parish (in Broadfield, for example, there were fourteen in the early fourteenth century; in King's Walden no less than thirty), and the holdings of individual farmers tended to be concentrated in the fields near their farms, rather than being more widely scattered (Roden 1973, 329). Separate groups of open fields were often associated with individual hamlets, especially those which had been established by late Saxon times (Roden 1973, 347–8). Almost always, however, such fields existed alongside areas of hedged closes which had been reclaimed directly from the 'waste'.

The dispersed settlement patterns (and irregular field systems) of the main, central and southern areas of Hertfordshire formed part of a much wider zone of 'ancient countryside' embracing most of south-eastern England and the southern parts of East Anglia. The 'champion' landscapes of north Hertfordshire similarly formed the edge of a more extensive region of nucleated settlement and 'regular' field systems that extended over much of the Midlands and into north-east England. Precisely why this marked regional dichotomy in landscape developed, and when, are matters of fierce debate among archaeologists and historians. But it is noteworthy that – in Hertfordshire, as elsewhere in England – 'champion' landscapes were found in two main kinds of terrain. Some corresponded with extensive areas of light, freely draining soil, such as the Chiltern escarpment. Here, farms were perhaps obliged to cluster together near springs and other supplies of running water. At the same time the need to manage the sheep flocks – which had to be systematically folded on these light, easily leached soils in order to maintain fertility – further encouraged communal agriculture and communal modes of living (Kerridge 1992, 26–34). Most 'champion' landscapes were not found on light land, however, but in areas of particularly difficult clay soils, poorly draining and easily damaged if worked wet – such as those in the clay vales at the far northern tip of Hertfordshire's two attenuated 'salients'. Here, rather different reasons for nucleated settlement and communal agriculture are apparent. In late Saxon times a heavier and larger plough came into general use, but it was expensive, and so too were the oxen (six or even eight in number) required to pull it. Peasant cultivators tended to share ploughs, each contributing oxen to the plough team. In areas of difficult, sticky soils it was particularly important that ploughs and teams could be assembled rapidly, in order to exploit every hour in which the ground was suitable for cultivation, especially during the short spring ploughing season; and farms tended to cluster together in villages in order to

Figure 57. Levens Green, Great Munden. Clusters of farms and cottages around diminutive greens are a typical feature of medieval settlement in north-east Hertfordshire especially. These small pockets of pasture may represent the truncated remains of far more extensive areas of common land (by courtesy of English Heritage).

facilitate this. It was also important that all who contributed to the common team should share equally in the benefits derived from it: hence the intermixture of holdings in a myriad of small intermingled strips in large fields, over which the plough would move in an ordered sequence, so that everybody had a reasonable chance of getting their land ploughed and harrowed in time for spring sowing (Williamson 2003, 141–59).

Although most of the county was, and is, characterised by 'ancient' rather than 'planned' countryside, different regions display particular variations on this basic theme. These, again, are largely related to aspects of the local environment, and the problems and opportunities which this presented to farmers as settlement expanded and woods and pastures were progressively ploughed in the course of the later Saxon and early post-Conquest periods. In the densely settled north-east of the county, as we have seen, large numbers of settlements already existed by late Saxon times. In the landscape of today many survive as villages, as 'hall–church complexes', or as moated farms or hamlets bearing the name of some Domesday vill and/or a name of archaic, Old English form. Such places are generally located – for reasons of water-supply – either in valley-floor locations or immediately *above* one of the valleys, on the edge of the boulder-clay plateau, which carried a perched water table. Either way, they were located next to the principal exposures of light valley soils on which the main areas of arable open fields had developed by early medieval times. Where the light soils were most extensive (in the valleys of the Rib, Stort, Ash and Quin) so too were the areas of open arable, and it was here that the largest nucleated settlements – places like Braughing or Standon – could be found, often displaying complex, somewhat rambling plans, in part perhaps because they developed from the fusion of two or more discrete hamlets.

In the higher reaches of the valleys of these rivers, and in those of their tributaries, areas of open field were less extensive and villages were correspondingly smaller and less tightly nucleated, often little more than a hall–church complex and a few farms or cottages. These higher reaches shade off imperceptibly into the level landscape of the clay plateau. On these heavy, poorly draining interfluves the settlement pattern consisted – and to a large extent still consists – of isolated farms, sometimes moated, and hamlets clustered around (and generally taking their name from) small commons or 'greens' (Figure 57).

Moated sites and greens are usually quite separate features of the landscape. The moated sites, and some of the isolated farms, can often be identified with new manors or substantial freehold farms carved out of woods and wood-pastures during the twelfth and thirteenth centuries. The green-edge settlements are different. They seldom include the sites of secondary manors, and appear to have developed in the twelfth and thirteenth centuries as small farms clustered at places where roads and droveways widened to enter some extensive tract of upland grazing, perhaps still partially wooded. In most cases, these large areas of 'waste' were subsequently converted to arable land or enclosed as managed woodland or deer parks, which were particularly numerous in this region (Rowe 2009, 15–20): the funnel entrance to the common, with its attendant houses, survived as a diminutive 'green'. Only in a minority of vills – often those associated with minor rather than major valleys, and containing a high proportion of level clay plateau within their bounds – did larger areas of common grazing remain, and in such circumstances they, rather than the manor house and church, often became the main focus for medieval settlement. The growth of a village on the old Saxon site was thus suppressed, and farms and

Figure 58. The river Chess, flowing through the middle of the photograph, forms the county boundary with Buckinghamshire. The sinuous shape of the field boundaries on the valley sides show that they were created through the early piecemeal enclosure of open-field strips, which themselves seem to have developed, in places, within a more ancient 'co-axial' framework. In the centre of the photograph earthworks of 'strip lynchets' – cultivation terraces, each the equivalent of an open-field strip – can be seen. They show that the steep slope here was cultivated in medieval times. To the right, the parish church stands almost isolated, settlement having been attracted to the common, on higher ground (top right), as the uplands were opened up for cultivation (© CUCAP).

cottages were in some cases attracted away from it, leading to the isolation or near-isolation of parish churches seen at places such as Sacombe. Areas of damp common could also be found on the floors of valleys, and here they often became the main articulating element in village plans, expansion of settlement occurring along their margins so that the parish church was left in a slightly peripheral position, as, for example, at Aspenden.

In some cases, 'green' hamlets on the clay plateau carry the names of lost Domesday vills, superficially suggesting that they had developed before the Conquest: the deserted site of Berkesdon Green in Aspenden (*Berchesdene* in

Domesday) is one example. But in most such cases it is clear that the name has been transferred from an older, 'manorial' site which has itself subsequently changed its name: greens and commons, as noted earlier, are generally areas of secondary, post-Conquest settlement. In the case of Berkesdon, the 'valley of the birches', the name seems a more appropriate term for the setting of Tannis Court, on a south-facing slope above a tributary of the Rib, than to the level plateau site 700 metres to the south once occupied by Berkesdon Green itself. Significantly, the parish church appears to have been located close to Tannis Court (Munby 1977, 126). The old hall–church complex, the site of the settlement described in Domesday, was evidently eclipsed by the growth of its later common-edge neighbour.

The development of settlement on the western edge of the Boulder Clay Plateau – the more difficult soils of the Stevenage–Welwyn Clays – was slightly different. Here, in addition to small greens, larger areas of common grazing more often survived on the 'uplands', partly because they corresponded with areas of particularly acid soils which were not worth cultivating, and these came to form foci around which extensive agglomerations of farmsteads developed, as at Rabley Heath or Mardley Heath. In many cases, as at Tewin or Digswell, these again suppressed the growth of settlement around the older Saxon site located on lower ground, in some cases leading to isolated or near-isolated churches.

The Chiltern Dipslope provides another variation on these same basic themes. Here, as we have seen, large estates and large vills still dominated the landscape at the time of Domesday, and extensive tracts of land on the clay-covered interfluves were but sparsely settled. This was, in consequence, a district of particularly large parishes: medieval churches are mainly located in the valleys of the principal rivers, leaving great tracts of upland territory quite devoid of them. Nevertheless, as we have seen, even in late Saxon times some farms or hamlets existed on the clay interfluves. Rapid population growth and subinfeudation ensured that the swine-woods and pastures here rapidly filled with settlements in the course of the early Middle Ages, creating a plethora of secondary manors, isolated farms and hamlets. The new manorial sites seldom had moats – these were difficult to construct where the clays were fairly porous and where there was no running surface water. The hamlets came in a variety of forms. Some clustered around small greens, such as Leverstock Green in Hemel Hempstead. Others, strung out irregularly along roads, were referred to as 'Rows', 'Ends' or, if located on the floor of one of

Figure 59. Little Gaddesden: another isolated church marking the original, Saxon, focus of settlement. Here, too, settlement seems to have drifted away to the common –

the narrow valleys dissecting the plateau, 'Bottoms'. In addition, there were once again a number of large commons, often associated with spreads of infertile sands and gravel. Some of these still remain as impressive incidents in the landscape: Chipperfield Common, Croxley Green, Sarratt Common and Harpenden Common are examples. As in other parts of the county, parishes with the most extensive commons – such as Sarratt or Gaddesden – tend to have isolated churches, presumably marking the sites of Saxon settlements on the plateau edge, beside the light soils of the valley sides (Figures 59, 60, 61). Once again, growth of settlement around the common presumably suppressed the development of a nucleated village on the older site, which was inconveniently situated as more and more of the forested uplands were opened up for cultivation. In one case, however – Harpenden – a secondary settlement itself eventually became the focus for a new parish: a new church, originally a chapelry of Wheathampstead, was erected at one end of the common (Page 1908, 311). On the higher ground to the north, immediately above the steep Chiltern escarpment, settlement was sparser and extensive

Figure 60. – which now forms the main focus of settlement in the parish.

tracts of wood-pasture survived well into the Middle Ages, either as wooded commons (such as the Frith in Berkhamsted) or deer parks (such as Ashridge). By the thirteenth century, however, the main areas of the interfluves were occupied by enclosed farmland, areas of enclosed coppiced woodland and small open fields.

Although the boulder clays of north-east Hertfordshire remained wealthier and more prosperous than the Chiltern Dipslope region, the differences between the two regions 'narrowed during the twelfth and thirteenth centuries, when rising population pressure and the growing demand for fuel and food in London resulted in some new settlement, the reduction of wood-pasture, and a shift towards arable farming in the latter area' (Bailey *et al.* 1998, xxi). As in the east of the county the larger areas of open field always occupied the tracts of light soils on the sides of the major valleys, and the more extensive the exposures of such soils, the more extensive the area of the open fields (Figure 59). A survey of Hemel Hempstead, dated 1523 but apparently based on a late medieval survey, describes around 7,000 acres of land, of which 3,000 lay in open fields,

Figure 61. Typical Chiltern dipslope countryside between St Albans and Hemel Hempstead, as shown on a map of Lord Grimston's estates, 1768. Note the scattered, isolated farms and the broadly 'co-axial' arrangement of fields and roads (by courtesy of HALS and with permission from the Earl of Verulam).

mainly occupying the slopes of the Gade valley (Munby 1977, 165). Where the terrain was very broken – where a number of exposures of light soil existed in a large parish, separated by tongues of clay-covered upland – open fields could be numerous: Great Gaddesden had as many as thirty individually named fields (Roden 1973, 329). As we have seen, both the enclosed fields on the uplands and the boundaries of the open-field furlongs on the valley sides often exhibited a marked co-axial layout, apparently because they developed within an earlier framework of transhumance tracks and associated boundaries (Figure 61).

Lastly, we may turn to the clay uplands in the south of the county, a sparsely peopled tract of woodland and pasture in late Saxon times although, as we have seen, by no means a wilderness. Here, too, settlement expanded in the centuries after Domesday, often forming long strings of farms and cottages along the ancient droves and tracks leading from the lower ground into the interior of the clay uplands. Some small greens and commons also existed, with associated girdles of settlement – Letchmore Heath in Aldenham, for example – while on the highest ground, where the London

Clay was capped with infertile sands and gravels laid down in Quaternary times, there were a number of particularly extensive commons, including Bushey Heath and Aldenham Common: farms and cottages were usually clustered close to the funnel-like entrances where roads and tracks entered them. Elsewhere, isolated farms were scattered across the landscape, often associated with pockets of lighter soils in stream valleys.

In spite of the progressive spread of settlement onto the interfluves, extensive remnants of the great woods and pastures of Saxon times survived, not only as large commons such as Bushey Heath but also as deer parks and woods. Hatfield Great Wood and its destruction have been described in an earlier chapter (above, pp. 160–1); it formed, well into post-medieval times, part of an almost continuous tract of woodland and common embracing some thirty square kilometres, which extended southwards as far as the county boundary with Middlesex and eastwards into Cheshunt, almost merging with the great areas of coppiced hornbeam woods around Broxbourne, Hoddesdon and Wormley on and immediately above the sides of the wide Lea valley. The more remote and level areas of upland were thus occupied by parks and commons, while the more intensively managed stands of woodland were found towards the major valleys, partly on sloping, lower ground. Many of the other large woods in this region were similarly located – towards the periphery of the main block of upland clays, immediately above valleys. It seems likely that, as the great tracts of waste were cleared for farmland (or degenerated through grazing to open common land) manorial lords chose to embank and preserve woodland in these positions because of the difficulties of transporting coppice wood and timber for long distances down the appalling clayland roads. A similar pattern can be discerned, if less clearly, on the boulder clays in the north-east of the county, and has been noted elsewhere in England, as for example in the Weald of Kent (Witney 1990).

Even in this late-settled district open fields seem to have been widespread in the Middle Ages, although particularly in or beside the valleys of the Lea and the Colne. Here, on occasions, they survived (if only in fragmentary form) well into the post-medieval period – in Wormley and Hoddesdon, for example, as late as the early nineteenth century (HALS B1444; HALS DSA 4 120/2). Even at a distance from these bands of lighter lands some open fields could be found (Figure 62), although for the most part the landscape was generally dominated by enclosed fields farmed in severalty. A survey of

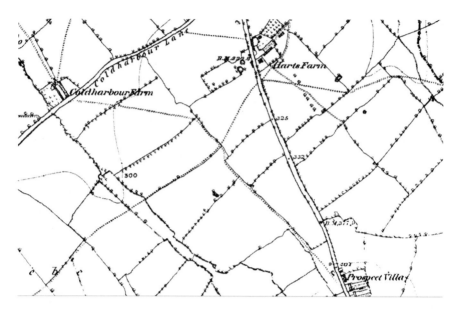

Figure 62. Open fields, albeit of 'irregular' form, appear to have been widespread throughout Hertfordshire in the Middle Ages. Even in the Southern Uplands they could be found wherever areas of lighter ground occurred. Here in Bushey the slightly sinuous shapes of the fields depicted on the first edition Ordnance Survey 6-inch maps show where pockets of open arable were gradually removed through informal, piecemeal enclosure.

1276 of the manor of Shenley, for example, shows that while the hall–church complex on the well-drained soils in the north of the parish, towards the Colne, was associated with three open fields, the rest of the parish lay in hedged fields which had presumably been enclosed direct from the 'waste' (Barton 1981).

It is noteworthy that in this district the close association of church and manor, so evident elsewhere in the county, tends to break down. Some hall–church complexes can certainly be found – as at Wormley – but many parishes, including Ridge, Northaw, Aldenham and Bushey, have churches which are not obviously associated with medieval manorial sites. Domesday does not list priests in the latter two vills, while Ridge and Northaw do not feature at all in the Survey, and, if they existed at all at this time, they were almost certainly too small to have gained churches of their own. In other words, in all these places churches were probably first erected only in the course of the twelfth century, by which time settlement had already expanded away from the valleys, along ancient droveways and tracks, far onto the clay-covered uplands. It is possible that local lords (in many cases St Albans Abbey) took the unusual step of erecting churches away from manorial complexes so that they could be more conveniently and centrally situated with respect to the farms and hamlets of the parish. Even where church and manor are in close association – as at Wormley or Shenley – the main focus of settlement generally lies on the higher, heavier ground.

By 1279, to judge from the *Taxatio Ecclesiastica*, churches had been established even in the most remote southern parts of the clay uplands, although most remained as dependent chapels until late in the Middle Ages or even beyond. That at East Barnet is largely of Norman date but it is a striking exception: most of the area's churches are either fifteenth-century structures, often extensively restored in the nineteenth century (Ridge, Shenley, Monken Hadley and Chipping Barnet); or else buildings entirely of eighteenth- or nineteenth-century construction (Elstree, Totteridge, Northaw). Before the end of the Middle Ages, the relative poverty of the parishes on these difficult soils ensured the erection of only modest structures, most of which were rendered redundant by later circumstances – in particular, by increases in wealth and population resulting from the district's proximity to London.

Indeed, in innumerable ways the development of Hertfordshire's medieval churches reflects the history of the communities they served. Eileen Roberts usefully divided them into five categories according to the complexity of their ground plans – 'primitive', 'simple', 'moderate', 'elaborate' and 'cruciform' (Roberts 1977). These variations were the consequence both of the original form of the church and of later developments, as individuals and communities added aisles, towers, porches and the rest. It is interesting to compare her lists and distribution maps with the discussion of the development of settlement and ecclesiastical organisation made in this and earlier chapters. By and large, the more complex plans ('moderate', 'elaborate' and 'cruciform') are associated with settlements in the principal valleys – larger villages, old estate centres. Churches on the upland interfluves, in contrast, tend to be of 'primitive' or 'simple' type. This pattern is particularly clear in the Chiltern Dipslope region, as Nicholas Doggett observed. Here 'the churches in the valleys have generally had the best opportunity to develop sophisticated plans as a result of serving long established, prosperous communities ... while upland churches have remained small to the present day' (Doggett 1981, 28). Interestingly, the pattern is not quite so marked in the north-east of the county. Here, while in general the more elaborate plans are associated with settlements in the major valleys, there are many exceptions – Ardeley, Aspenden and Barley, for example. The wealth which could be generated on these fertile soils evidently allowed quite small communities and individual families to add and rebuild in lavish style during the course of the Middle Ages.

Yet it is, paradoxically, on these same soils that the majority of Hertfordshire's 'deserted medieval villages' are found, especially in the district around Buntingford (Rutherford Davis 1973). The inverted commas are important. The county has very few *real* deserted villages, in the sense in which this term is used in the Midlands: that is, moderately large nucleated settlements abandoned, or intentionally depopulated for sheep farming, in the period between the late fourteenth and early sixteenth centuries, or cleared to make way for parks in the period up to the nineteenth century. Pendley, in the west of the county, and possibly Mimms, in the south, were examples of villages removed for emparking, but the majority of Hertfordshire's deserted sites, which are found on these boulder-clay soils, were very different. Berkesdon and Wakeley were settlements with their own churches, parishes in their own right, but all the others appear to have been small hamlets which never achieved parochial status. Many appear in Domesday but fall into the third category of vills, as defined in the previous chapter. They were small places, mostly located on the poorly draining interfluves, and their shrinkage to single farms or (more rarely) their complete disappearance in late medieval times was probably the consequence of a combination of economic and demographic factors. As population fell in the wake of the Black Death, farmers migrated away from settlements on these difficult soils in order to take up holdings elsewhere, on the more easily cultivated, lighter land in the neighbouring valleys. And as the economy became more specialised in the fifteenth and sixteenth centuries, the surviving farms in these 'upland' areas reverted to their earlier function, as cattle-grazing enterprises (Figure 63).

The growth of towns

Although more settlements with urban characteristics may have existed by the time of the Conquest than Domesday superficially suggests, there is no doubt that the following three centuries saw a significant increase in the number of such places, and by the early fourteenth century more than twenty places in

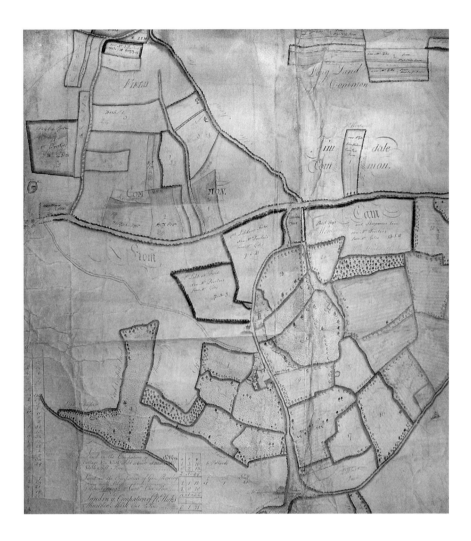

Figure 63. Extract from a map of 1778 of an estate in Standon, showing the typical boulder-clay landscape of north-east Hertfordshire. Areas of irregular fields, on the higher ground, indicate tracts of former wood-pasture lying beyond the main areas of open-field arable in the principal valleys. Some of these open fields still survived as late as this (towards the top of the picture) but many had been removed in the course of the post-medieval period by informal, piecemeal enclosure, creating closes with slightly sinuous boundaries. Note the green-edge settlement towards the bottom of the picture (by courtesy of HALS).

Hertfordshire had regular markets (Bailey 2008, 46–7). While some of these remained little more than villages others had clear urban functions and a recognisable urban topography (Slater 2008). Medieval historians have generally emphasised the importance of lordly foundations – 'planted' towns – in the urban experience of the Middle Ages. While, as we have seen, it is likely

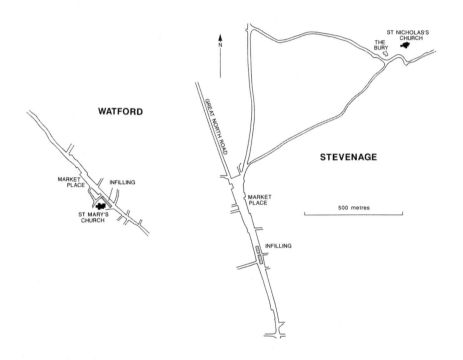

Figure 64. Later towns and marketplaces in Hertfordshire. Left: Watford, a narrow marketplace (little more than a widening in the main road to London) established in the twelfth century beside the parish church. Right: Stevenage, a market established on a strip of common land in the later thirteenth century, some way from the church and manor house.

that in some cases medieval lords simply recognised and encouraged an existing market or fair by obtaining a royal charter and providing appropriate facilities, in others – especially in the post-Conquest period – they clearly took the initiative, laying out a marketplace and plots on which shops and workshops could be erected at places which had formerly been empty sites or little more than hamlets. Baldock, for example, does not appear in Domesday. The Knights Templars were granted land here in 1140 (hence the town's name, a corruption of 'Baghdad') and by 1189 a market was in existence and confirmed by royal grant. The town occupies a site where two Roman roads met, just to the south of the Icknield Way. Its plan comprised two marketplaces which met at right angles, both formed by diverting and then widening one of the two roads. A church was erected in the angle between them (Munby 1977, 98–9; Beresford 1967, 195, 261). Royston was in some ways similar. Here a priory, founded close to the junction of Ermine Street and the Icknield Way, obtained a market grant in 1189, and in 1224 Ermine Street was realigned, an event probably marking the establishment of the two marketplaces here in their present form (Plowman 2008): one to the north and one to the south of the Icknield Way, a layout probably chosen because one lay in the county of Cambridgeshire and the other in Hertfordshire – such was the artificiality of this urban creation. Indeed, although Royston was recognised as a distinct vill by the early fourteenth century it did not become a separate parish until 1540, remaining divided between Barkway, Reed and Therfield (in Hertfordshire) and Melbourne and Kneesworth (in Cambridgeshire), although the town was served by a chapelry from the 1160s or 70s (Plowman 2008; Munby 1977, 97–8).

Both Baldock and Royston were equipped with large or double markets, like those associated with pre-Conquest urban centres. Most of the towns which (so far as the evidence goes) first came into existence during the post-Conquest period, however, are rather different in layout. At Berkhamsted, established beside the new castle some time after the Conquest; Hemel Hempstead, where a market was being held by *c.*1300; Watford, where a market was probably established on the Abbot of St Albans' manor in the early twelfth century (Figure 64); Bushey, where there was a market by 1200; and Barkway, established before 1270; the marketplace was no more than a simple widening of a major road, perhaps a small pre-existing green or common, commandeered for the purpose (it is certainly noteworthy that, with the exception of Sawbridgeworth, most Hertfordshire markets are triangular or irregular in form, often with routeways entering at each corner, and thus resembling areas of common land rather than spaces specially created for the purpose (Smith 1992, 136–42; Page 1920; Slater 2008, 81–3)). Nevertheless, the close spatial association of marketplace and parish church is still much in evidence, although obscured to varying extents by later infilling (Figure 64). But there is another important feature which distinguishes most twelfth- and early-thirteenth-century towns from earlier urban centres: fewer were associated with places of ancient importance. Hemel, although a large manor, had no very distinguished antecedents; Bushey and Barkway appear as rather minor places in Domesday; Watford, Baldock and Royston do not appear there at all (Forsyth 2008, 277–8; Bailey 2008; Slater 2008).

Town formation continued into the later thirteenth and fourteenth centuries, but the trends already noted intensified. Not only did almost all these relatively late creations have fairly small marketplaces, occupying slight widenings in major roads but, in addition, the spatial association of church and marketplace, so obvious in earlier towns, is now much less evident. At King's Langley, for example, the marketplace, now the High Street, is parallel to the line of the old main road running along the Gade valley (it was called New Chipping in a document of 1416) and thus some way from the parish church (Smith 1992, 138–40). Stevenage is perhaps the most dramatic case. A market grant was received in 1281: the marketplace was located on what was in the process of becoming the Great North Road. It was fairly large by contemporary standards, but was nearly a kilometre away from what was presumably the site of the Domesday manor, and probable original focus of settlement in the parish, beside the parish church of St Nicholas (Figure 64) (Munby 1977, 99–100; Slater 2008, 81–3). In the more crowded and cluttered world of the later thirteenth and fourteenth centuries it was more difficult to create open spaces where none had existed before, particularly in symbolically significant locations, and markets and associated plots frequently had to be slotted into any available space, often (as here) an area of common land sometimes lying at a significant distance from existing settlement, church or manor.

These later towns were even less closely associated with places of ancient importance than those which appeared in the twelfth and early thirteenth centuries. Nor were they usually established on the manors of great magnates and prelates. Town-making was now mainly the work of minor local lords, who often had more optimism than sound economic sense. The lord of Popes Hall manor in Buckland, on Ermine Street in east Hertfordshire, obtained the right to hold a market and a three-day fair at a place called 'New Chipping' (from the Old English *ciepping*, market) in 1252. The enterprise was a failure and Chipping remains today a minor hamlet on the A10. The site had no clear advantages which would draw trade from Royston, only seven kilometres to the north. Whether markets had ceased to be held here before 1258, when the lord of Buckland manor obtained a grant to establish a market a little further north along Ermine Street, in Buckland village, remains unclear; but this attempt, similarly, met with little success. Instead a town developed at Buntingford, some eleven kilometres to the south of Royston, at a point where Ermine Street crosses the River Rib, and is itself crossed by an east–west route leading from Baldock to the Pelhams. No vill of this name appears in Domesday Book and in 1288 the place was described as a hamlet, but by 1292 a chapel to St John the Baptist had been erected here. A marketplace was created in a widening of Ermine Street and the town prospered, but only later became a separate parish, carved out of Aspenden, Layston, Throcking and Wyddial (Munby 1977, 100–1).

The earlier, abortive attempts to create a town on Ermine Street were not unusual: and compared with towns established before *c.*1250 relatively few of the places receiving market grants or charters in the later thirteenth or fourteenth centuries were particularly successful. Stevenage, Sawbridgeworth, Hatfield and Tring had great futures ahead of them but settlements such as Codicote, Bygrave, Eastwick, Digswell and King's Langley always remained as little more than villages. Most towns created before *c.*1250 grew up (or were established) at places of ancient importance and/or occupied locations of particular economic significance in the landscape, such as the highest point of navigation on major rivers (Hertford) or the junctions of major routeways (Royston). The newer creations, in contrast, were often much more artificial beasts and – like Chipping, or Buckland – had to compete with well-established, more advantageously positioned neighbours. The fate of towns was shaped by wide economic and geographical factors, not simply by the whims of their founders, and location was the key to success or failure.

In this context, it is noteworthy that most of the towns which were established in the post-Conquest period were on major roads to London – many functioned primarily as collecting centres for grain, livestock and other produce destined for the capital. By the later Middle Ages most of the principal markets were on one of the three main roads leading through and out of the county: the present A411 (Bushey, Watford, King's Langley, Hemel, Berkhamsted, Tring); the Great North Road (Chipping Barnet, Hatfield, Stevenage, Baldock); and Ermine Street (Cheshunt, Hoddesdon, Ware, Buntingford, Royston) (Bailey 2008, 52–5; Smith 1992, 136). But the proximity of London served to constrain as much as to stimulate urban development: the large numbers of roads passing through the county *en route* for the capital ensured that most of its urban centres remained small – in the early fourteenth century St Albans was the only Hertfordshire town of any real size (Bailey *et al.* 1998, xxv; Bailey 2008, 55–6). Transport by road, however, especially of heavy or bulky goods, was more difficult than transport by river, and while many of the county's rivers might be locally navigable by small boats, large commercial craft could only use the Lea, navigable as far as Hertford. This presumably explains the particularly tight cluster of urban centres which developed in the east of the county: Hertford, Ware and Stanstead Abbots, with a penumbra of smaller centres at Cheshunt, Hoddesdon and Sawbridgeworth. Grain for London, grown on the rich soils of eastern Hertfordshire and western Essex, was a key commodity, and in 1247 London merchants erected a granary at Stanstead St Margaret's, from which wheat and barley could be taken by boats to the metropolis (Kiln and Partridge 1995, 109).

Navigable rivers drew trade from many miles around, and the highest navigable point on any river was of critical economic significance, hence the significance of the dispute between Hertford and Ware in 1274, when the bailiffs at Ware were said to have deliberately neglected the weirs there, so that boats could no longer pass upriver. This was part of a long and complex history of rivalry between the two towns. Ware was better placed in terms not only of river traffic, but also of terrestrial, as it stood on Ermine Street, the main road from London to the north-east. The bridge across the Lea had disappeared some time in the early post-Roman period, encouraging traffic to divert to Hertford, where the Lea could be more easily forded. It is unclear when a bridge was re-established here, but in 1191 there is a reference to the bridge here 'having been broken down by the men of Hertford', while in 1211–14 Sayer de Quincey, Justiciar of England and lord of the manor of Ware, removed the blocks and chains which the bailiff of Hertford had erected to obstruct the bridge (Kiln and Partridge 1995, 108–14).

After the Middle Ages

This is not the place to discuss the development of Hertfordshire, its people and its landscape in the period after the Middle Ages. It is sufficient to say that London's steady growth ensured that its impact on the county, and on the lives of its inhabitants, increased inexorably, further stimulating the expansion of towns and villages on the main roads leading to it, influencing the development of its agricultural economy and much else. This influence was strongest in the south of the county, and by the eighteenth century affected the landscape in many ways – most notably perhaps in the high density of landscape parks and gentleman's residences to be found there (Williamson 2007; Spooner 2009). Of course, many other factors combined with the proximity of the capital to mould Hertfordshire's geography, in particular variations in soil type, which had an important effect on farming practices. Thus the development of the Chiltern Dipslope, with its emphasis on sheep and grain production, diverged from that of the Southern Uplands, whose heavy soils (and proximity to London) continued to encourage an emphasis on pastoral farming (and eventually hay production), or the dissected Boulder Clay Plateau, where grain-growing (increasingly barley for malting, an industry still so evident in the architecture of Hertford or Ware) was combined with both sheep and cattle farming.

Yet among such factors we must include the continuing influence of the geographical structures established before the Norman Conquest. Many of the county's principal eighteenth-century towns, for example – Berkhamsted, Bishop's Stortford, Cheshunt, Hertford, Hitchin, St Albans, Ware and Welwyn – had probably been important central places, the centres of great estates, in the middle Saxon period. Some had arguably first risen to a kind of prominence in Roman times, or even before. Equally influential in moulding the character of the county in the post-medieval centuries was the enduring contrast between vale, scarp and valley on the one hand, and clay-covered uplands on the other. Almost all the principal urban settlements of the eighteenth century were thus in 'primary' locations, in vale or valley: only Stevenage, and to some extent Watford, break the ancient pattern. The largest villages also tended to remain in the main valleys, with the clay uplands continuing to be characterised, as they had long been, by more scattered, dispersed settlement.

The contrast between 'river and wold' was not at first lessened by the admittedly muted impact of industrialisation upon Hertfordshire. The county's main industries, brewing, malting and paper-making, needed large amounts of water and were therefore valley-based (Johnson 1970, 28–61), leading by the mid nineteenth century to the striking contrast between, for example, the valley of the Gade to the south of Hemel Hempstead, with its mills and factories, and the more rural aspect of the adjacent plateaux. The first railway line in Hertfordshire – the London–Birmingham–Manchester line, opened in 1837 – followed this same valley. Later lines, however, tended to strike out from the valleys, cutting dramatically across the interfluves. By the end of the nineteenth century the rail network, together with steady improvements to the principal roads to London, was encouraging the spread of new suburbs in the south of the county, especially on the poor soils of the Southern Uplands. Indeed, a marked contrast steadily developed in this respect between the south-west and the north-east of the county. When the Victoria County History was published at the start of the twentieth century

Barnet had become the terminus of the electric tramway to Highgate, and many new houses had lately been erected there (Page 1908, 329): in contrast, at Clothall and Bygrave, in the far north of the county, the medieval open fields still remained unenclosed. Expansion of population in what had earlier been the most sparsely settled regions of the county led to the disruption of traditional administrative structures, with the upgrading of old chapelries to independent parishes and the appearance in some cases of entirely new parishes, both ecclesiastical and civil.

By 1941 the same dichotomy between the north-east and south-west of the county was highlighted by the authors of the Land Utilisation Survey for Hertfordshire. Watford and Barnet were 'largely dormitory areas for London in which the dwellers owe little allegiance to the old centres on the fringe of which they now reside'. Other market towns in the west had 'entered a new phase: fast and efficient transport to London and to the Midlands combined with a local labour supply have attracted many light industries and much of south-west Hertfordshire has thus become greatly industrialised' (Cameron 1941, 336). In contrast, factories and dormitory settlement were 'less marked in the eastern two-thirds of Hertfordshire', although there were signs of change, with the development in the first half of the century of the two Garden Cities of Letchworth and Welwyn – arguably two of the most important features of Hertfordshire's historic landscape heritage.

The post-war period saw the development of New Towns at Hatfield, Hemel Hempstead and Stevenage, a steady increase in car ownership and improvements in the road network which culminated in the opening of the M11 in 1980; this, together with the development of Stansted as London's third airport, further eroded the isolation of the north-east. This area nevertheless remains the most rural part of the county, even if changes in farming (especially an ever-increasing concentration on purely arable production, mechanisation and a steady growth in farm size) have ensured that much of its ancient landscape has been simplified by the removal of hedges, copses and ancient meadows, and that many of its former farms are now the homes of well-to-do London commuters (Figure 65).

In spite of such changes, the fabric of the ancient landscape often remains remarkably intact here. Yet even in the more urbanised south the patterns of the past endure, often in surprising ways. Some of the roads in Hemel Hempstead New Town have fossilised the ancient co-axial patterns of the countryside they replaced. The names of modern housing estates, such as

Figure 65. Typical rolling boulder-clay countryside in north-east Hertfordshire. This remains the most rural part of the county.

Meriden in Watford, preserve those of obscure Saxon farms and hamlets. Even the names of the new local authorities established in the 1970s sometimes refer back to antiquity: that of Dacorum, for example, carries an echo of the transient Danish occupation of west Hertfordshire in the late ninth century.

Continuity with the past is all around us: and continuity is what this book has emphasised, perhaps over-emphasised, throughout. Even in a patently artificial county like Hertfordshire many of the essential structures of medieval geography were established in the Saxon period: some first emerged before the Roman Conquest. Continuity does not mean stasis, however: some features of human geography have, for a variety of reasons, proved more persistent than others. St Albans maintained into the late Middle Ages the role it had first developed in the late Iron Age – that of great cult centre (Figure 66). Braughing, in contrast, important Iron Age *oppidum* and second most important settlement in Roman Hertfordshire, was by late medieval times not much more than a village. Nevertheless, in Hertfordshire, as elsewhere, successive societies have seldom begun from scratch, creating

Figure 66. The medieval church of St Albans Abbey viewed through the walls of Roman Verulamium: a striking image of continuity.

new spatial patterns unrelated to what has gone before. Radically new social forms might develop, but they generally did so within ancient frameworks – partly because of essential conservatism, partly because of the constancy of the constraints imposed by environment and topography.

In some ways this book has been a sustained exercise in speculation. Where the evidence is thin, we either say nothing or go rather further beyond it than we might like. And when we turn our back for a second, statements that began life as tentative hypotheses soon pick up the nasty habit of masquerading as facts. In this revised edition, while a number of suggestions made in the original book (2000) have been confirmed by new evidence, others have not, and have thus either been downplayed or quietly dropped altogether. As the researches of Hertfordshire's many able historians and archaeologists continue, other suggestions made here will doubtless need to be revised or rejected. Indeed, I hope this volume may encourage others to examine the long and complex interplay between society and topography, stasis and change, that have made Hertfordshire what it is today.

Bibliography

Ager, B.M. (1989) 'The Anglo-Saxon cemetery', in I. Stead and V. Rigby (eds), *Verulamium: the King Harry Lane site* (London), 219–39.

Applebaum, E.S. (1949) 'Excavations at Wilbury Hill, an Iron Age hill-fort near Letchworth, Herts, 1933', *Archaeological Journal*, 106, 12–45.

Astle, T., Ayscough, S. and Caley, J. (eds) (1802) *Taxatio Ecclesiastica Angliae et Walliae Auctoritate P.Nicholai IV circa AD 1291* (London).

Austin, P. (1995) 'Hatfield Great Wood and its enclosure', *Hertfordshire's Past*, 38, 2–7.

Bailey, K. (1989) 'The Middle Saxons', in S.J. Bassett (ed.), *The origins of Anglo-Saxon kingdoms* (Leicester), 108–22.

Bailey, M. (2008) 'The economy of towns and markets, 1100–1500', in T. Slater and N. Goose (eds), *A county of small towns: the development of Hertfordshire's urban landscape to 1800* (Hatfield), 46–66.

Bailey, M., Brooker, J. and Flood, S. (1998) *Hertfordshire Lay Subsidy Rolls 1307 and 1334* (Hertford).

Baker, J. (2006) *Cultural transition in the Chilterns and Essex region, 350 AD to 650 AD* (Hatfield).

Baring, F.F. (1898) 'The Conqueror's footprints in Domesday', *English Historical Review*, 19, 17–25.

Barton, P. (1981) *Manorial economy and society in Shenley: a Hertfordshire manor in the 13th and 14th centuries* (Hertford).

Bassett, S.J. (1989) 'In search of the origins of Anglo-Saxon kingdoms', in S.J. Bassett (ed.), *The origins of Anglo-Saxon kingdoms* (Leicester), 3–27.

Beresford, M. (1967) *New towns of the Middle Ages* (London).

Biddle, M. and Kjolbye-Biddle, B. (1981) 'England's premier abbey: the medieval chapter house of St Albans and its excavation in 1978', *Hertfordshire's Past*, 11, 3–29.

Biddle, M. and Kjolbye-Biddle, B. (2001) 'The origins of St Albans Abbey: Romano-British cemetery and Anglo-Saxon monastery', in M. Henig and P. Lindley (eds), *Alban and St Albans: Roman and medieval architecture, art and archaeology* (Leeds), 45–77.

Birch, W. de Gray (1885–9) *Cartularium Saxonicum: a collection of charters relating to Anglo-Saxon history*, 4 vols (London).

Blair, J. (1985) 'Secular minster churches in Domesday Book', in P. Sawyer (ed.), *Domesday Book: a reassessment* (London), 104–42.

Blair, J. (1988) 'Minsters in the landscape', in D. Hooke (ed.), *Anglo-Saxon Settlements* (Oxford), 35–58.

Blair, J. (2005) *The church in Anglo-Saxon England* (Oxford).

Borrill, H. (1981) 'Hertford: early settlement and recent excavations', *Hertfordshire's Past*, 10, 15–20.

Branigan, K. (1985) *The Catuvellauni* (London).

Branigan, K. and Niblett, R. (2005) *The Roman Chilterns* (Great Missenden).

Brooks, H. and Bedwin, O. (1989) *Archaeology at the airport: the Stansted archaeological project 1985–1989* (Chelmsford).

Brown, W. Newman (1992) 'A Roman settlement in Aldenham?', *Hertfordshire's Past*, 33, 34–5.

Bryant, S. (1995) 'The late Bronze Age to the middle Iron Age of the north Chilterns', in R. Holgate (ed.), *Chiltern archaeology: recent work* (Dunstable), 17–27.

Bryant, S. and Burleigh, G. (1995) 'Late prehistoric dykes of the eastern Chilterns', in R. Holgate (ed.), *Chiltern archaeology: recent work* (Dunstable), 92–5.

Bryant, S. and Niblett, R. (1997) 'The late Iron Age in Hertfordshire and the north Chilterns', in A. Gwilt and C. Haselgrove (eds), *Reconstructing Iron Age societies* (Oxford), 271–81.

Bryant, S., Perry, B. and Williamson, T. (2005) 'A "relict landscape" in south-east Hertfordshire: archaeological and topographic investigations in the Wormley area', *Landscape History* 27, 5–15.

Buckler, I.C. and Buckler, C.A. (1847) *A history of the architecture of the abbey church of St Alban* (London).

Burleigh, G.R. (1980) 'Excavations at the Mile Ditches, near Royston, 1978', *Hertfordshire's Past* 12, 3–18.

Burleigh, G.R. (1982) 'Excavations at Baldock, 1980–81', *Hertfordshire's Past*, 12, 3–12.

Burleigh, G.R. (1995) 'A late Iron Age *oppidum* at Baldock, Hertfordshire', in R. Holgate (ed.), *Chiltern archaeology: recent work* (Dunstable), 103–12.

Burnham, B.C. and Wacher, J. (1990) *The 'small towns' of Roman Britain* (London).

Cam, H.H. (1930) *The hundred and the hundred rolls* (London).

Cameron, L.G. (1941) *The land of Britain, Part 80: Hertfordshire* (London).

Campbell, B. (2000) *English seigniorial agriculture 1250–1450* (Cambridge).

Campbell, E.M. (1962) 'Hertfordshire', in H.C. Darby and E.M. Campbell (eds), *The Domesday geography of south-east England* (Cambridge).

Catt, J. (1978) 'The contribution of loess to soils in lowland Britain', in S. Limbrey and J.G. Evans (eds), *The effects of man on the landscape: the lowland zone*, CBA Research Report 21 (London).

Chauncy, Sir H. (1700) *The historical antiquities of Hertfordshire* (London).

Colgrave, B. and Mynors, R.A.B. (1991) *Bede's ecclesiastical history of the English people*, revised edn (Oxford).

Crick, J. (ed.) (2007) *Charters of St Albans* (Oxford).

Cunliffe, B. (1968) *Iron Age communities in Britain* (London).

Cunliffe, B. (1995) *Iron Age Britain* (London).

Curry, D. (1992) 'Tertiary', in D. Duff and A. Smith (eds), *The geology of England and Wales* (London).

Cushion, B. (2008) *Braughing: woodland archaeological earthwork surveys*, unpublished report for Hertfordshire County Council Environmental Department.

Darby, H.C. (1977) *Domesday England* (Cambridge).

Dark, K. (1994) *Civitas to kingdom: British political continuity 300–800* (Leicester).

Darvill, T. (1996) *Prehistoric Britain* (London).

Davies, W. and Vierck, H. (1974) 'The contexts of the Tribal Hidage: social aggregates and settlement patterns', *Fruhmittelalterliche Studia* 8, 223–93.

Davis, R.H.C. (1982) 'Alfred and Guthrum's frontier', *English Historical Review*, 97, 803–10.

Doggett, N. (1981) 'The parish churches of Dacorum: how they reflect social history', *Hertfordshire's Past*, 11, 28–36.

Doggett, N. (1988) 'Medieval church dedications in Hertfordshire', *Hertfordshire's Past*, 25, 22–30.

Doggett, N. (1989) 'Medieval church dedications in Hertfordshire (concluded)', *Hertfordshire's Past*, 26, 9–16.

Doggett, N. (1993) 'Medieval church dedications: two early eighteenth-century lists', *Hertfordshire's Past*, 35, 14–17.

Doggett, N. and Hunn, J. (1985) 'The origins and development of medieval Berkhamsted', *Hertfordshire's Past*, 18, 18–36.

Drury, P. and Rodwell, W. (1980) 'Settlement in the later Iron Age and Roman periods', in D.G. Buckley (ed.), *The Archaeology of Essex to AD 1500*, CBA Research Report 34 (London), 59–75.

Dumville, D. (1989) 'Essex, Middle Anglia, and the expansion of Mercia in the south-east Midlands', in S.J. Bassett (ed.), *The origins of Anglo-Saxon kingdoms* (Leicester), 123–40.

Dumville, D. (1992) *Wessex and England from Alfred to Edgar: six essays in political, cultural and ecclesiastical revival* (Woodbridge).

Dyer, J.F. (1961) 'Dray's Ditches, Bedfordshire, and early Iron Age territorial boundaries in the Chilterns', *Antiquaries Journal*, 118, 32–43.

Dyer, J.F. (1963) 'The Chiltern Grim's Ditch', *Antiquity* 37, 46–9.

Dyer, J.F. (1976) 'Ravensburgh Castle, Hertfordshire', in D.W. Harding (ed.), *Hillforts: later prehistoric earthworks in Britain and Ireland* (London), 153–9.

Ekwall, E. (1928) *English River Names* (Oxford).

Ely, K.D. and Edwards, K. (2003) *Cheshunt Park, Hertfordshire. An archaeological investigation by the Time Team*. Unpublished report, Bristol.

Everitt, A. (1977) 'River and wold: reflections on the historical origins of regions and *pays*', *Journal of Historical Geography*, 3, 1–19.

Everitt, A. (1979) 'Country, county and town: patterns of regional evolution in England', *Transactions of the Royal Historical Society*, 5th series, 29, 79–108.

Everitt, A. (1986) *Continuity and colonisation: the evolution of Kentish settlement* (Leicester).

Faith, R. (1997) *The English peasantry and the growth of lordship* (Leicester).

Fleming, A. (1978) 'The prehistoric landscape of Dartmoor, Part 1: South Dartmoor', *Proceedings of the Prehistoric Society*, 44, 97–124.

Fleming, A. (1983) 'The prehistoric landscape of Dartmoor, Part 2: North and East Dartmoor', *Proceedings of the Prehistoric Society,* 49, 195–241.

Fleming, A. (1984) 'The prehistoric landscape of Dartmoor: wider implications', *Landscape History,* 6, 5–19.

Fleming, A. (1988) *The Dartmoor Reaves* (London).

Fleming, R. (1986) 'Domesday Book and the tenurial revolution', *Proceedings of the Battle Conference,* 9, 87–101.

Fleming, R. (1991) *Kings and lords in conquest England* (Cambridge).

Forsyth, M. (2008) 'The establishment and development of Watford', in T. Slater and N. Goose (eds), *A county of small towns: the development of Hertfordshire's urban landscape to 1800* (Hatfield), 276–300.

Freeman, I. (1977) 'The boundary hedge of Saxon Wheathampstead', *Hertfordshire's Past,* 4, 14–22.

Frere, S.S. (1972) *Verulamium excavations, volume I,* Society of Antiquaries Research Report 28 (London).

Frere, S.S. (1983) *Verulamium excavations, volume II,* Society of Antiquaries Research Report 40 (London).

Frere, S.S. (1984) *Verulamium excavations, volume III,* Oxford University Archaeological Committee Monograph 1 (Oxford).

Friel, I. (1982) 'The Hicce – an Anglo-Saxon tribe of the Hitchin area', *Hertfordshire's Past,* 13, 2–18.

Gardiner, H.W. (1967) *A survey of the agriculture of Hertfordshire,* Royal Agricultural Society of England County Agricultural Surveys 5 (London).

Garfi, S. (1995) 'Appendix A: the Hertford burghs – a survey of the evidence', in R.J. Kiln and C.R. Partridge (eds), *Ware and Hertford: the story of two towns from birth to middle age* (Welwyn Garden City), 115–27.

Gelling, M. (1975) 'Further thoughts on pagan place names', in K. Cameron (ed.), *Place name evidence for the Anglo-Saxon invasions and the Scandinavian settlements* (Nottingham).

Gelling, M. (1978) *Signposts to the Past* (London).

Gelling, M. (1979) *The early charters of the Thames valley* (Leicester).

Gelling, M. (1984) *Place names in the landscape* (London).

Giles, J.A. (ed.) (1866) *William of Malmesbury's chronicle of the kings of England* (London).

Golding, B. (1986) 'Wealth and artistic patronage at twelfth-century St Albans', in S. Macready and F.H. Thompson (eds) *Art and Patronage in the English Romanesque* (London).

Goodburn, R. (1976) 'Roman Britain in 1975', *Britannia,* 7, 290–377.

Gover, J.E.B., Mawer, A. and Stenton, F.M. (1938) *The place-names of Hertfordshire* (Cambridge).

Hamerow, H. (1991) 'Settlement mobility and the "middle Saxon shift": rural settlements and settlement patterns in Anglo-Saxon England', *Anglo-Saxon England,* 20, 1–17.

Handford, S.A. (ed.) (1951) *Caesar: the conquest of Gaul* (Harmondsworth).

Harrison, S. (2003) 'The Icknield Way: some queries', *Archaeological Journal,* 160, 1–22.

Hart, C. (1971) 'The Tribal Hidage', *Transactions of the Royal Historical Society,* 21, 133–57.

Hart, C. (1977) 'The kingdom of Mercia', in A. Dornier (ed.), *Mercian studies* (Leicester), 43–62.

Haselgrove, C. and Millett, M. (1997) 'Verlamion reconsidered', in A. Gwilt and C. Haselgrove (eds), *Reconstructing Iron Age societies* (Oxford), 282–96.

Higham, N. (1995) *An English empire: Bede and the early Anglo-Saxon kings* (Manchester).

Hill, J.D. (1995) *Ritual and rubbish in the Iron Age of Wessex*, BAR British Series 242 (Oxford).

Hill, J.D. (1999) 'Settlement, landscape and regionality: Norfolk and Suffolk in the pre-Roman Iron Age of Britain and beyond', in J. Davies and T. Williamson (eds), *Land of the Iceni: the Iron Age of northern East Anglia* (Norwich), 185–205.

Hills, C. (1998) 'Early historic Britain', in J. Hunter and I. Ralston (eds), *The archaeology of Britain: an introduction from the upper Palaeolithic to the Industrial Revolution* (London), 176–93.

Hines, J. (1984) *The Scandinavian character of Anglian England in the pre-Viking period*, BAR British Series 124 (Oxford).

Hingley, R. (1984) 'Towards social analysis in archaeology: Celtic society in the Iron Age of the upper Thames valley', in B.W. Cunliffe and D. Miles (eds), *Aspects of the Iron Age in central southern Britain* (Oxford).

Hodder, I. (1979) 'Pre-Roman and Romano-British tribal economies', in B. Burnham and H. Johnson (eds), *Invasion and response: the case of Roman Britain*, BAR British Series 73 (Oxford), 197–210.

Hodge, C., Burton, R., Corbett, W., Evans, R. and Seale, R. (1984) *Soils and their uses in Eastern England* (Harpenden).

Hodges, R. (1989) *The Anglo-Saxon achievement: archaeology and the beginnings of English society* (London).

Holgate, R. (1988) *Neolithic settlement of the Thames valley*, BAR British Series 194 (Oxford).

Holgate, R. (1995) 'Early prehistoric settlement of the Chilterns', in R. Holgate (ed.), *Chiltern archaeology: recent work* (Dunstable), 3–16.

Holmes, J. and Frend, W. (1959) 'A Belgic chieftain's grave at Hertford Heath', *Transactions of the East Hertfordshire Archaeological Society,* 14, 1–19.

Hooke, D. (1981) *Anglo-Saxon landscapes of the West Midlands: the charter evidence*, BAR British Series 95 (Oxford).

Hooke, D. (1998) *The landscape of Anglo-Saxon England* (Leicester).

Howlett, B. (2008) 'Manorial estate and market town: the early development of Hitchin', in T. Slater and N. Goose (eds), *A county of small towns: the development of Hertfordshire's urban landscape to 1800* (Hatfield), 188–223.

Hunn, J.R. (1994) *Reconstruction and measurement of landscape change*, BAR British Series 236 (Oxford).

Hunn, J.R. (1996) *Settlement patterns in Hertfordshire: a review of the typology and function of enclosures in the Iron Age and Roman landscape*, BAR British Series 249 (Oxford).

Hunn, J.R. (2004) *Tytenhanger: excavation and survey in the parish of Ridge*, BAR British Series (Oxford).

Jacobi, R.M. (1978) 'Population and landscape in Mesolithic lowland Britain', in S. Limbrey and J.C. Evans (eds), *The effects of man on the landscape: the lowland zone*, CBA Research Report 21 (London).

Jacobi, R.M. (1980) 'The upper Palaeolithic of Britain with special reference to Wales', in J.A. Taylor (ed.), *Culture and environment in prehistoric Wales*, BAR British Series 76 (Oxford), 15–100.

Javes, G.A. (1992) 'The medieval Barnets', *Hertfordshire's Past*, 33, 1–6.

Jewell, H. (1972) *English local administration in the Middle Ages* (Newton Abbot).

Johnson, W. Branch (1970) *The industrial archaeology of Hertfordshire* (Newton Abbot).

Jones, G. (1971) 'The multiple estate as a model framework for tracing early stages in the evolution of rural settlement', in F. Dussart (ed.), *L'Habitat at les Paysages Rureaux d'Europe* (Liege), 251–67.

Jones, G. (1979) 'Multiple estates and early settlement', in P. Sawyer (ed.), *English medieval settlement* (London), 9–34.

Jones, G. (2007) *Saints in the landscape* (Stroud).

Kerridge, E. (1992) *The common fields of England* (Manchester).

Keynes, S. (1993) 'A lost cartulary of St Albans Abbey', *Anglo-Saxon England*, 22, 253–79.

Keynes, S. (1998) 'King Alfred and the Mercians', in M.A.S. Blackburn and D.N. Dumville (eds), *Kings, currency and alliances: history and coinage of southern England in the ninth century* (Woodbridge), 1– 45.

Kiln, R.J. and Partridge, C.R. (1995) *Ware and Hertford: the story of two towns from birth to middle age* (Welwyn Garden City).

Kirby, D. (1991) *The earliest English kings* (London).

Landon, M. (2009) 'Making a mint: the archaeology of a late Iron Age industry', *Current Archaeology*, 234, 5.

Le Quesne, C., Capon, L. and Stevens, T. (2001) *Post-excavation assessment of The Grove Estate, Watford*, Unpublished report, Hertfordshire County Council Environmental Department.

Levett, A.E. (1938) *Studies in manorial history* (Oxford).

Levison, W. (1941) 'St Albans and St Alban', *Antiquity*, 15, 337–59.

Liddiard, R. (2000) *Landscapes of lordship: Norman castles and the countryside in medieval Norfolk, 1066–1200*, BAR British Series 309 (Oxford).

Lilley, K. (2002) *Urban life in the Middle Ages* (Basingstoke).

Longman, G. (1976) 'The origins of Watford', *Hertfordshire's Past*, 2, 7–11.

Luard, H.R. (ed.) (1872) *The Chronica Majora of Matthew of Paris* (London).

Lucy, S. (2000) *The Anglo-Saxon way of death: burial rites in early England* (Stroud).

MacDonald, T. (1995) 'The A41 project, Hertfordshire Archaeological Trust', in R. Holgate (ed.), *Chiltern archaeology: recent work* (Dunstable), 120–3.

Maitland, F.W. (1897) *Domesday Book and beyond* (Cambridge).

Mawer, A. and Stenton, F.M. (1926) *The place-names of Bedfordshire and Huntingdonshire* (Cambridge).

Millward, D., Ellison, R.A., Lake, R.D. and Loorlock, B.S. (1987) *The geology of the country around Epping: memoir for the 1:50,000 Sheet 240 of the British Geological Survey* (London).

Morris, M. and Wainwright, A. (1995) 'Iron Age and Romano-British settlement and economy in the Upper Bulbourne Valley, Hertfordshire', in R. Holgate (ed.), *Chiltern archaeology: recent work* (Dunstable).

Morris, R. (1989) *Churches in the landscape* (London).

Moss Eccardt, J. (1988) 'Archaeological investigations in the Letchworth area, 1958–1974', *Proceedings of the Cambridgeshire Antiquarian Society,* 77, 35–103.

Munby, L. (ed.) (1973) *The settlement of Wheathampstead and Harpenden* (Harpenden).

Munby, L. (1977) *The Hertfordshire landscape* (London).

Myres, J.N.L. (1960) 'Pelagius and the end of Roman rule in Britain', *Journal of Roman Studies,* 50, 21–36.

Neal, D.S., Wardle, A. and Hunn, J. (1990) *Excavations of the Iron Age, Roman and medieval settlement at Gorhambury, St Albans,* English Heritage Archaeological Reports 14 (London).

Niblett, R. (1992) 'A Catauvellaunian chieftain's burial from St Albans', *Antiquity,* 66, 917–29.

Niblett, R. (1993) 'Verulamium since the Wheelers', in S.J. Greep (ed.), *Roman towns, the Wheeler inheritance: a review of fifty years' research,* CBA Research Report 93 (London), 78–93.

Niblett, R. (1995a) 'A new site at Verulamium (St Albans)', in R. Holgate (ed.), *Chiltern archaeology: recent work* (Dunstable), 96–102.

Niblett, R. (1995b) *Roman Hertfordshire* (Wimbourne).

Niblett, R. (1999) *The excavation of a ceremonial site at Folly Lane, Verulamium,* Britannia Monograph 14 (London).

Niblett, R. and Thompson, I. (2005) *Alban's buried towns: an assessment of St Albans' archaeology to AD 1600* (Oxford).

Ollard, S.L, Crosse, G. and Bond, M. (1948) *A dictionary of English church history,* 3rd edn (London).

Page, W. (1905–6) 'Kingsbury Castle', *Transactions of the St Albans and Hertfordshire Architectural and Archaeological Society,* 2, 149–57.

Page, W. (1908) *The Victoria History of the County of Hertford,* vol. II (London).

Page, W. (1912) *The Victoria History of the County of Hertford,* vol. III (London).

Page, W. (1920) 'The origins and forms of Hertfordshire towns and villages', *Archaeologia,* 69, 47–60.

Parker Pearson, M. (1993) *Bronze Age Britain* (London).

Parker Pearson, M., van de Noort, R. and Woolf, A. (1993) 'Three men and a boat: Sutton Hoo and the East Anglian kingdom', *Anglo-Saxon England,* 22, 27–50.

Partridge, C. (1977) 'Excavations and fieldwork at Braughing 1968–73', *Hertfordshire Archaeology,* 5, 22–108.

Partridge, C. (1979) 'Excavations at Puckeridge and Braughing 1975–79', *Hertfordshire Archaeology,* 7, 28–132.

Partridge, C. (1980) 'Late Bronze Age artefacts from Hertford Heath, Hertfordshire', *Hertfordshire Archaeology,* 7, 1–9.

Partridge, C. (1981) *Skeleton Green: a late Iron Age and Romano-British site,* Britannia Monograph 2 (London).

Partridge, C. (1989) *Foxholes Farm: a multi-period gravel site,* Hertfordshire Archaeological Trust Monograph (Hertford).

Partridge, C. (2008) 'Hertford and Ware: archaeological perspectives from birth to middle age', in T. Slater and N. Goose (eds), *A county of small towns: the development of Hertfordshire's urban landscape to 1800* (Hatfield), 127–58.

Pevsner, N. and Cherry, B. (1977) *The buildings of England: Hertfordshire*, 2nd edn (Harmondsworth).

Phythian-Adams, C. (1987) *Rethinking English local history* (Leicester).

Phythian-Adams, C. (1993) *Societies, cultures and kinship 1580–1850: cultural provinces and English local history* (Leicester).

Plowman, D. (2008) 'Royston: a thirteenth-century planned town?', in T. Slater and N. Goose (eds), *A county of small towns: the development of Hertfordshire's urban landscape to 1800* (Hatfield), 173–87.

Rackham, O. (1976) *Trees and woodland in the British landscape* (London).

Rackham, O. (1986) *The history of the countryside* (London).

Renn, D. (1971) *Medieval castles in Hertfordshire* (Chichester).

Riley, H.T. (ed.) (1867) *Gesta Abbatum Monasterii S.Albani*, vols I and II (London).

Riley, H.T. (ed.) (1908) *Ingulph's chronicle of the Abbey of Croyland* (London).

Roberts, E. (1977) 'Parish church studies: an analysis of Hertfordshire plans', *Hertfordshire's Past*, 4, 22–7.

Roden, D. (1973) 'Field systems of the Chiltern Hills and their environs', in A.H.R. Baker and R.A. Butlin (eds), *Studies of field systems in the British Isles* (Cambridge), 325–76.

Rodwell, W. (1975) 'Trinovantian towns in their setting', in R. Rodwell and T. Rowley (eds), *The small towns of Roman Britain*, BAR British Series 15 (Oxford), 85–102.

Rodwell, W. (1978) 'Relict landscapes in Essex', in H.C. Bowen and P.J. Fowler (eds), *Early land allotment*, BAR 48 (London), 89–98.

Roe, D.A. (1981) *The lower and middle Palaeolithic periods in Britain* (London).

Rook, A.G. (1968) 'Investigations of a Belgic occupation site at Crookhams, Welwyn Garden City', *Hertfordshire Archaeology*, 1, 51–65.

Rook, A.G. (1970a) 'A Belgic and Roman site at Brickwall Hill, Welwyn Garden City', *Hertfordshire Archaeology*, 2, 23–30.

Rook, A.G. (1970b) 'Investigation of a Belgic site at Grubs Barn, Welwyn Garden City', *Hertfordshire Archaeology*, 2, 31–6.

Rook, A.G. (1974) 'Welch's Farm', *Hertfordshire Archaeological Review*, 9, 170.

Rook, A.G. (1986) 'The Roman villa site at Dicket Mead, Lockleys, Welwyn', *Hertfordshire Archaeology*, 9, 79–176.

Rowe, A. (2009) *Medieval parks of Hertfordshire* (Hatfield).

Rumble, A.R. (1977) 'The Wheathampstead (Herts) charter bounds, 1060: a corrected note and text on the boundary-points', *Journal of English Place-Name Studies*, 9, 6–11.

Rutherford Davis, K. (1973) *The deserted medieval villages of Hertfordshire* (Chichester).

Rutherford Davis, K. (1982) *Britons and Saxons: the Chiltern region 400–700* (Chichester).

Saunders, C. (1982) 'Some thoughts on the oppida at Wheathampstead and Verulamium', *Hertfordshire Archaeology*, 8, 31–9.

Saunders, C. and Havercroft, A.B. (1982a) 'Excavations on the line of the Wheathampstead by-pass, 1974 and 1977', *Hertfordshire Archaeology*, 8, 11–30.

Saunders, C. and Havercroft, A.B. (1982b) 'Excavations at St Helen's Church, Wheathampstead', *Hertfordshire Archaeology*, 8, 102–10.

Sawyer, P.H. (ed.) (1979) *English medieval settlement* (London).

Sayers, J. (1976) 'Monastic archdeacons', in C.N.L. Brooke (ed.) *Church and government in the Middle Ages* (Cambridge).

Sharpe, R. (2001) 'The late Passion of St Alban', in M. Henig and P. Lindley (eds), *Alban and St Albans: Roman and medieval architecture, art and archaeology* (Leeds), 30–7.

Sherlock, R.L. (1962) *British regional geology: London and the Thames valley* (London).

Sherwood, J. (2008) 'Influences on the growth and development of medieval and early modern Berkhamsted', in T. Slater and N. Goose (eds), *A county of small towns: the development of Hertfordshire's urban landscape to 1800* (Hatfield), 224–48.

Short, D. (1988) 'Braughing: a possible Saxon estate?', *Hertfordshire's Past*, 23, 8–15.

Short, D. (2008) 'Ashwell: an example of Anglo-Saxon town planning', in T. Slater and N. Goose (eds), *A county of small towns: the development of Hertfordshire's urban landscape to 1800* (Hatfield), 159–72.

Slater, T. (2008) 'Roads, commons and boundaries in the topography of Hertfordshire towns', in T. Slater and N. Goose (eds), *A county of small towns: the development of Hertfordshire's urban landscape to 1800* (Hatfield), 67–95.

Smith, J.T. (1992) *English houses 1200–1800: the Hertfordshire evidence* (London).

Smith, R.P. (1987) *Roadside settlements in lowland Roman Britain: a gazetteer and study of their origins, growth and decline*, BAR British Series 157 (Oxford).

Smith, T.P. (1973) *The Anglo-Saxon churches of Hertfordshire* (Chichester).

Spooner, S. (2009) 'Rural landscapes and urban mentalities in the eighteenth century', *Landscapes*, 10/1, 101–22.

Spratt, D. (1989) *The linear earthworks of the Tabular Hills, North Yorks.* (Sheffield).

Stainton, B. (1995) 'Field work by the Chess Valley Archaeological and Historical Society (CVAHS) in the Buckinghamshire Chilterns', in R. Holgate (ed.), *Chiltern archaeology: recent work* (Dunstable), 124–30.

Stead, I. and Rigby, V. (1986) *Baldock: the excavation of a Roman and pre-Roman settlement 1968–75*, Britannia Monograph 7 (London).

Stenton, F.M. (1971) *Anglo-Saxon England* (Oxford).

Stevenson, J. (ed.) (1864) *Florence of Worcester's history of the kings of England* (London).

Swanton, M. (ed.) (1996) *The Anglo-Saxon chronicle* (London).

Taylor, H.M. and Taylor, J. (1965) *Anglo-Saxon architecture* (Cambridge).

Taylor, P. (1995) 'Boundaries and margins: Barnet, Finchley and Totteridge', in M.J. Franklin and C. Harper-Bill (eds), *Medieval ecclesiastical studies in honour of Dorothy M. Owen* (Woodbridge), 259–79.

Taylor, P. (2008) 'Boundaries, margins and the delineation of the urban: the case of Barnet', in T. Slater and N. Goose (eds), *A county of small towns: the development of Hertfordshire's urban landscape to 1800* (Hatfield), 249–75.

Thomasson, A.J. (1969) 'Some aspects of the drift deposits and geomorphology of south-east Hertfordshire', *Proceedings of the Geological Association*, 72, 287–302.

Thomasson, A.J. and Avery, B.W. (1970) *The Soils of Hertfordshire,* (Harpenden).

Thompson, A. and Holland, E. (1977) 'Excavation of an Iron Age site at Dellfield, Berkhamsted', *Hertfordshire Archaeology*, 4, 137–48.

Weale, C. (1987) 'Churches and clergy in the Hertfordshire Domesday', *Hertfordshire's Past*, 23, 3–8.

Westell, W.P. (1931) 'A Romano-British cemetery at Baldock, Hertfordshire', *Archaeological Journal*, 88, 247–301.

Wheeler, R.E.M. (1935) *London and the Saxons* (London).

Wheeler, R.E.M. and Wheeler, T.V. (1936) *Verulamium: a Belgic and two Roman cities*, Society of Antiquaries Research Report (London).

Whitelock, D. (ed.) (1968) *The will of Æthelgifu* (Oxford).

Williamson, T. (1986) 'The development of settlement in north-west Essex: the results of a recent field survey', *Essex Archaeology and History*, 17, 120–32.

Williamson, T. (1987) 'Early co-axial field systems on the East Anglian boulder clays', *Proceedings of the Prehistoric Society*, 53, 419–31.

Williamson, T. (1988) 'Settlement, hierarchy and economy: a case study in north-west Essex', in K. Branigan and D. Miles (eds), *The economies of Romano-British villas* (Sheffield).

Williamson, T. (1993) *The origins of Norfolk* (Manchester).

Williamson, T. (1998) 'The "Scole–Dickleburgh Field System" revisited', *Landscape History*, 20, 19–28.

Williamson, T. (2003) *Shaping medieval landscapes* (Macclesfield).

Williamson, T. (2007) 'The character of Hertfordshire's parks and gardens', in A. Rowe (ed.) *Hertfordshire garden history: a miscellany* (Hatfield), 1–25.

Williamson, T. (2008) 'Co-axial landscapes: time and topography', in P. Rainbird (ed.) *Monuments in the landscape* (Stroud), 123–35.

Wilson, D.R. (1975) 'Causewayed camps and interrupted ditch systems', *Antiquity*, 49, 178–86.

Winchester, A. (1990) *Discovering parish boundaries* (Princes Risborough).

Wingfield, C. (1995) 'The Anglo-Saxon settlement of Bedfordshire and Hertfordshire: the archaeological view', in R. Holgate (ed.), *Chiltern archaeology: recent work* (Dunstable), 31–43.

Winterbottom, M. (ed.) (1978) *Gildas: the ruin of Britain and other works* (Chichester).

Witney, K.P. (1990) 'The woodland economy of Kent, 1066–1348', *Agricultural History Review*, 38, 20–39.

Wooldridge, S.W. and Hutchings, G.E. (1957) *London's Countryside* (London).

Yorke, B. (1990) *Kings and kingdoms of early Anglo-Saxon England* (London).

Index

Entries in italics refer to the illustrations